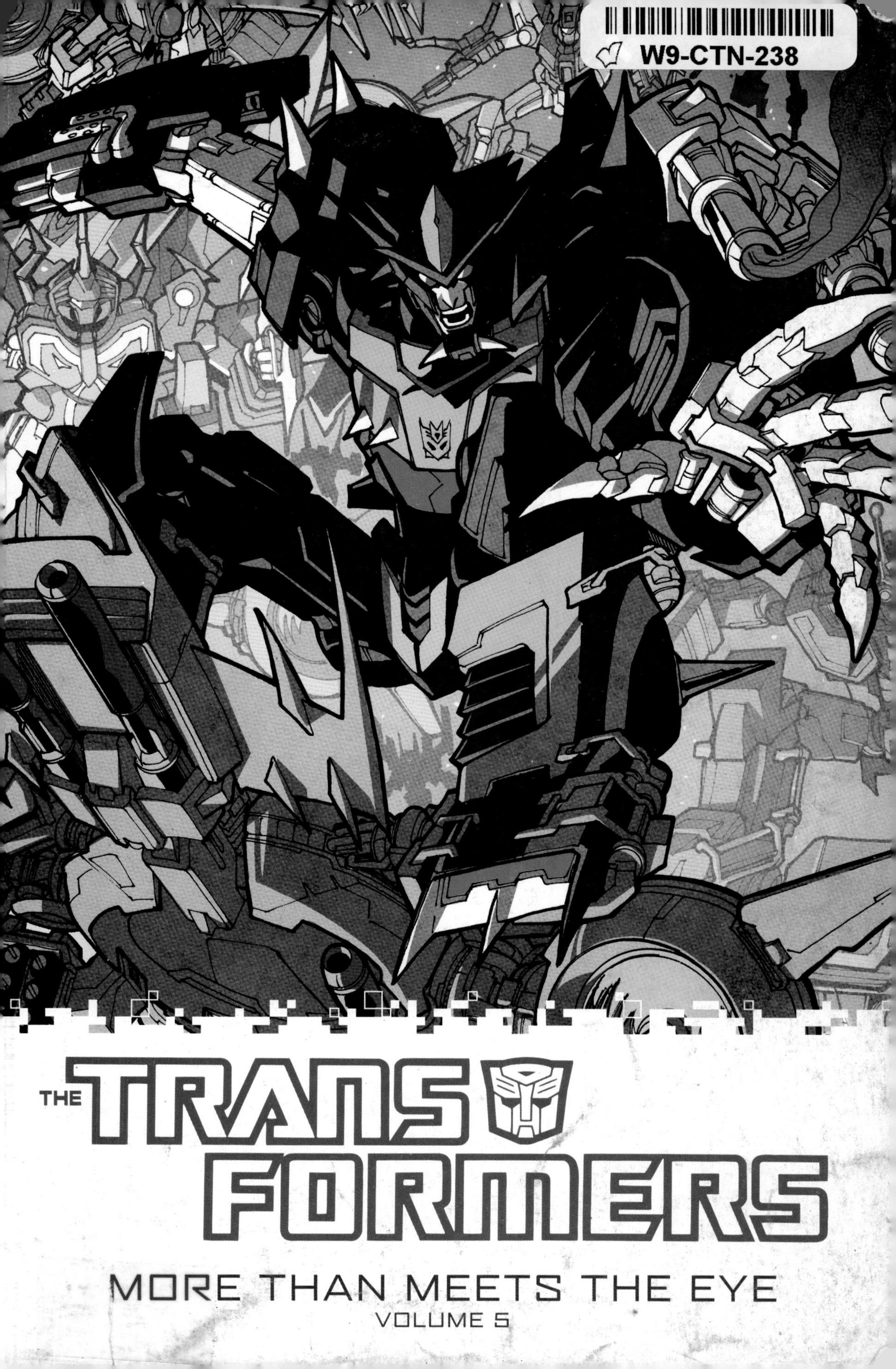

THE TRANSFORMERS

MORE THAN MEETS THE EYE

VOLUME 5

Series Edits by John Barber
Editorial Assistance by Toni Korde, Mariel Romero, and Kevin Smead
Collection Edits by Justin Eisinger and Alonzo Simon
Collection Design by Chris Mowry

Special thanks to Hasbro's Clint Chapman, Jerry Jivoin, Joshua Lamb, Ed Lane, Joe Furfaro, Heather Hopkins, and Michael Kelly for their invaluable assistance.

IDW founded by Ted Adams, Alex Garner, Kris Oprisko, and Robbie Robbins |

ISBN: 978-1-61377-802-9   16 15 14 13   1 2 3 4

 IDW ®

Licensed By:

Ted Adams, CEO & Publisher
Greg Goldstein, President & COO
Robbie Robbins, EVP/Sr. Graphic Artist
Chris Ryall, Chief Creative Officer/Editor-in-Chief
Matthew Ruzicka, CPA, Chief Financial Officer
Alan Payne, VP of Sales
Dirk Wood, VP of Marketing
Lorelei Bunjes, VP of Digital Services

Become our fan on Facebook facebook.com/idwpublishing
Follow us on Twitter @idwpublishing
Check us out on YouTube youtube.com/idwpublishing
www.IDWPUBLISHING.com

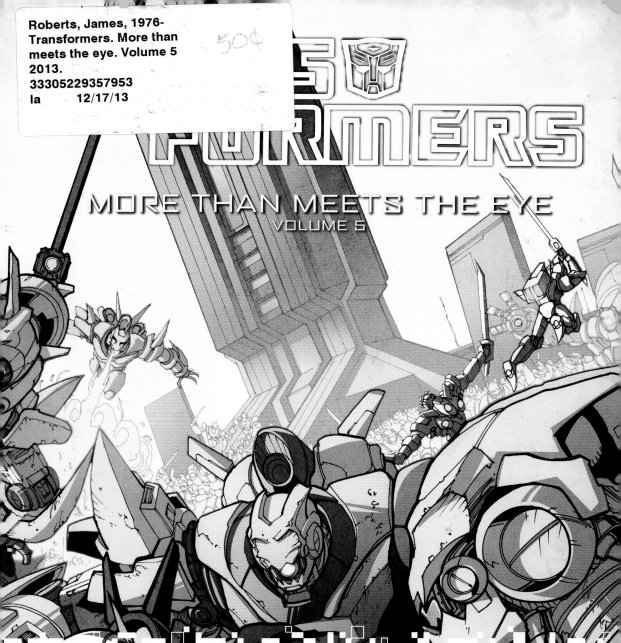

TRANSFORMERS
MORE THAN MEETS THE EYE
VOLUME 5

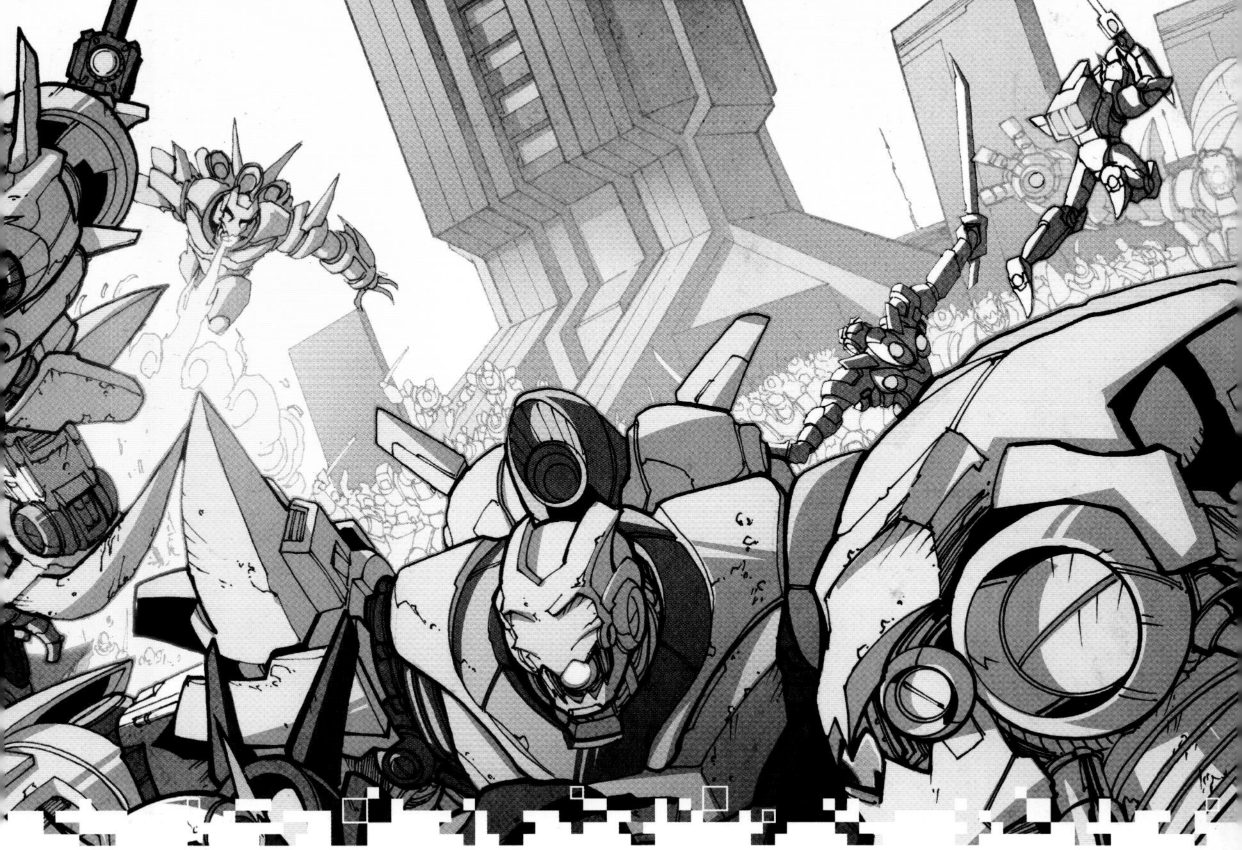

WRITTEN BY **JAMES ROBERTS**

PENCILS BY **ALEX MILNE** AND **JAMES RAIZ**

INKS BY **BRIAN SHEARER, ALEX MILNE,** AND **JAMES RAIZ**

COLORS BY **JOSH BURCHAM**

COLOR ASSIST BY **JOHN-PAUL BOVE** AND **JOANA LAFUENTE**

LETTERS BY **TOM B. LONG**

COVER BY **ALEX MILNE**
COVER COLORS BY **JOSH PEREZ**

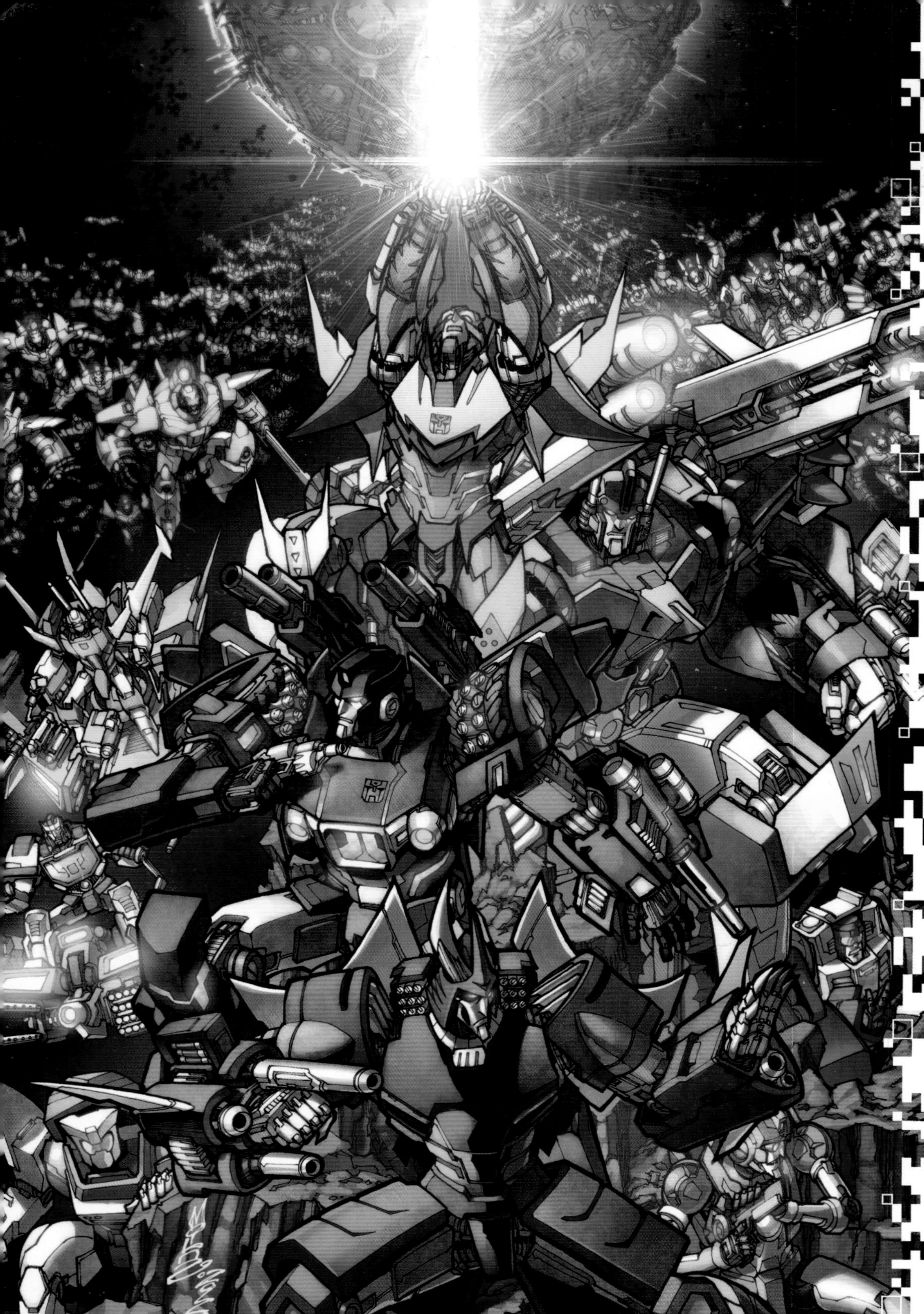

MORE THAN MEETS THE EYE #17 COVER A

by **ALEX MILNE** Colors by **JOSH PEREZ**

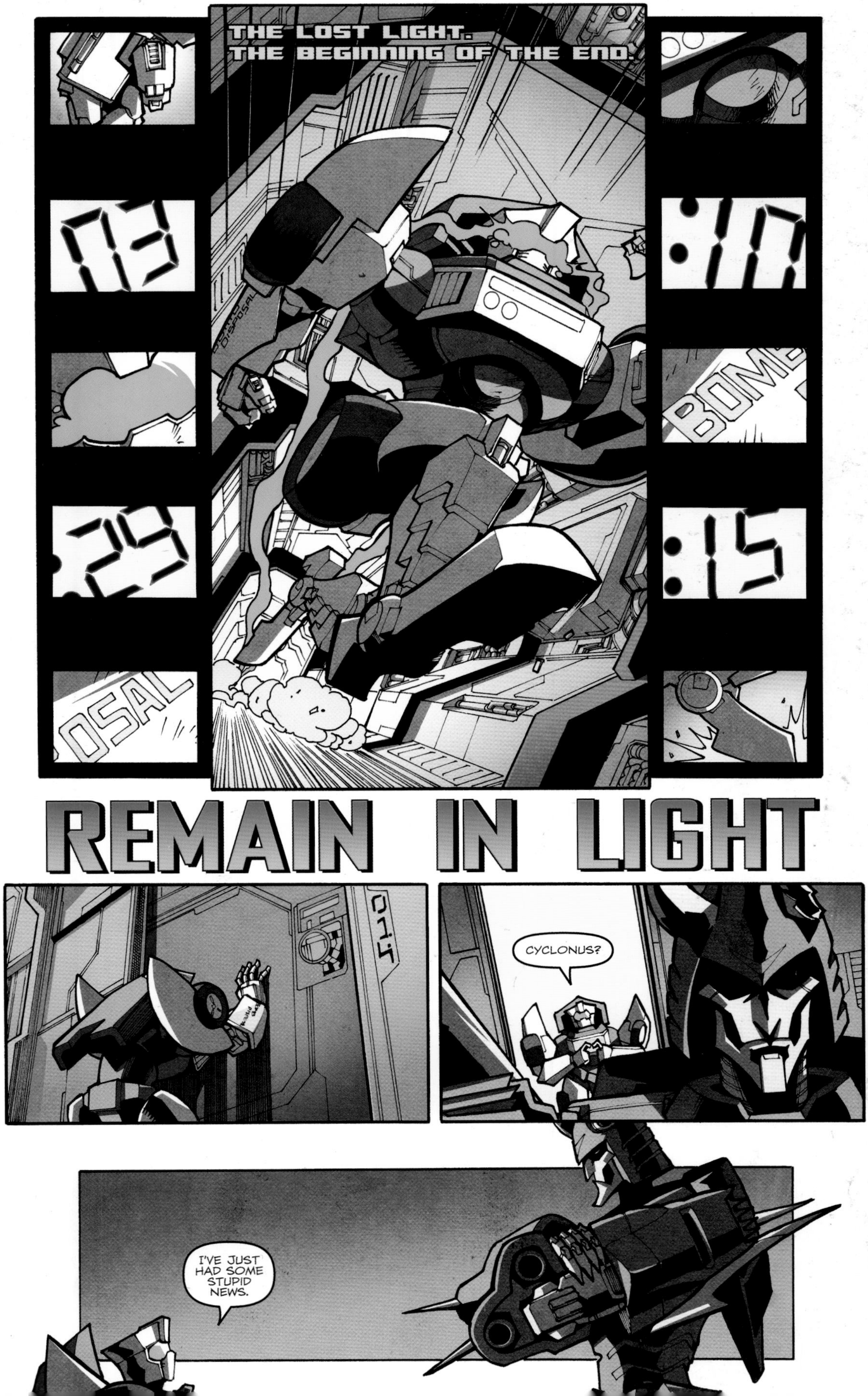
THE LOST LIGHT.
THE BEGINNING OF THE END.
03
:10
:24
:15
BOMB
OSAL
REMAIN IN LIGHT
CYCLONUS?
I'VE JUST HAD SOME STUPID NEWS.

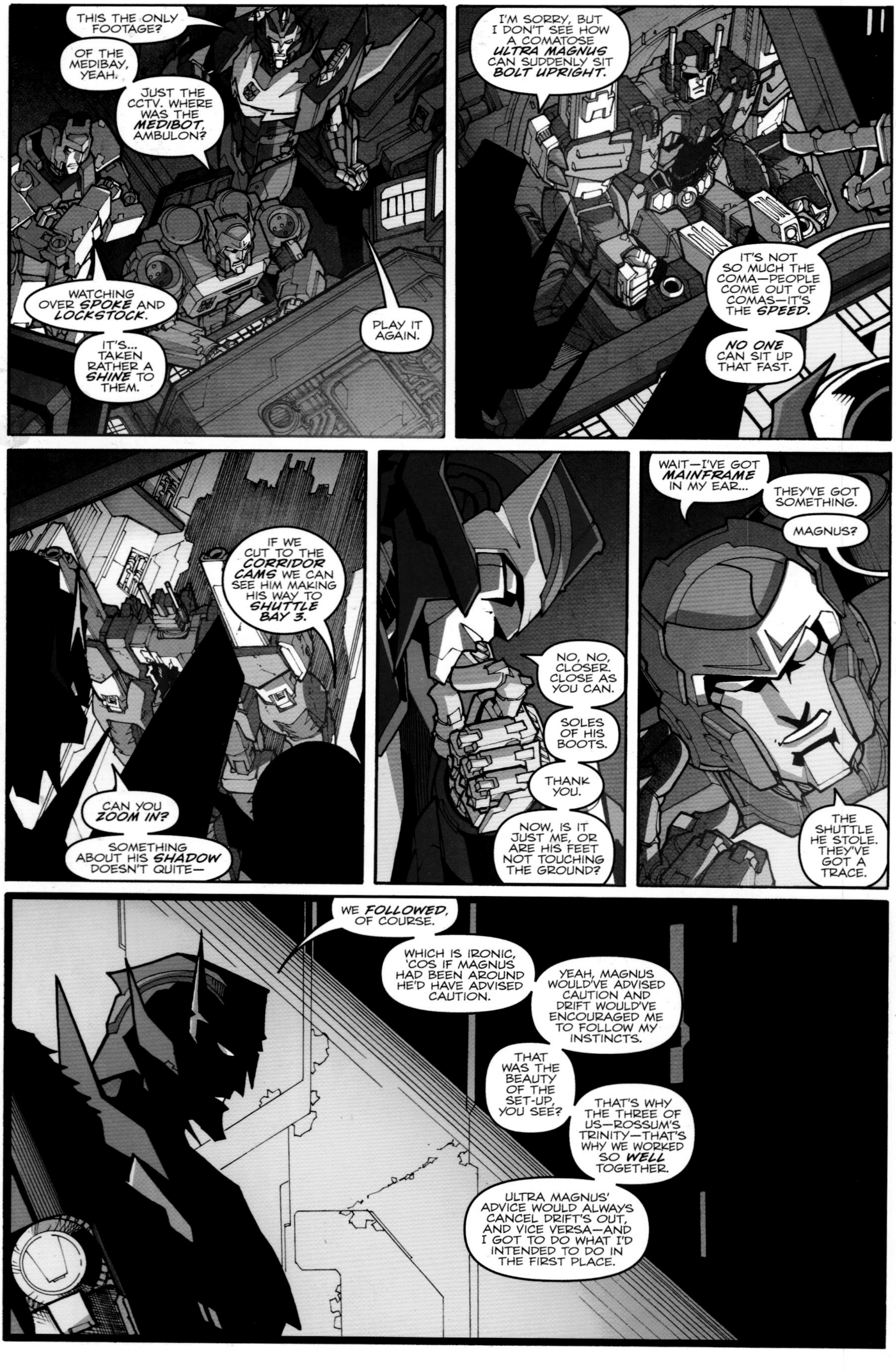
THIS THE ONLY FOOTAGE?
OF THE MEDIBAY, YEAH.
JUST THE CCTV. WHERE WAS THE MEDIBOT, AMBULON?
WATCHING OVER SPOKE AND LOCKSTOCK.
IT'S... TAKEN RATHER A SHINE TO THEM.
PLAY IT AGAIN.
I'M SORRY, BUT I DON'T SEE HOW A COMATOSE ULTRA MAGNUS CAN SUDDENLY SIT BOLT UPRIGHT.
IT'S NOT SO MUCH THE COMA—PEOPLE COME OUT OF COMAS—IT'S THE SPEED.
NO ONE CAN SIT UP THAT FAST.
IF WE CUT TO THE CORRIDOR CAMS WE CAN SEE HIM MAKING HIS WAY TO SHUTTLE BAY 3.
CAN YOU ZOOM IN?
SOMETHING ABOUT HIS SHADOW DOESN'T QUITE—
NO, NO, CLOSER. CLOSE AS YOU CAN.
SOLES OF HIS BOOTS.
THANK YOU.
NOW, IS IT JUST ME, OR ARE HIS FEET NOT TOUCHING THE GROUND?
WAIT—I'VE GOT MAINFRAME IN MY EAR...
THEY'VE GOT SOMETHING.
MAGNUS?
THE SHUTTLE HE STOLE. THEY'VE GOT A TRACE.
WE FOLLOWED, OF COURSE.
WHICH IS IRONIC, 'COS IF MAGNUS HAD BEEN AROUND HE'D HAVE ADVISED CAUTION.
YEAH, MAGNUS WOULD'VE ADVISED CAUTION AND DRIFT WOULD'VE ENCOURAGED ME TO FOLLOW MY INSTINCTS.
THAT WAS THE BEAUTY OF THE SET-UP, YOU SEE?
THAT'S WHY THE THREE OF US—ROSSUM'S TRINITY—THAT'S WHY WE WORKED SO WELL TOGETHER.
ULTRA MAGNUS' ADVICE WOULD ALWAYS CANCEL DRIFT'S OUT, AND VICE VERSA—AND I GOT TO DO WHAT I'D INTENDED TO DO IN THE FIRST PLACE.

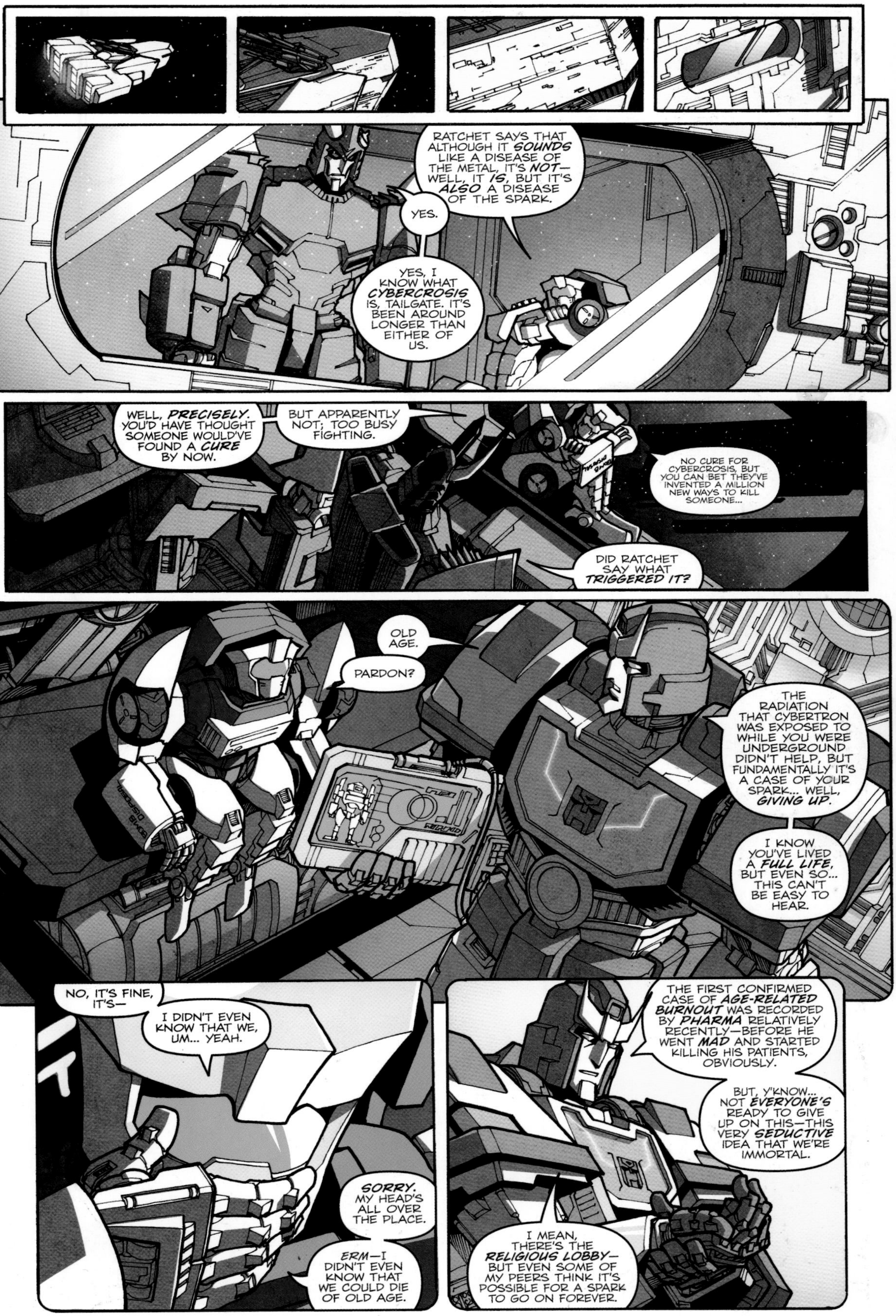
RATCHET SAYS THAT ALTHOUGH IT SOUNDS LIKE A DISEASE OF THE METAL, IT'S NOT— WELL, IT IS, BUT IT'S ALSO A DISEASE OF THE SPARK.
YES.
YES, I KNOW WHAT CYBERCROSIS IS, TAILGATE. IT'S BEEN AROUND LONGER THAN EITHER OF US.
WELL, PRECISELY. YOU'D HAVE THOUGHT SOMEONE WOULD'VE FOUND A CURE BY NOW.
BUT APPARENTLY NOT; TOO BUSY FIGHTING.
NO CURE FOR CYBERCROSIS, BUT YOU CAN BET THEY'VE INVENTED A MILLION NEW WAYS TO KILL SOMEONE...
DID RATCHET SAY WHAT TRIGGERED IT?
OLD AGE.
PARDON?
THE RADIATION THAT CYBERTRON WAS EXPOSED TO WHILE YOU WERE UNDERGROUND DIDN'T HELP, BUT FUNDAMENTALLY IT'S A CASE OF YOUR SPARK... WELL, GIVING UP.
I KNOW YOU'VE LIVED A FULL LIFE, BUT EVEN SO... THIS CAN'T BE EASY TO HEAR.
NO, IT'S FINE, IT'S—
I DIDN'T EVEN KNOW THAT WE, UM... YEAH.
SORRY. MY HEAD'S ALL OVER THE PLACE.
ERM—I DIDN'T EVEN KNOW THAT WE COULD DIE OF OLD AGE.
THE FIRST CONFIRMED CASE OF AGE-RELATED BURNOUT WAS RECORDED BY PHARMA RELATIVELY RECENTLY—BEFORE HE WENT MAD AND STARTED KILLING HIS PATIENTS, OBVIOUSLY.
BUT, Y'KNOW... NOT EVERYONE'S READY TO GIVE UP ON THIS—THIS VERY SEDUCTIVE IDEA THAT WE'RE IMMORTAL.
I MEAN, THERE'S THE RELIGIOUS LOBBY— BUT EVEN SOME OF MY PEERS THINK IT'S POSSIBLE FOR A SPARK TO GO ON FOREVER.

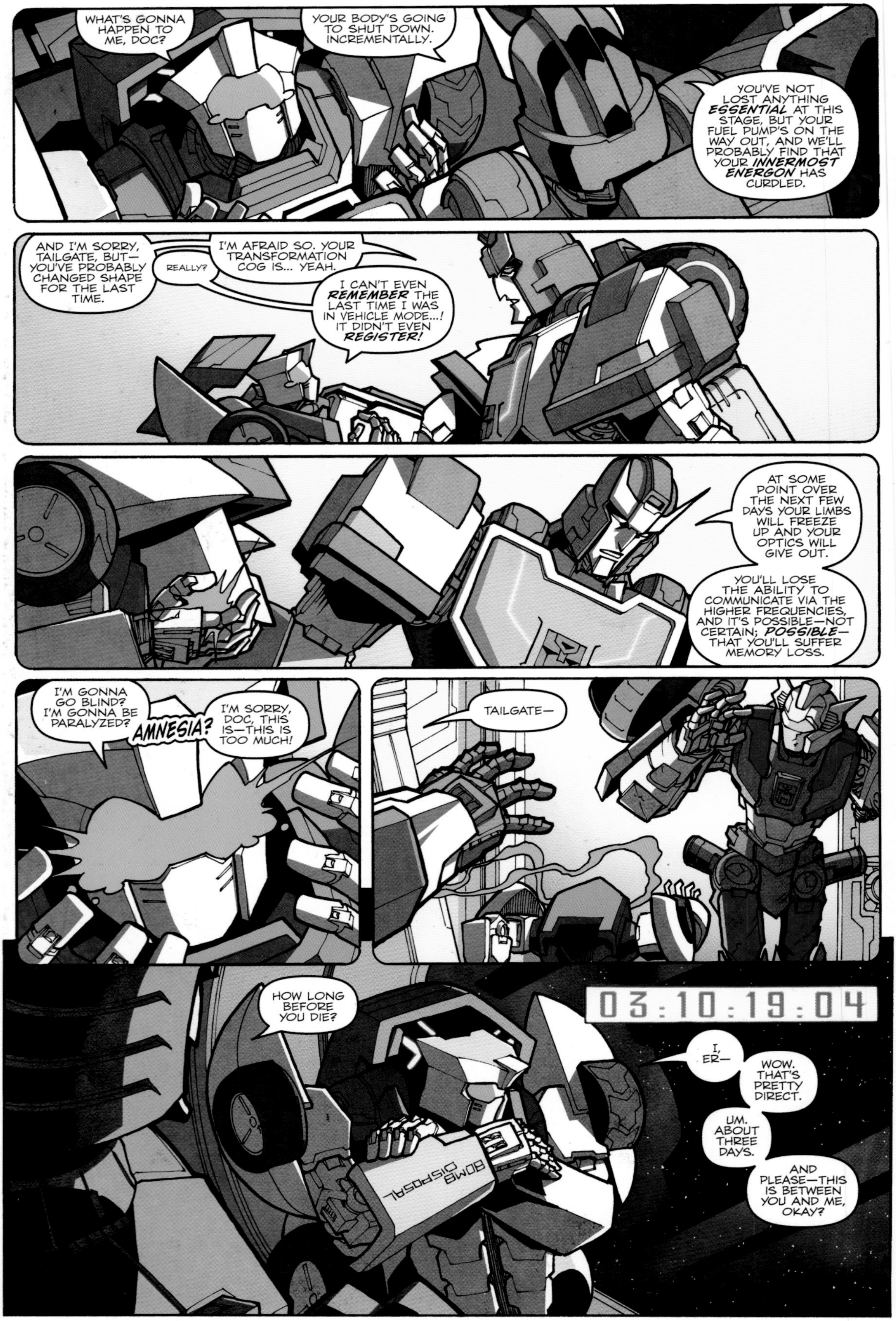
WHAT'S GONNA HAPPEN TO ME, DOC?
YOUR BODY'S GOING TO SHUT DOWN. INCREMENTALLY.
YOU'VE NOT LOST ANYTHING ESSENTIAL AT THIS STAGE, BUT YOUR FUEL PUMP'S ON THE WAY OUT, AND WE'LL PROBABLY FIND THAT YOUR INNERMOST ENERGON HAS CURDLED.
AND I'M SORRY, TAILGATE, BUT— YOU'VE PROBABLY CHANGED SHAPE FOR THE LAST TIME.
REALLY?
I'M AFRAID SO. YOUR TRANSFORMATION COG IS... YEAH.
I CAN'T EVEN REMEMBER THE LAST TIME I WAS IN VEHICLE MODE...! IT DIDN'T EVEN REGISTER!
AT SOME POINT OVER THE NEXT FEW DAYS YOUR LIMBS WILL FREEZE UP AND YOUR OPTICS WILL GIVE OUT.
YOU'LL LOSE THE ABILITY TO COMMUNICATE VIA THE HIGHER FREQUENCIES, AND IT'S POSSIBLE—NOT CERTAIN; POSSIBLE— THAT YOU'LL SUFFER MEMORY LOSS.
I'M GONNA GO BLIND? I'M GONNA BE PARALYZED? AMNESIA?
I'M SORRY, DOC, THIS IS—THIS IS TOO MUCH!
TAILGATE—
HOW LONG BEFORE YOU DIE?
03:10:19:04
I, ER—
WOW. THAT'S PRETTY DIRECT.
UM. ABOUT THREE DAYS.
AND PLEASE—THIS IS BETWEEN YOU AND ME, OKAY?
BOMB DISPOSAL

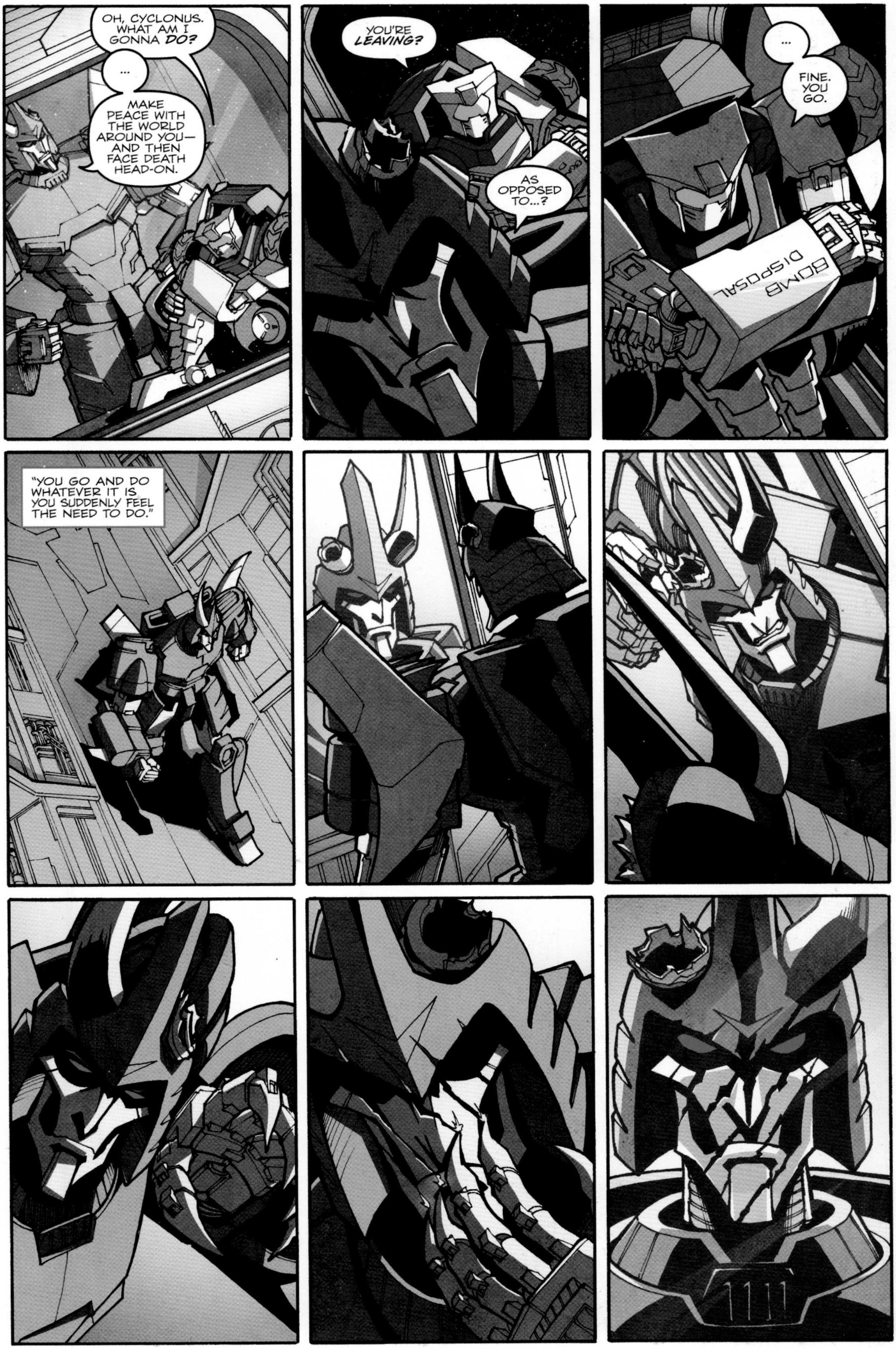
OH, CYCLONUS. WHAT AM I GONNA DO?
...
MAKE PEACE WITH THE WORLD AROUND YOU— AND THEN FACE DEATH HEAD-ON.
YOU'RE LEAVING?
AS OPPOSED TO...?
...
FINE. YOU GO.
BOMB DISPOSAL
"YOU GO AND DO WHATEVER IT IS YOU SUDDENLY FEEL THE NEED TO DO."

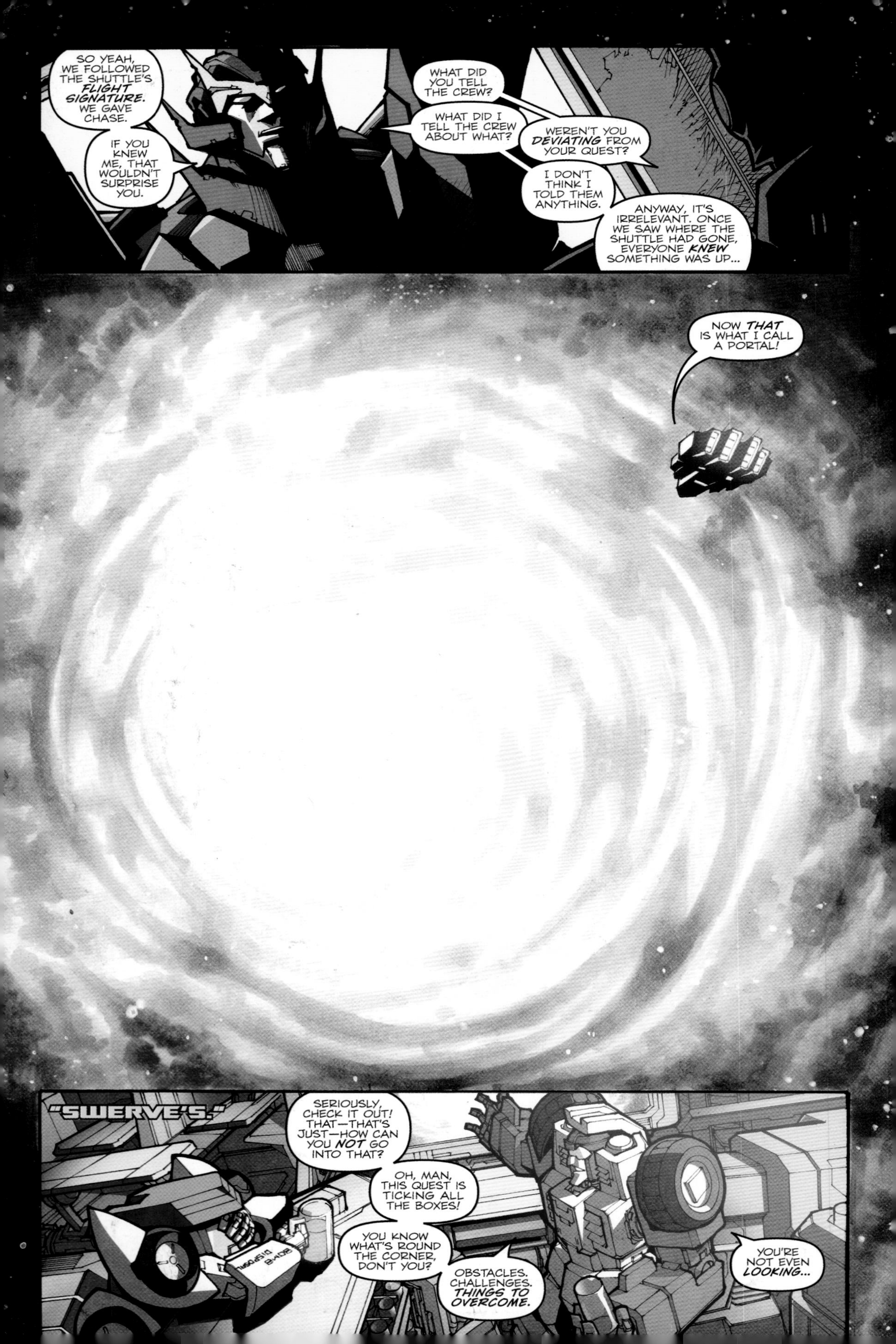
SO YEAH, WE FOLLOWED THE SHUTTLE'S FLIGHT SIGNATURE. WE GAVE CHASE.
IF YOU KNEW ME, THAT WOULDN'T SURPRISE YOU.
WHAT DID YOU TELL THE CREW?
WHAT DID I TELL THE CREW ABOUT WHAT?
WEREN'T YOU DEVIATING FROM YOUR QUEST?
I DON'T THINK I TOLD THEM ANYTHING.
ANYWAY, IT'S IRRELEVANT. ONCE WE SAW WHERE THE SHUTTLE HAD GONE, EVERYONE KNEW SOMETHING WAS UP...
NOW THAT IS WHAT I CALL A PORTAL!
"SWERVE'S."
SERIOUSLY, CHECK IT OUT! THAT—THAT'S JUST—HOW CAN YOU NOT GO INTO THAT?
OH, MAN, THIS QUEST IS TICKING ALL THE BOXES!
YOU KNOW WHAT'S ROUND THE CORNER, DON'T YOU?
OBSTACLES. CHALLENGES. THINGS TO OVERCOME.
YOU'RE NOT EVEN LOOKING...

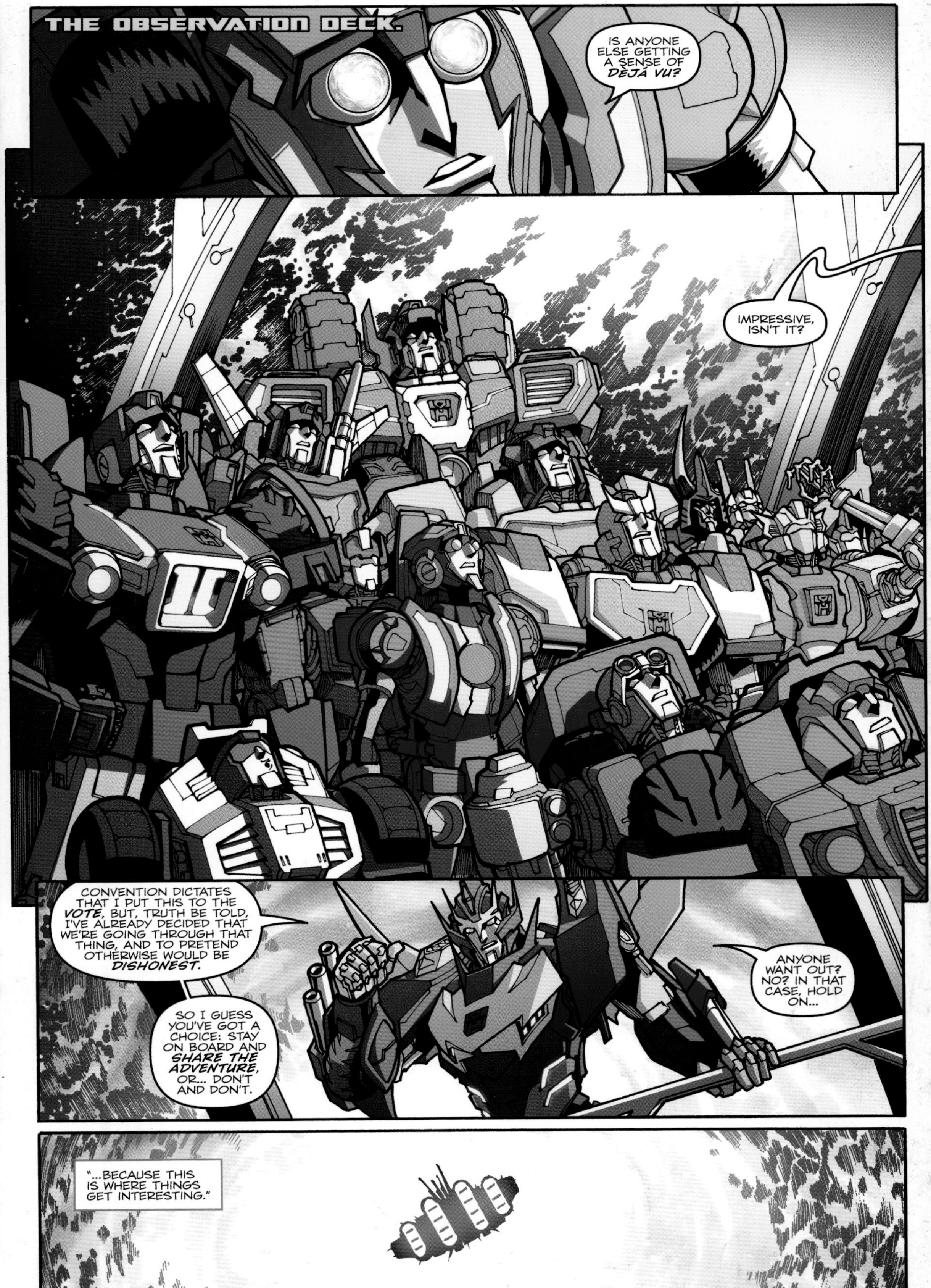
THE OBSERVATION DECK.
IS ANYONE ELSE GETTING A SENSE OF DÉJÀ VU?
IMPRESSIVE, ISN'T IT?
CONVENTION DICTATES THAT I PUT THIS TO THE VOTE, BUT, TRUTH BE TOLD, I'VE ALREADY DECIDED THAT WE'RE GOING THROUGH THAT THING, AND TO PRETEND OTHERWISE WOULD BE DISHONEST.
SO I GUESS YOU'VE GOT A CHOICE: STAY ON BOARD AND SHARE THE ADVENTURE, OR... DON'T AND DON'T.
ANYONE WANT OUT? NO? IN THAT CASE, HOLD ON...
"...BECAUSE THIS IS WHERE THINGS GET INTERESTING."

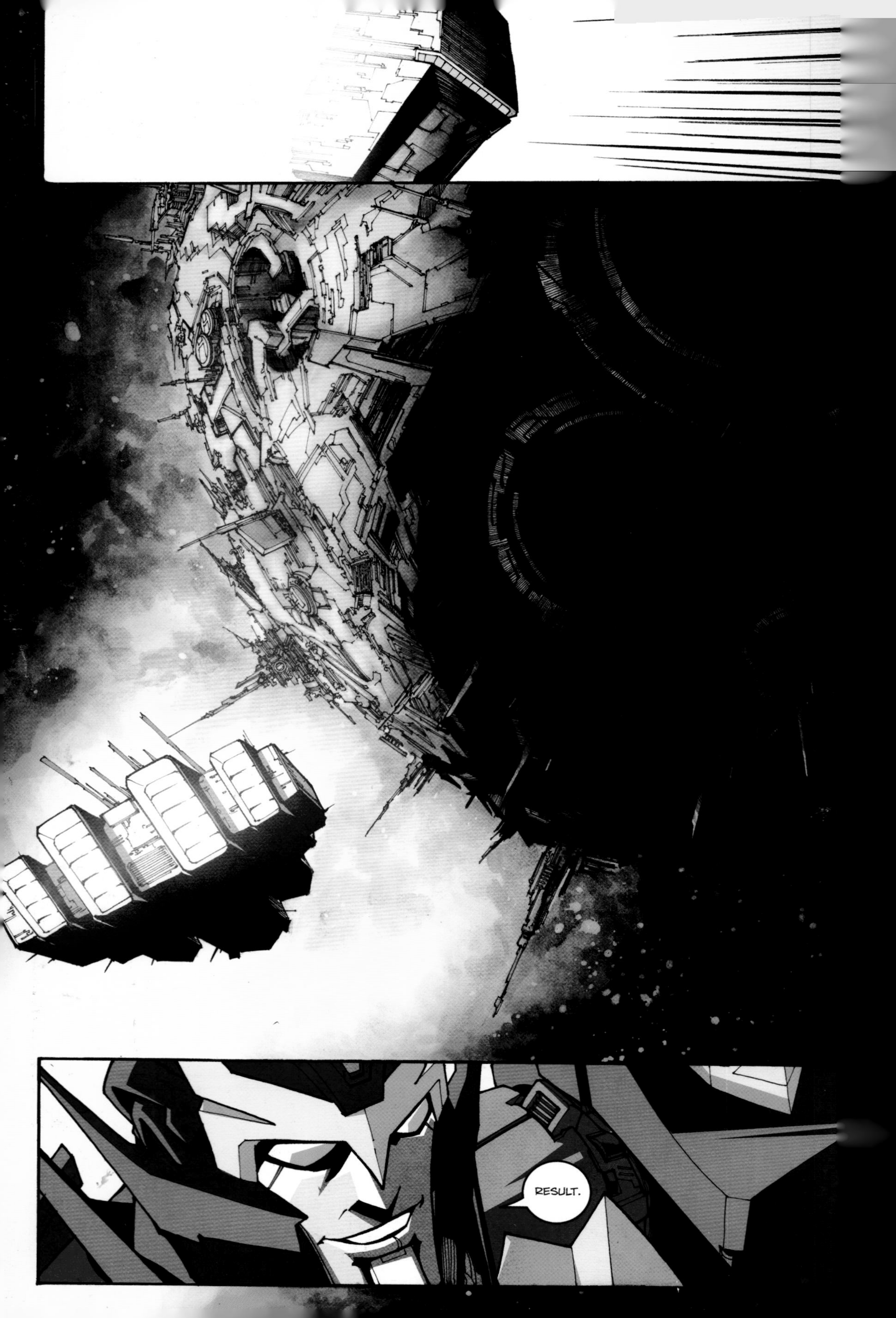
RESULT.

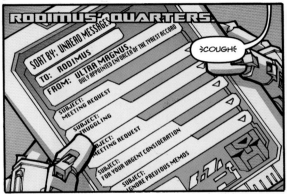

SORT BY: UNREAD MESSAGES

TO: RODIMUS

FROM: ULTRA MAGNUS,
DULY APPOINTED ENFORCER OF THE TYREST ACCORD

SUBJECT:
MEETING REQUEST

SUBJECT:
SMUGGLING

SUBJECT:
MEETING REQUEST

SUBJECT:
FOR YOUR URGENT CONSIDERATION

SUBJECT:
IGNORE PREVIOUS MEMOS

≥COUGH≤

WELL? IS IT *LUNA 1?*

EVERYTHING WOULD SUGGEST YES.

I *KNEW* IT.

LUNA 1, PERCEPTOR! THE *MIRACLE MOON!*

EVERYTHING YOU COULD EVER WANT TO FIND, ALL IN ONE PLACE!

I'M WELL AWARE OF ITS POSITION IN THE POPULAR CONSCIOUSNESS.

THE ANSWER TO EVERYTHING, EVER. AREN'T YOU *EXCITED?*

VERY.

LONG-RANGE VISUAL. IT LOOKS *DESERTED.*

NO OBVIOUS SETTLEMENTS. NO LIGHTS. COURSE, THERE'S ALWAYS *UNDERGROUND.*

ACTUALLY, SCANS SUGGEST THAT IT'S LARGELY SOLID—MUCH LIKE LUNA 2.

HAVE YOU SCANNED FOR *LIFE SIGNS?*

I'M RE-SCANNING, YES.

RIGHT. YOU WEREN'T HAPPY WITH THE RESULTS OF THE FIRST SCAN?

NOT PARTICULARLY, NO.

OKAY. SO... HOW ABOUT YOU GIVE THEM TO ME ANYWAY, AND I'LL DECIDE IF I'M HAPPY WITH THEM OR NOT.

WELL, ACCORDING TO WHAT IS ALMOST CERTAINLY A *FLAWED FIRST READING...*

YES?

LUNA 1 IS HOME TO A BILLION PEOPLE.

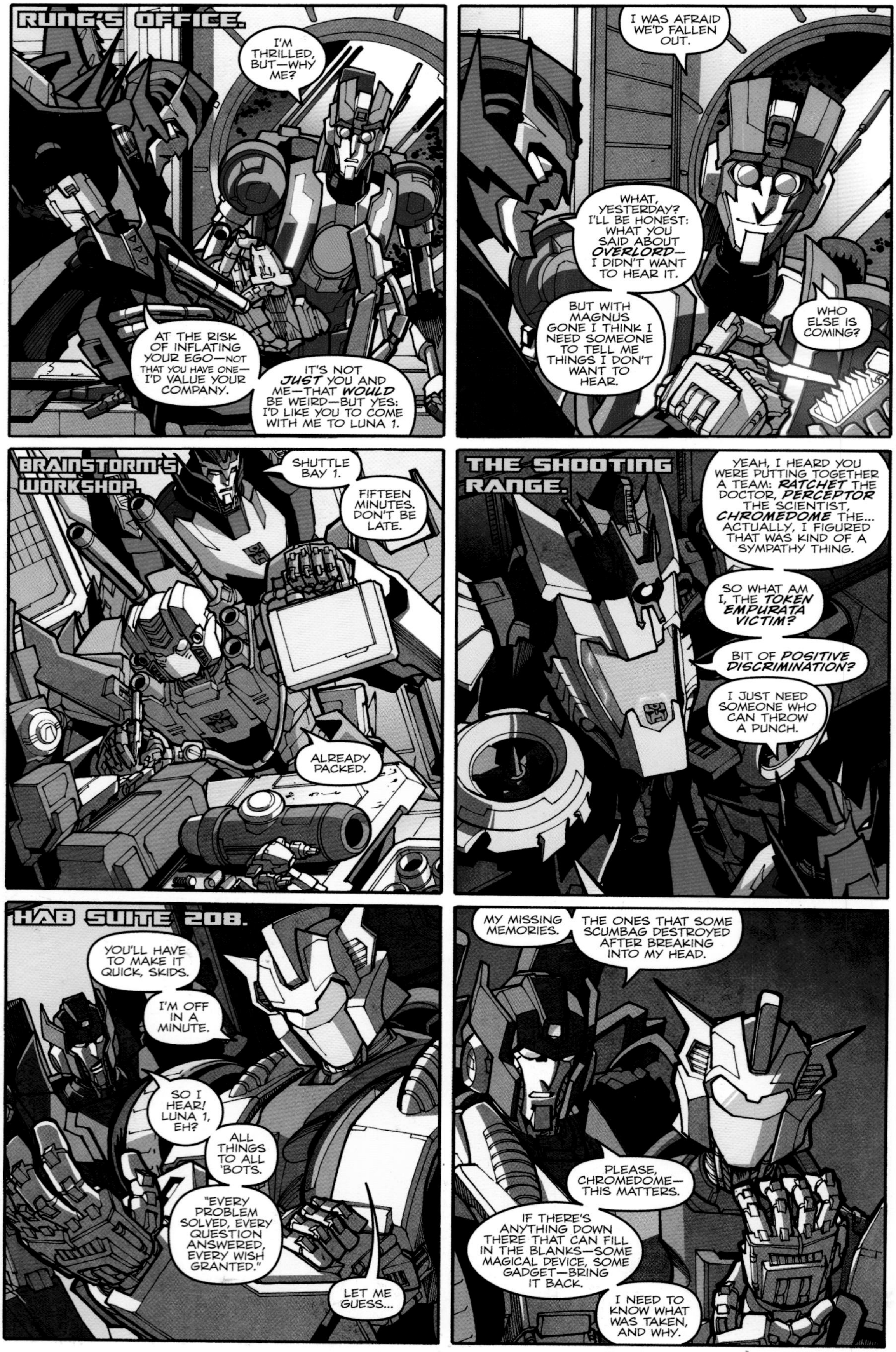
RUNG'S OFFICE.
I'M THRILLED, BUT—WHY ME?
AT THE RISK OF INFLATING YOUR EGO—NOT THAT YOU HAVE ONE—I'D VALUE YOUR COMPANY.
IT'S NOT JUST YOU AND ME—THAT WOULD BE WEIRD—BUT YES: I'D LIKE YOU TO COME WITH ME TO LUNA 1.
I WAS AFRAID WE'D FALLEN OUT.
WHAT, YESTERDAY? I'LL BE HONEST: WHAT YOU SAID ABOUT OVERLORD—I DIDN'T WANT TO HEAR IT.
BUT WITH MAGNUS GONE I THINK I NEED SOMEONE TO TELL ME THINGS I DON'T WANT TO HEAR.
WHO ELSE IS COMING?
BRAINSTORM'S WORKSHOP.
SHUTTLE BAY 1.
FIFTEEN MINUTES. DON'T BE LATE.
ALREADY PACKED.
THE SHOOTING RANGE.
YEAH, I HEARD YOU WERE PUTTING TOGETHER A TEAM: RATCHET THE DOCTOR, PERCEPTOR THE SCIENTIST, CHROMEDOME THE... ACTUALLY, I FIGURED THAT WAS KIND OF A SYMPATHY THING.
SO WHAT AM I, THE TOKEN EMPURATA VICTIM?
BIT OF POSITIVE DISCRIMINATION?
I JUST NEED SOMEONE WHO CAN THROW A PUNCH.
HAB SUITE 208.
YOU'LL HAVE TO MAKE IT QUICK, SKIDS.
I'M OFF IN A MINUTE.
SO I HEAR! LUNA 1, EH?
ALL THINGS TO ALL 'BOTS.
"EVERY PROBLEM SOLVED, EVERY QUESTION ANSWERED, EVERY WISH GRANTED."
LET ME GUESS...
MY MISSING MEMORIES.
THE ONES THAT SOME SCUMBAG DESTROYED AFTER BREAKING INTO MY HEAD.
PLEASE, CHROMEDOME—THIS MATTERS.
IF THERE'S ANYTHING DOWN THERE THAT CAN FILL IN THE BLANKS—SOME MAGICAL DEVICE, SOME GADGET—BRING IT BACK.
I NEED TO KNOW WHAT WAS TAKEN, AND WHY.

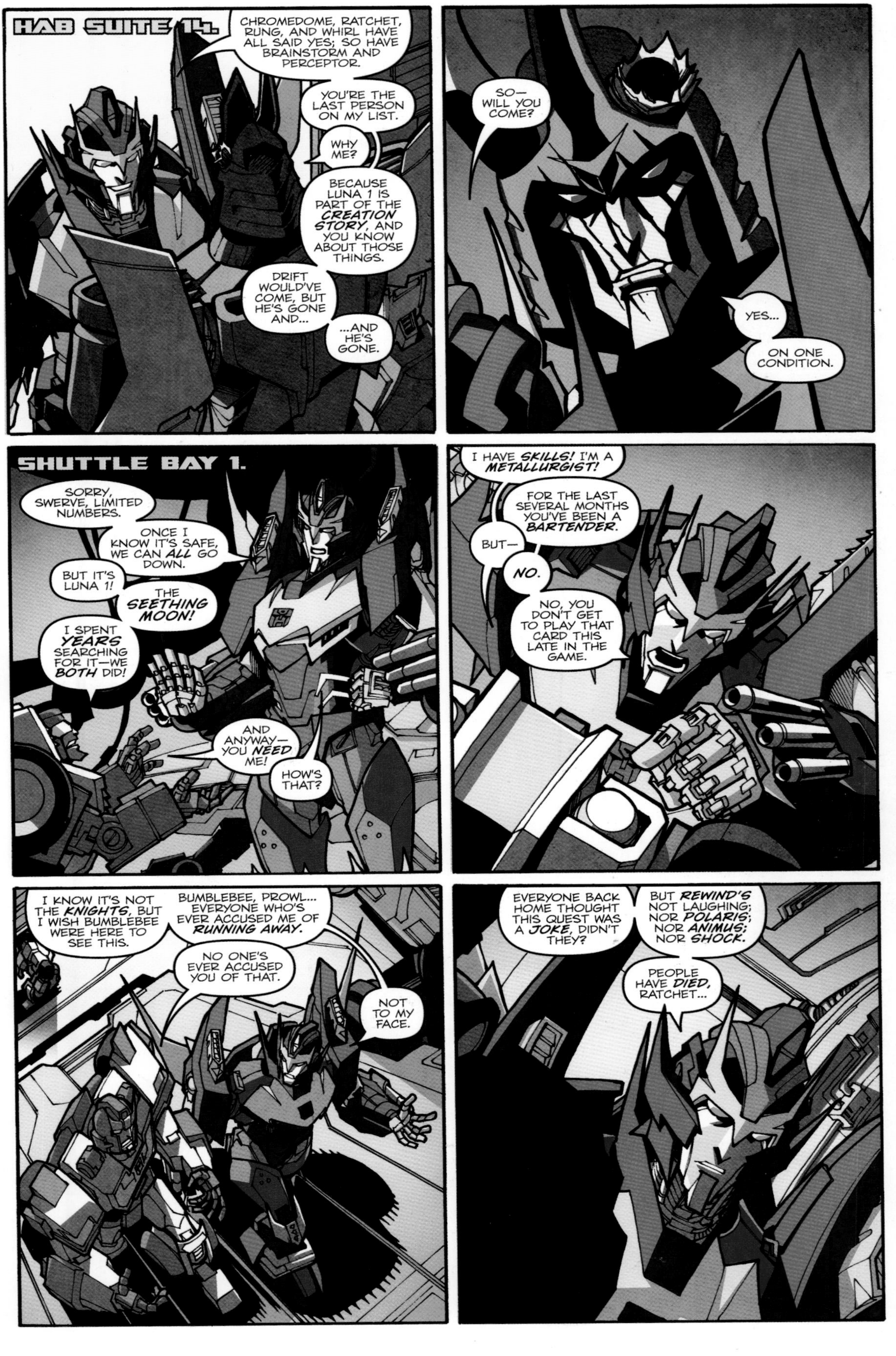
HAB SUITE 14.
CHROMEDOME, RATCHET, RUNG, AND WHIRL HAVE ALL SAID YES; SO HAVE BRAINSTORM AND PERCEPTOR.
YOU'RE THE LAST PERSON ON MY LIST.
WHY ME?
BECAUSE LUNA 1 IS PART OF THE CREATION STORY, AND YOU KNOW ABOUT THOSE THINGS.
DRIFT WOULD'VE COME, BUT HE'S GONE AND...
...AND HE'S GONE.
SO— WILL YOU COME?
YES...
ON ONE CONDITION.
SHUTTLE BAY 1.
SORRY, SWERVE, LIMITED NUMBERS.
ONCE I KNOW IT'S SAFE, WE CAN ALL GO DOWN.
BUT IT'S LUNA 1!
THE SEETHING MOON!
I SPENT YEARS SEARCHING FOR IT—WE BOTH DID!
AND ANYWAY— YOU NEED ME!
HOW'S THAT?
I HAVE SKILLS! I'M A METALLURGIST!
FOR THE LAST SEVERAL MONTHS YOU'VE BEEN A BARTENDER.
BUT—
NO.
NO, YOU DON'T GET TO PLAY THAT CARD THIS LATE IN THE GAME.
I KNOW IT'S NOT THE KNIGHTS, BUT I WISH BUMBLEBEE WERE HERE TO SEE THIS.
BUMBLEBEE, PROWL... EVERYONE WHO'S EVER ACCUSED ME OF RUNNING AWAY.
NO ONE'S EVER ACCUSED YOU OF THAT.
NOT TO MY FACE.
EVERYONE BACK HOME THOUGHT THIS QUEST WAS A JOKE, DIDN'T THEY?
BUT REWIND'S NOT LAUGHING; NOR POLARIS; NOR ANIMUS; NOR SHOCK.
PEOPLE HAVE DIED, RATCHET...

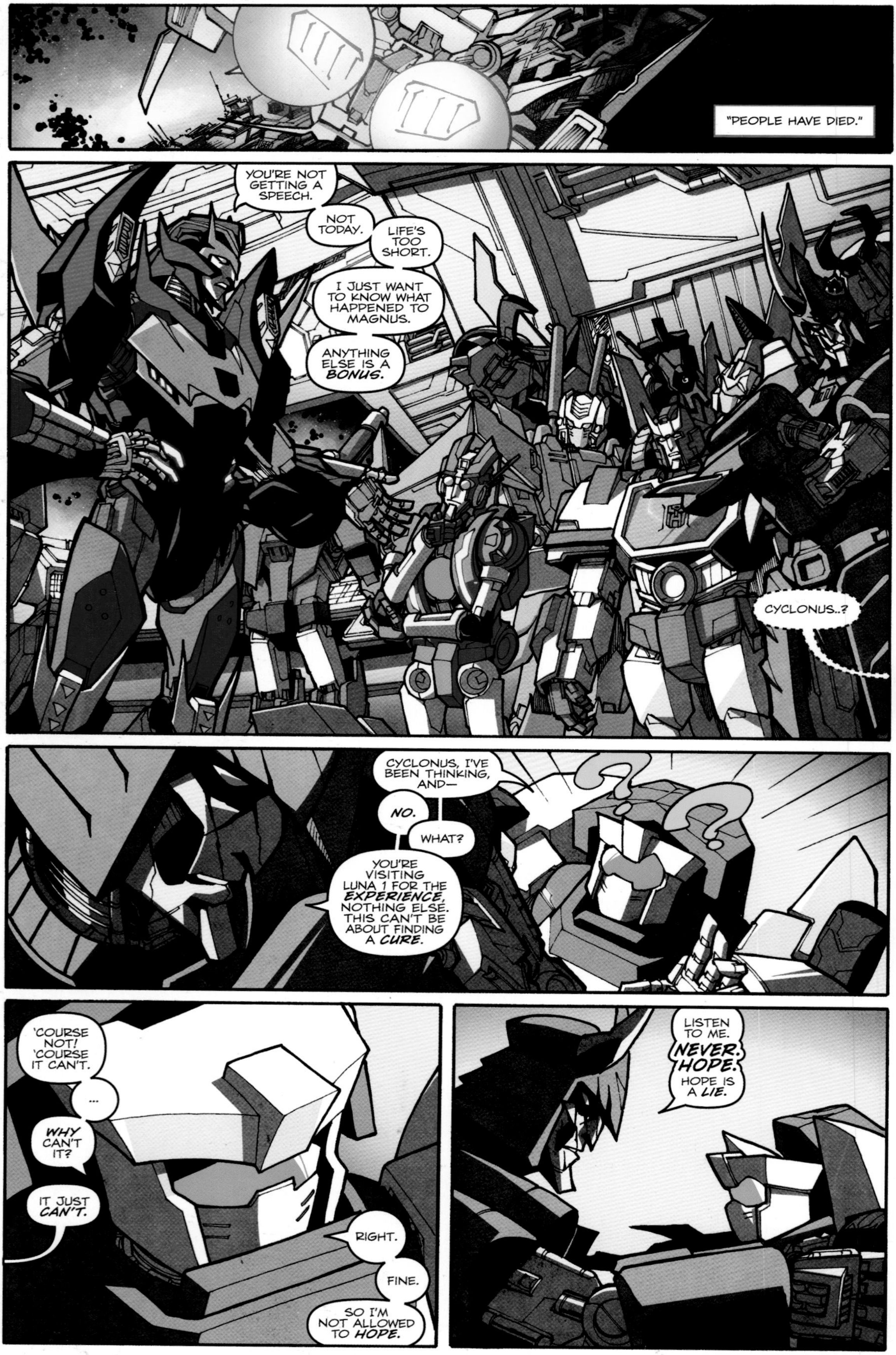
"PEOPLE HAVE DIED."
YOU'RE NOT GETTING A SPEECH.
NOT TODAY.
LIFE'S TOO SHORT.
I JUST WANT TO KNOW WHAT HAPPENED TO MAGNUS.
ANYTHING ELSE IS A BONUS.
CYCLONUS..?
CYCLONUS, I'VE BEEN THINKING, AND—
NO.
WHAT?
YOU'RE VISITING LUNA 1 FOR THE EXPERIENCE, NOTHING ELSE. THIS CAN'T BE ABOUT FINDING A CURE.
'COURSE NOT! 'COURSE IT CAN'T.
...
WHY CAN'T IT?
IT JUST CAN'T.
RIGHT.
FINE.
SO I'M NOT ALLOWED TO HOPE.
LISTEN TO ME. NEVER. HOPE. HOPE IS A LIE.

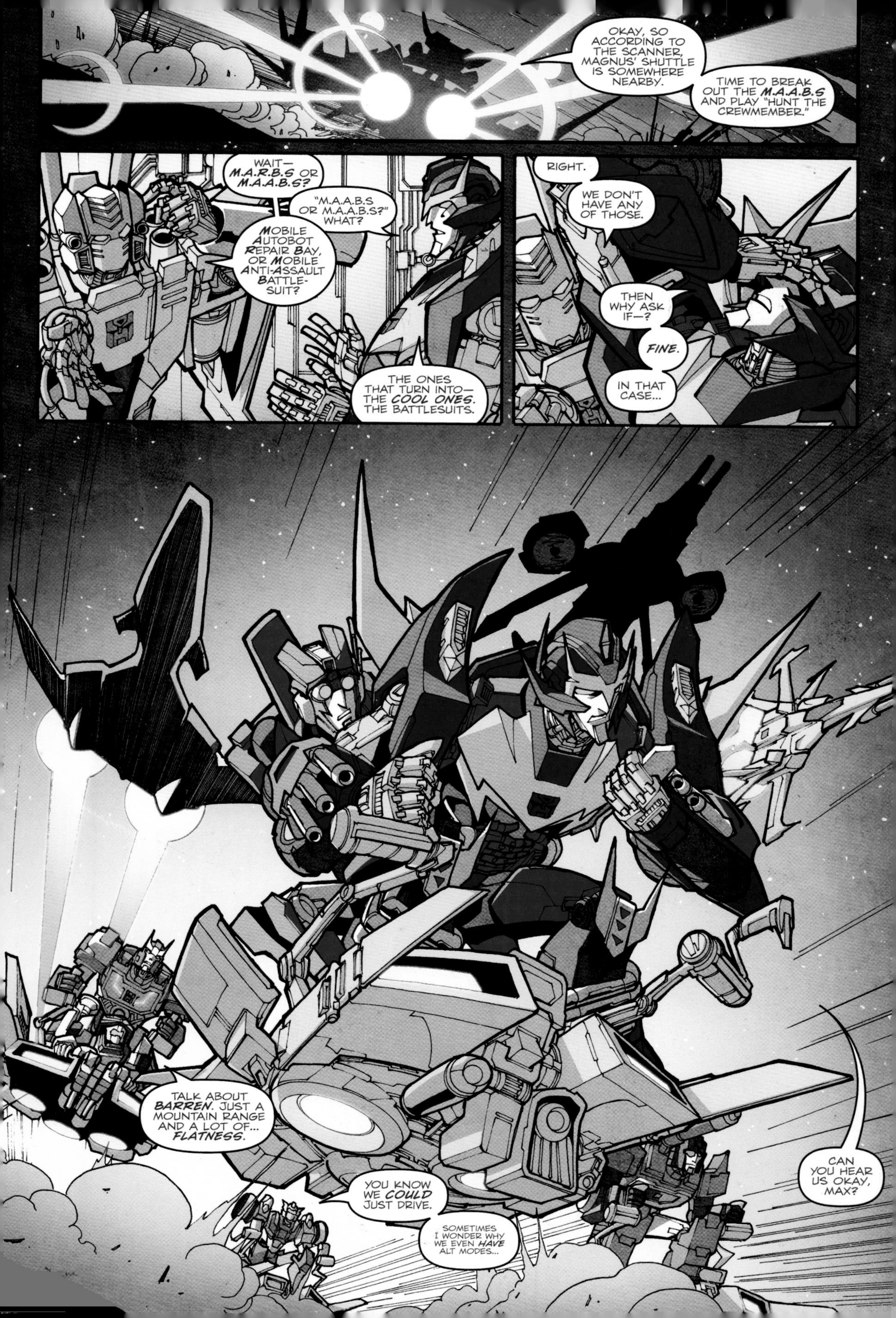

OKAY, SO ACCORDING TO THE SCANNER, MAGNUS' SHUTTLE IS SOMEWHERE NEARBY.
TIME TO BREAK OUT THE M.A.A.B.S AND PLAY "HUNT THE CREWMEMBER."
WAIT— M.A.R.B.S OR M.A.A.B.S?
"M.A.A.B.S OR M.A.A.B.S?" WHAT?
MOBILE AUTOBOT REPAIR BAY, OR MOBILE ANTI-ASSAULT BATTLE-SUIT?
THE ONES THAT TURN INTO— THE COOL ONES. THE BATTLESUITS.
RIGHT.
WE DON'T HAVE ANY OF THOSE.
THEN WHY ASK IF—?
FINE.
IN THAT CASE...
TALK ABOUT BARREN. JUST A MOUNTAIN RANGE AND A LOT OF... FLATNESS.
YOU KNOW WE COULD JUST DRIVE.
SOMETIMES I WONDER WHY WE EVEN HAVE ALT MODES...
CAN YOU HEAR US OKAY, MAX?

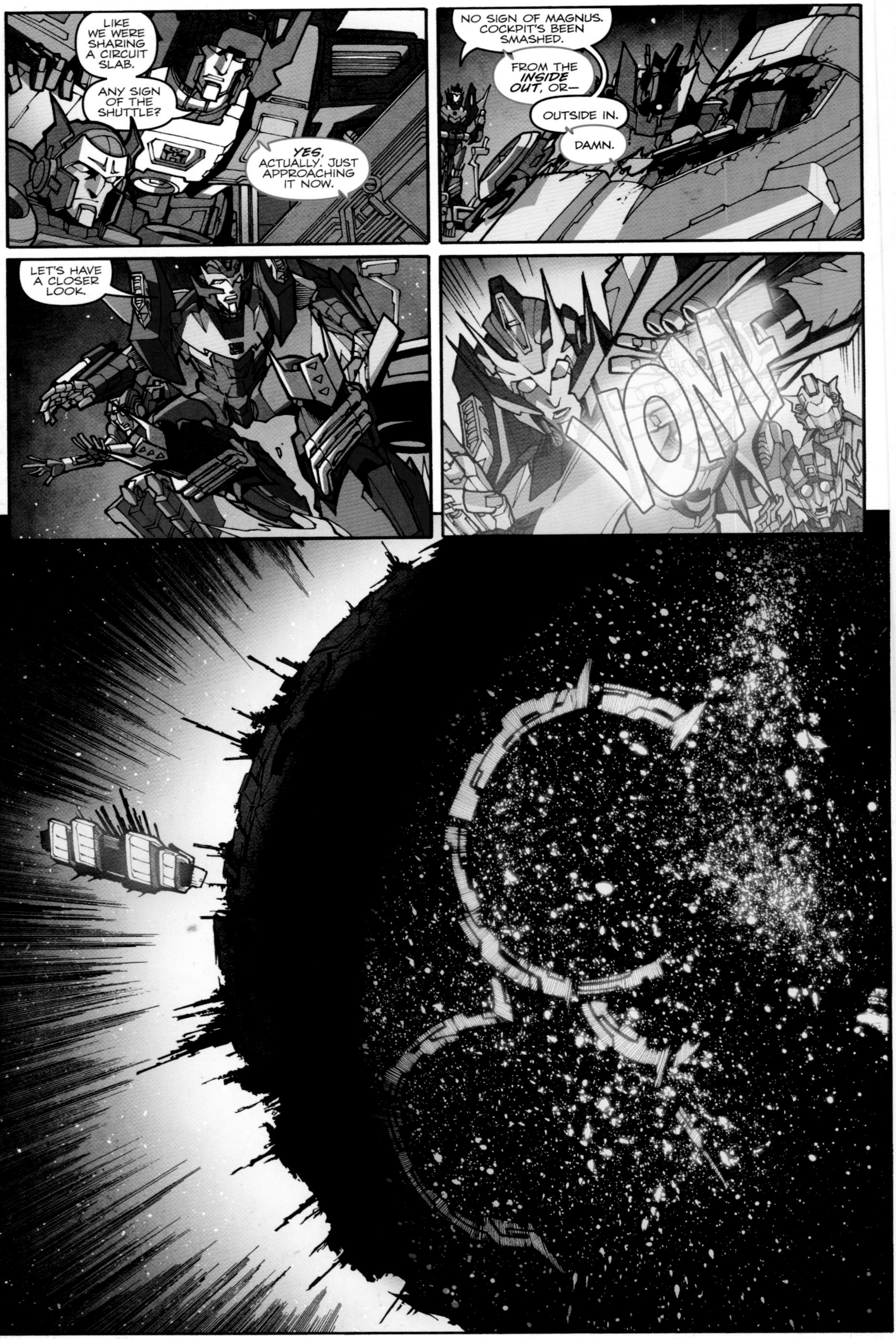

LIKE WE WERE SHARING A CIRCUIT SLAB.
ANY SIGN OF THE SHUTTLE?
YES, ACTUALLY. JUST APPROACHING IT NOW.
NO SIGN OF MAGNUS. COCKPIT'S BEEN SMASHED.
FROM THE INSIDE OUT, OR—
OUTSIDE IN.
DAMN.
LET'S HAVE A CLOSER LOOK.
VOM!

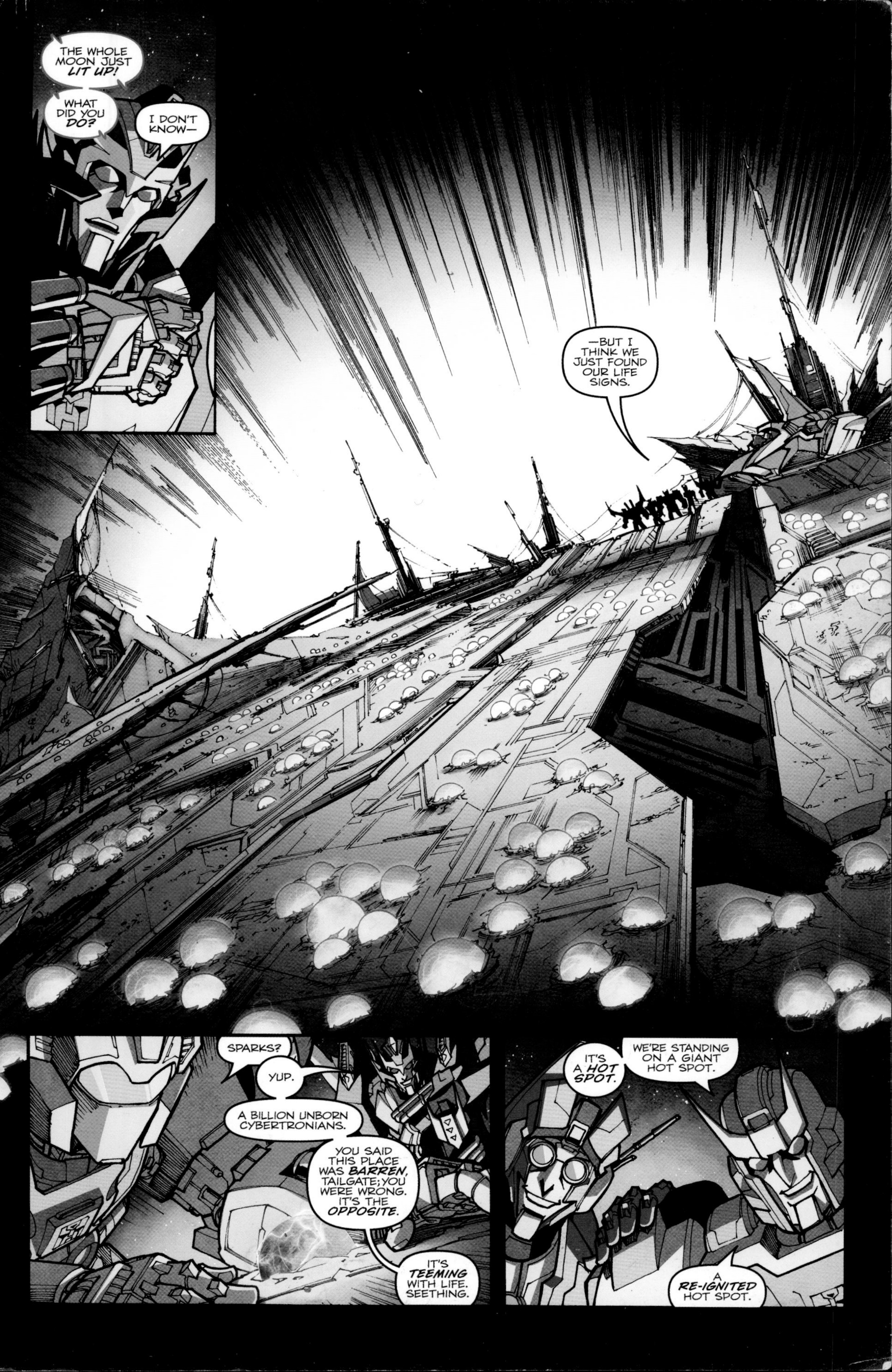
THE WHOLE MOON JUST LIT UP!
WHAT DID YOU DO?
I DON'T KNOW—
—BUT I THINK WE JUST FOUND OUR LIFE SIGNS.
SPARKS?
YUP.
A BILLION UNBORN CYBERTRONIANS.
YOU SAID THIS PLACE WAS BARREN, TAILGATE; YOU WERE WRONG. IT'S THE OPPOSITE.
IT'S TEEMING WITH LIFE. SEETHING.
IT'S A HOT SPOT.
WE'RE STANDING ON A GIANT HOT SPOT.
A RE-IGNITED HOT SPOT.

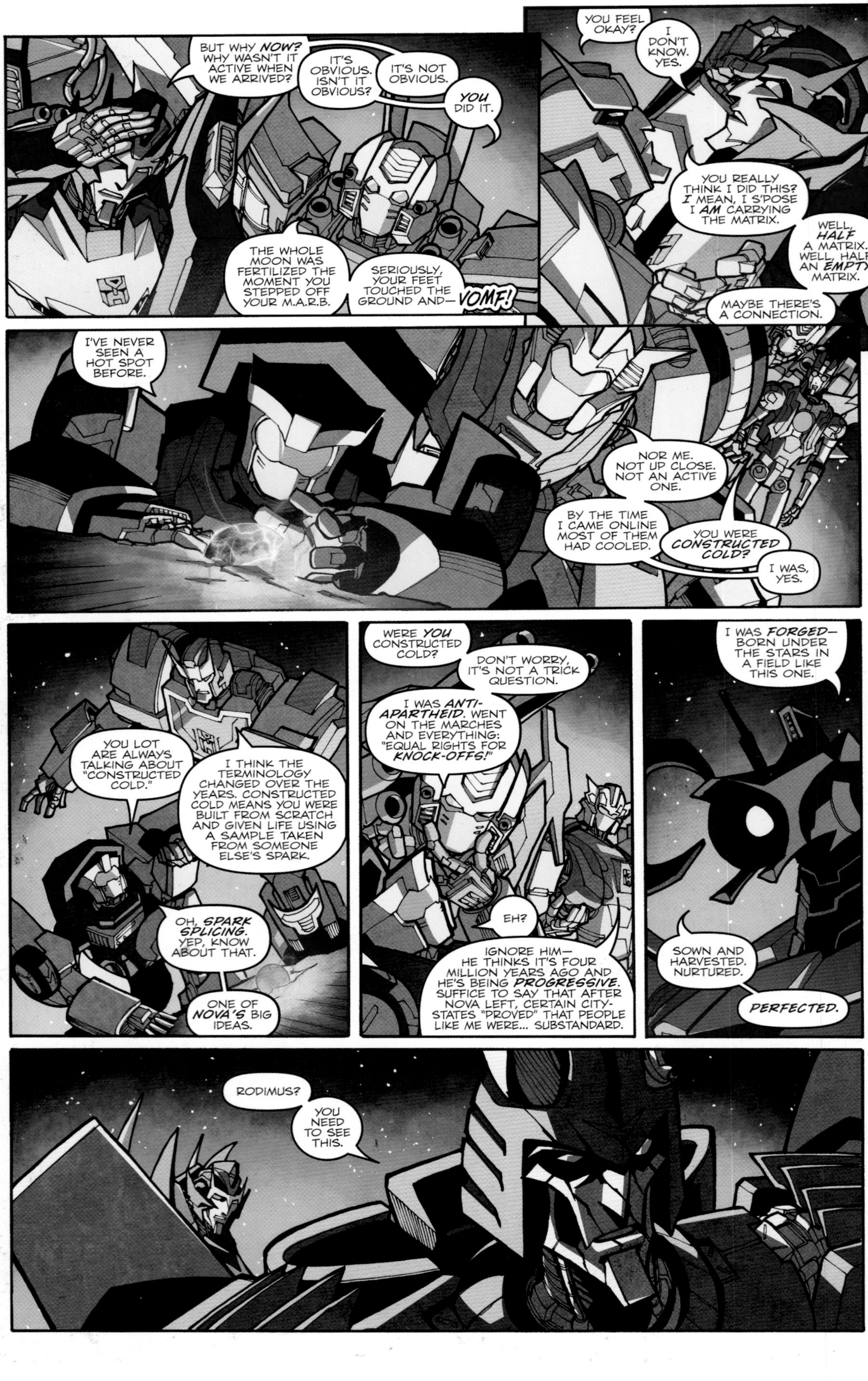

BUT WHY NOW? WHY WASN'T IT ACTIVE WHEN WE ARRIVED?
IT'S OBVIOUS. ISN'T IT OBVIOUS?
IT'S NOT OBVIOUS.
YOU DID IT.
THE WHOLE MOON WAS FERTILIZED THE MOMENT YOU STEPPED OFF YOUR M.A.R.B.
SERIOUSLY, YOUR FEET TOUCHED THE GROUND AND—VOMF!
YOU FEEL OKAY?
I DON'T KNOW. YES.
YOU REALLY THINK I DID THIS? I MEAN, I S'POSE I AM CARRYING THE MATRIX.
WELL, HALF A MATRIX. WELL, HALF AN EMPTY MATRIX.
MAYBE THERE'S A CONNECTION.
I'VE NEVER SEEN A HOT SPOT BEFORE.
NOR ME. NOT UP CLOSE. NOT AN ACTIVE ONE.
BY THE TIME I CAME ONLINE MOST OF THEM HAD COOLED.
YOU WERE CONSTRUCTED COLD?
I WAS, YES.
YOU LOT ARE ALWAYS TALKING ABOUT "CONSTRUCTED COLD."
I THINK THE TERMINOLOGY CHANGED OVER THE YEARS. CONSTRUCTED COLD MEANS YOU WERE BUILT FROM SCRATCH AND GIVEN LIFE USING A SAMPLE TAKEN FROM SOMEONE ELSE'S SPARK.
OH, SPARK SPLICING. YEP, KNOW ABOUT THAT.
ONE OF NOVA'S BIG IDEAS.
WERE YOU CONSTRUCTED COLD?
DON'T WORRY, IT'S NOT A TRICK QUESTION.
I WAS ANTI-APARTHEID. WENT ON THE MARCHES AND EVERYTHING: "EQUAL RIGHTS FOR KNOCK-OFFS!"
EH?
IGNORE HIM— HE THINKS IT'S FOUR MILLION YEARS AGO AND HE'S BEING PROGRESSIVE. SUFFICE TO SAY THAT AFTER NOVA LEFT, CERTAIN CITY-STATES "PROVED" THAT PEOPLE LIKE ME WERE... SUBSTANDARD.
I WAS FORGED— BORN UNDER THE STARS IN A FIELD LIKE THIS ONE.
SOWN AND HARVESTED. NURTURED.
PERFECTED.
RODIMUS?
YOU NEED TO SEE THIS.

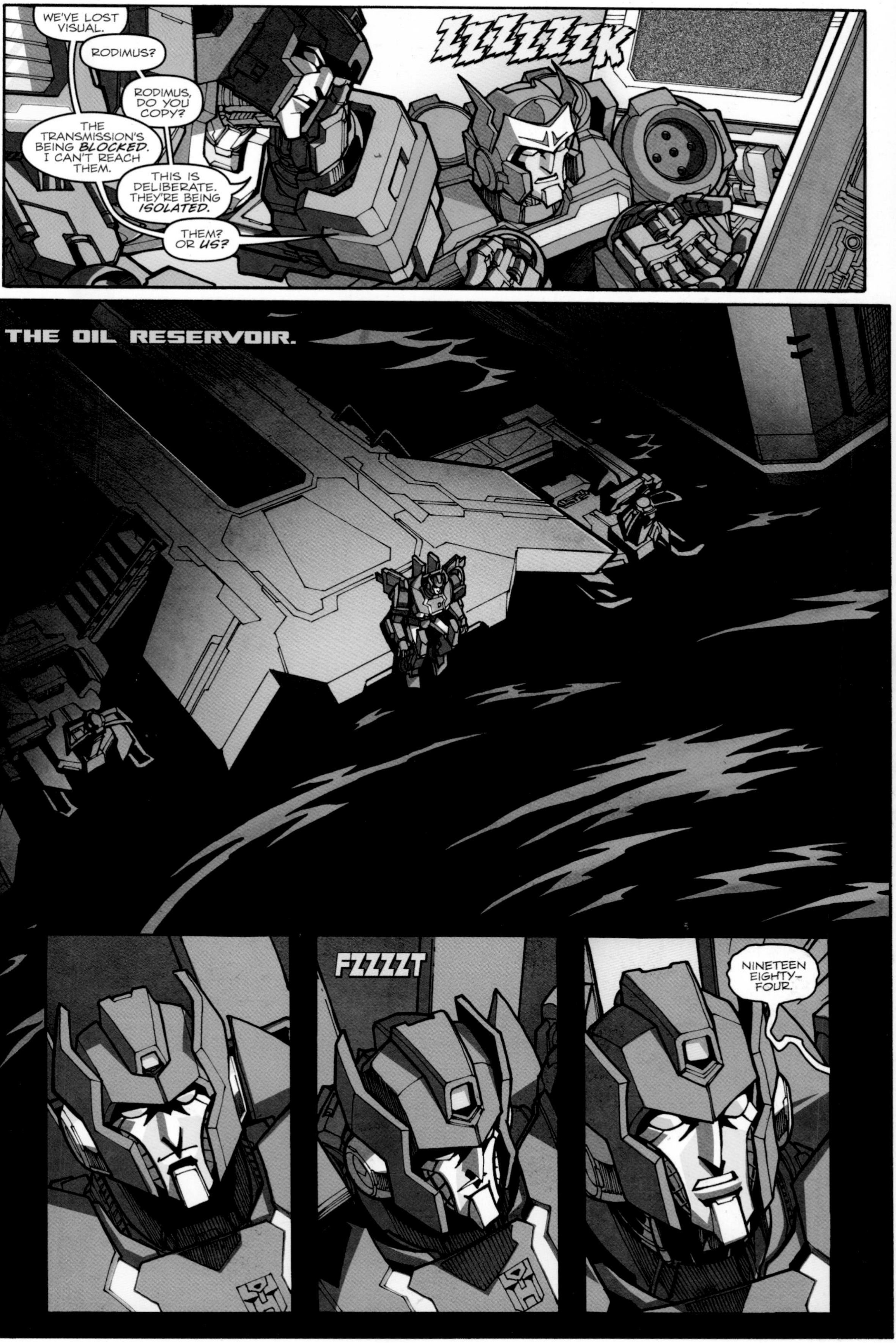
WE'VE LOST VISUAL.
RODIMUS?
RODIMUS, DO YOU COPY?
THE TRANSMISSION'S BEING BLOCKED. I CAN'T REACH THEM.
THIS IS DELIBERATE. THEY'RE BEING ISOLATED.
THEM? OR US?
ZZZZZZK
THE OIL RESERVOIR.
FZZZZT
NINETEEN EIGHTY-FOUR.

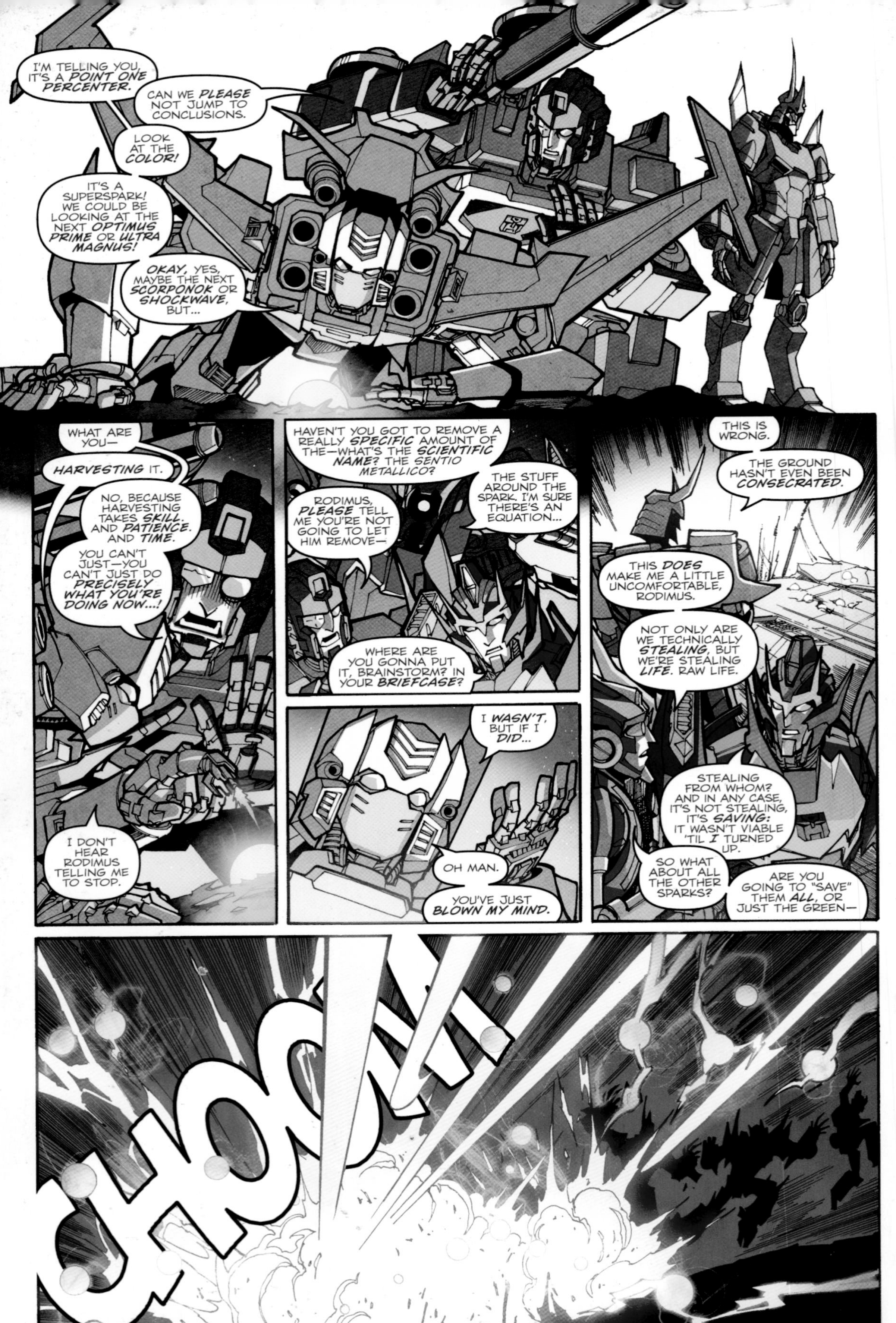
I'M TELLING YOU, IT'S A POINT ONE PERCENTER.
CAN WE PLEASE NOT JUMP TO CONCLUSIONS.
LOOK AT THE COLOR!
IT'S A SUPERSPARK! WE COULD BE LOOKING AT THE NEXT OPTIMUS PRIME OR ULTRA MAGNUS!
OKAY, YES, MAYBE THE NEXT SCORPONOK OR SHOCKWAVE, BUT...
WHAT ARE YOU—
HARVESTING IT.
NO, BECAUSE HARVESTING TAKES SKILL. AND PATIENCE. AND TIME.
YOU CAN'T JUST—YOU CAN'T JUST DO PRECISELY WHAT YOU'RE DOING NOW...!
I DON'T HEAR RODIMUS TELLING ME TO STOP.
HAVEN'T YOU GOT TO REMOVE A REALLY SPECIFIC AMOUNT OF THE—WHAT'S THE SCIENTIFIC NAME? THE SENTIO METALLICO?
THE STUFF AROUND THE SPARK. I'M SURE THERE'S AN EQUATION...
RODIMUS, PLEASE TELL ME YOU'RE NOT GOING TO LET HIM REMOVE—
WHERE ARE YOU GONNA PUT IT, BRAINSTORM? IN YOUR BRIEFCASE?
I WASN'T, BUT IF I DID...
OH MAN.
YOU'VE JUST BLOWN MY MIND.
THIS IS WRONG.
THE GROUND HASN'T EVEN BEEN CONSECRATED.
THIS DOES MAKE ME A LITTLE UNCOMFORTABLE, RODIMUS.
NOT ONLY ARE WE TECHNICALLY STEALING, BUT WE'RE STEALING LIFE. RAW LIFE.
STEALING FROM WHOM? AND IN ANY CASE, IT'S NOT STEALING, IT'S SAVING: IT WASN'T VIABLE 'TIL I TURNED UP.
SO WHAT ABOUT ALL THE OTHER SPARKS?
ARE YOU GOING TO "SAVE" THEM ALL, OR JUST THE GREEN—
CHOOM!

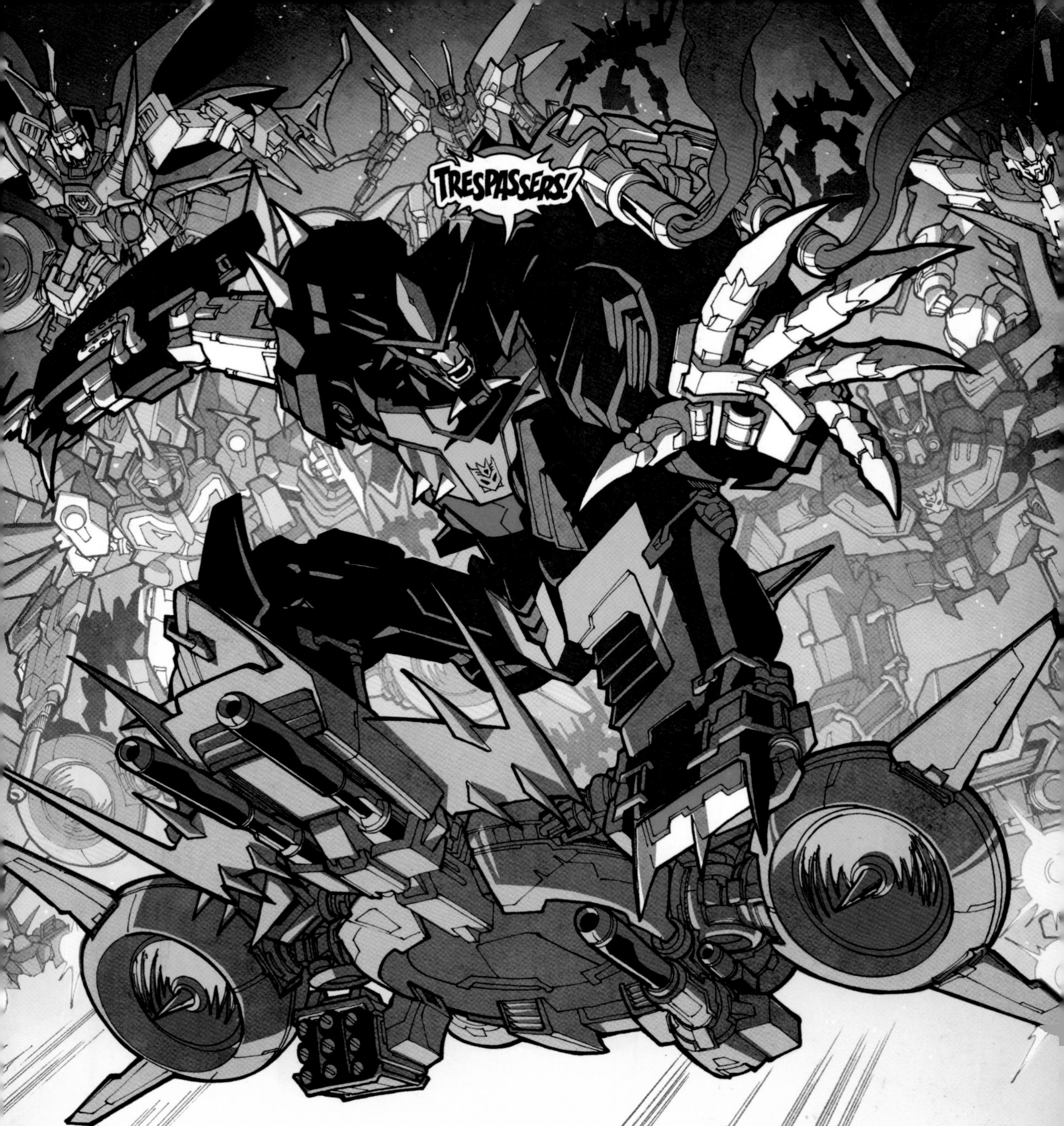
TRESPASSERS!

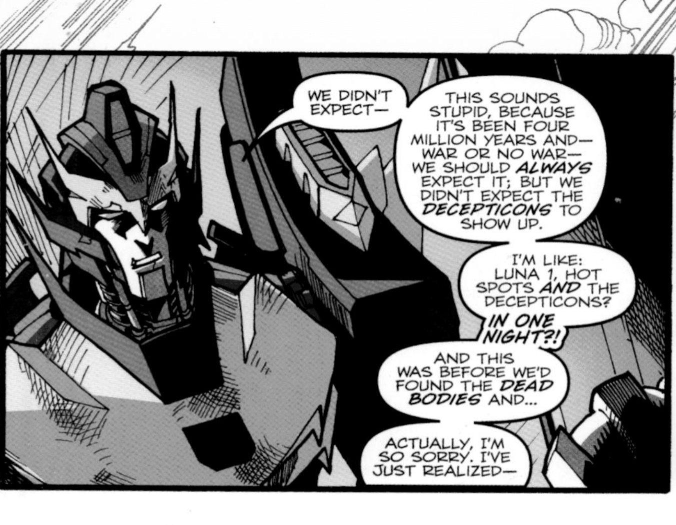
WE DIDN'T EXPECT—
THIS SOUNDS STUPID, BECAUSE IT'S BEEN FOUR MILLION YEARS AND—WAR OR NO WAR—WE SHOULD *ALWAYS* EXPECT IT; BUT WE DIDN'T EXPECT THE *DECEPTICONS* TO SHOW UP.
I'M LIKE: LUNA 1, HOT SPOTS *AND* THE DECEPTICONS? *IN ONE NIGHT?!*
AND THIS WAS BEFORE WE'D FOUND THE *DEAD BODIES* AND...
ACTUALLY, I'M SO SORRY. I'VE JUST REALIZED—

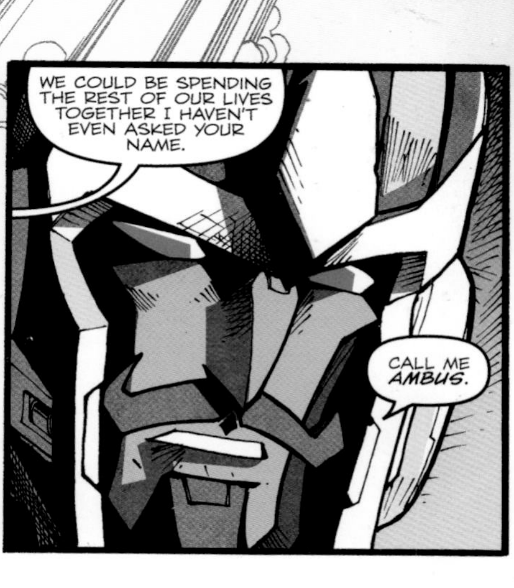
WE COULD BE SPENDING THE REST OF OUR LIVES TOGETHER I HAVEN'T EVEN ASKED YOUR NAME.
CALL ME *AMBUS*.

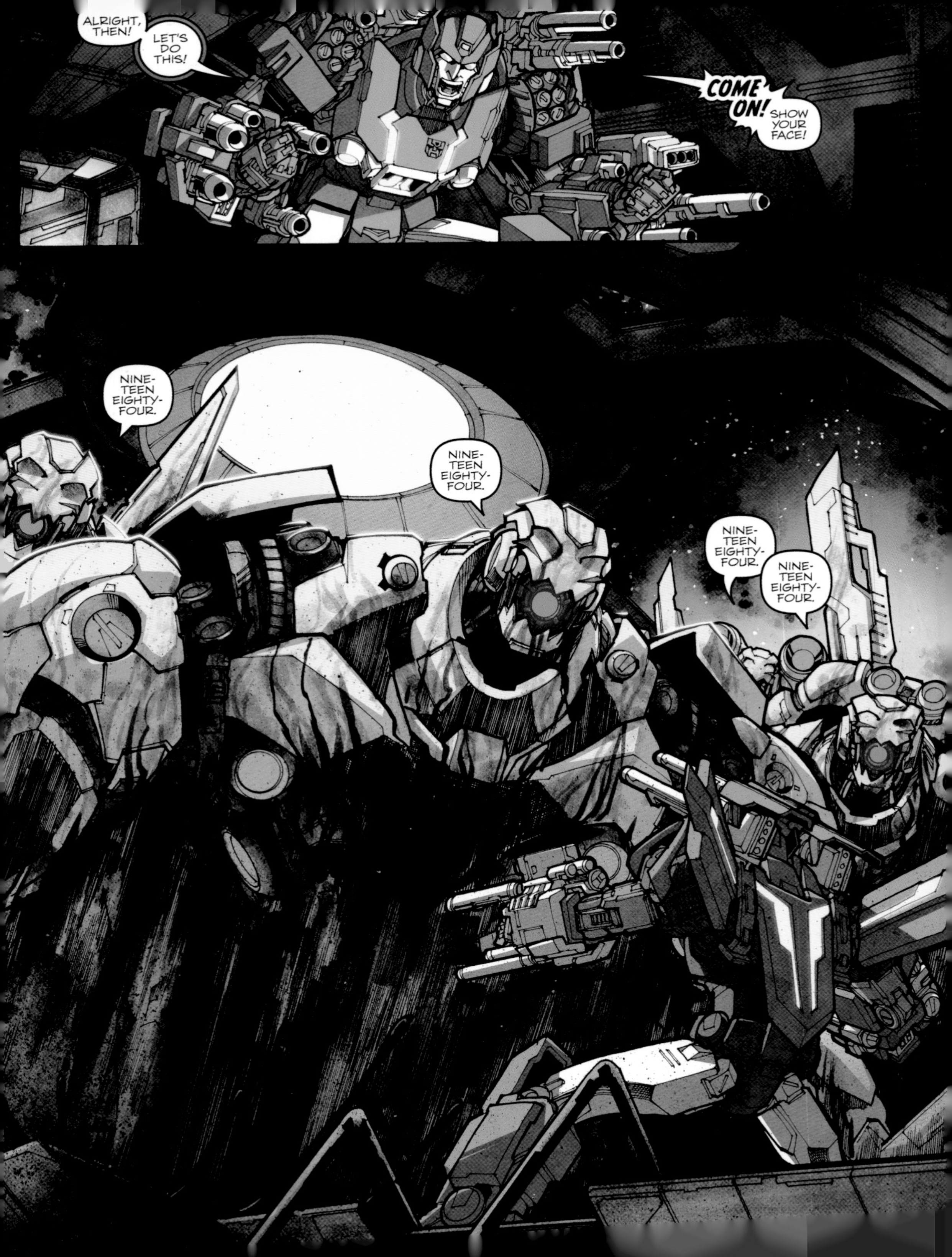
ALRIGHT, THEN!
LET'S DO THIS!
COME ON! SHOW YOUR FACE!
NINE-TEEN EIGHTY-FOUR.
NINE-TEEN EIGHTY-FOUR.
NINE-TEEN EIGHTY-FOUR.
NINE-TEEN EIGHTY-FOUR.

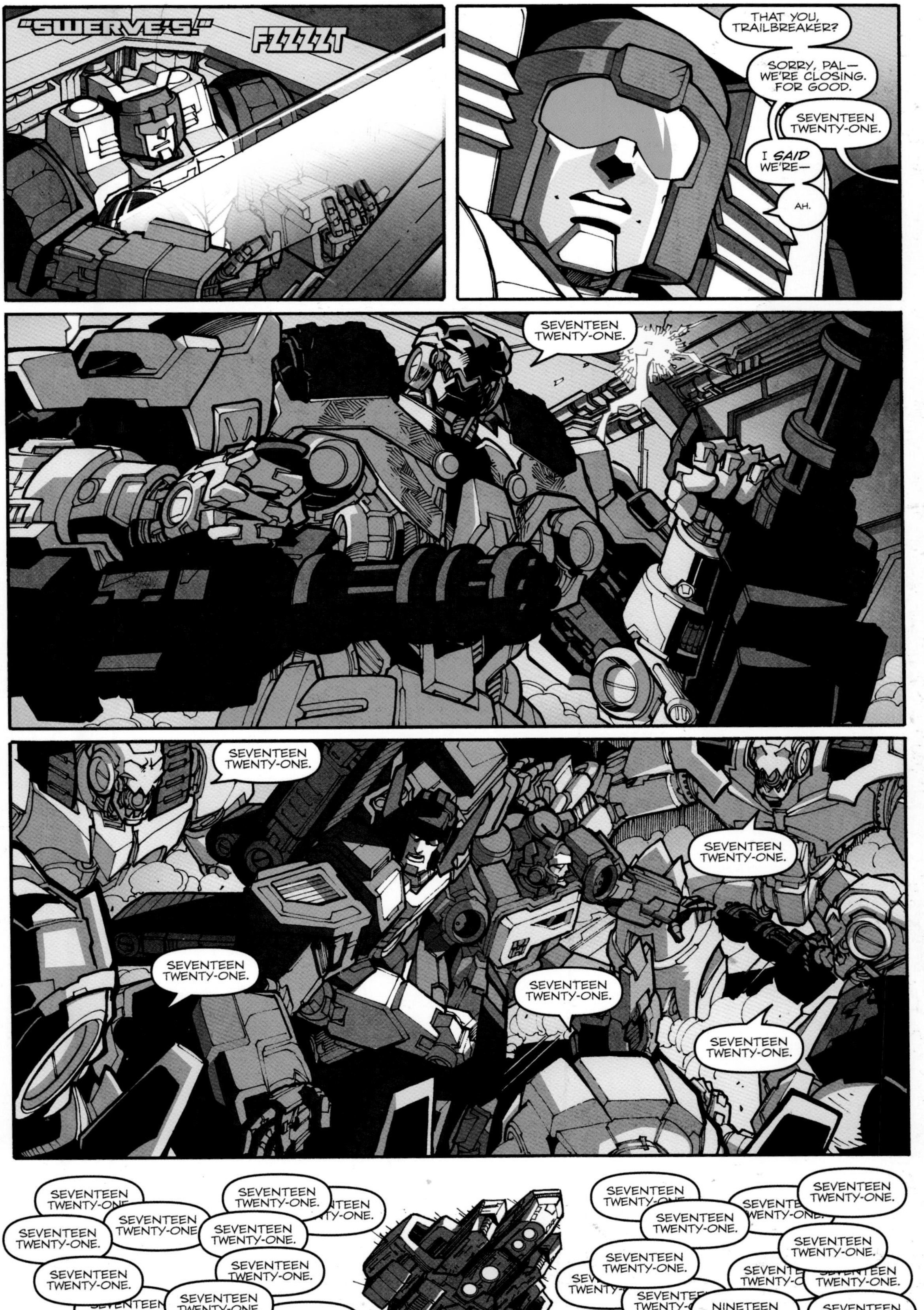
"SWERVE'S."
FZZZZT
THAT YOU, TRAILBREAKER?
SORRY, PAL— WE'RE CLOSING. FOR GOOD.
SEVENTEEN TWENTY-ONE.
I *SAID* WE'RE—
AH.
SEVENTEEN TWENTY-ONE.
SEVENTEEN TWENTY-ONE.
SEVENTEEN TWENTY-ONE.
SEVENTEEN TWENTY-ONE.
SEVENTEEN TWENTY-ONE.
SEVENTEEN TWENTY-ONE.
SEVENTEEN TWENTY-ONE.
SEVENTEEN TWENTY-ONE.
SEVENTEEN TWENTY-ONE.
SEVENTEEN TWENTY-ONE.
SEVENTEEN TWENTY-ONE.
SEVENTEEN TWENTY-ONE.
SEVENTEEN TWENTY-ONE.
SEVENTEEN TWENTY-ONE.
SEVENTEEN TWENTY-ONE.
SEVENTEEN TWENTY-ONE.
SEVENTEEN TWENTY-ONE.
SEVENTEEN TWENTY-ONE.
NINETEEN EIGHTY-FOUR.
SEVENTEEN TWENTY-ONE.
SEVENTEEN TWENTY-ONE.

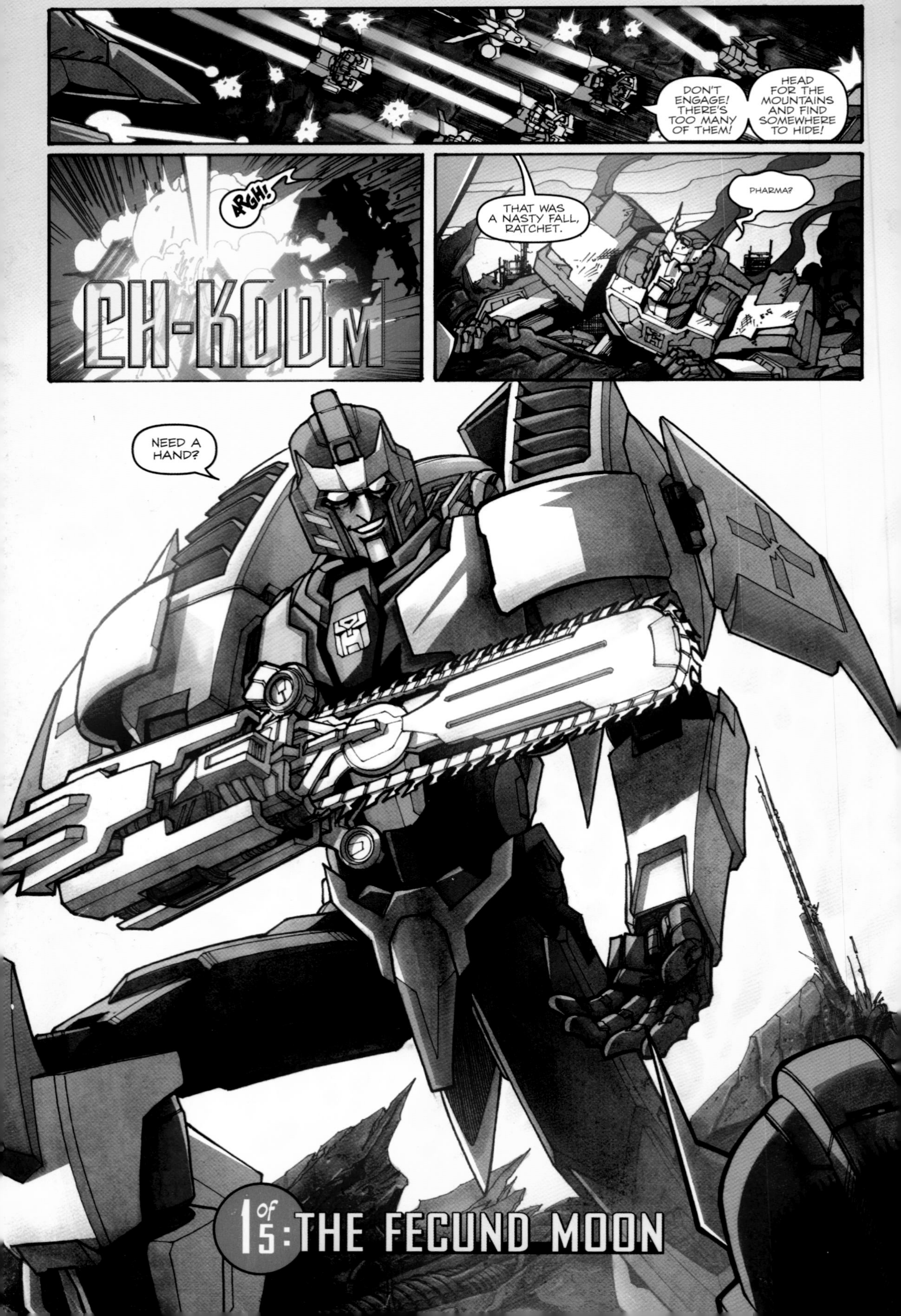
DON'T ENGAGE! THERE'S TOO MANY OF THEM!
HEAD FOR THE MOUNTAINS AND FIND SOMEWHERE TO HIDE!
ARGH!
CH-KOOM
THAT WAS A NASTY FALL, RATCHET.
PHARMA?
NEED A HAND?
1 of 5: THE FECUND MOON

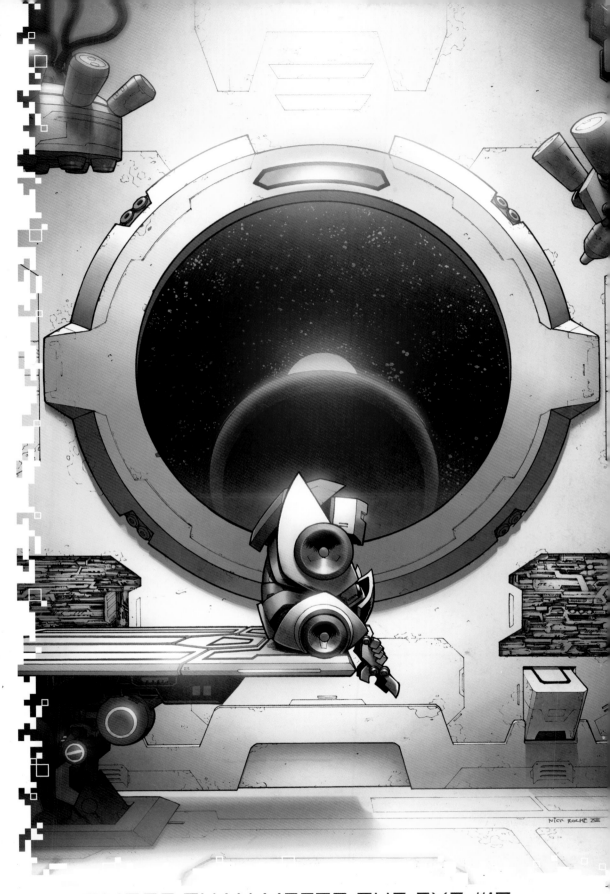

□MORE THAN MEETS THE EYE #17 COVER RI
by **NICK ROCHE** Colors by **JOSH PEREZ**

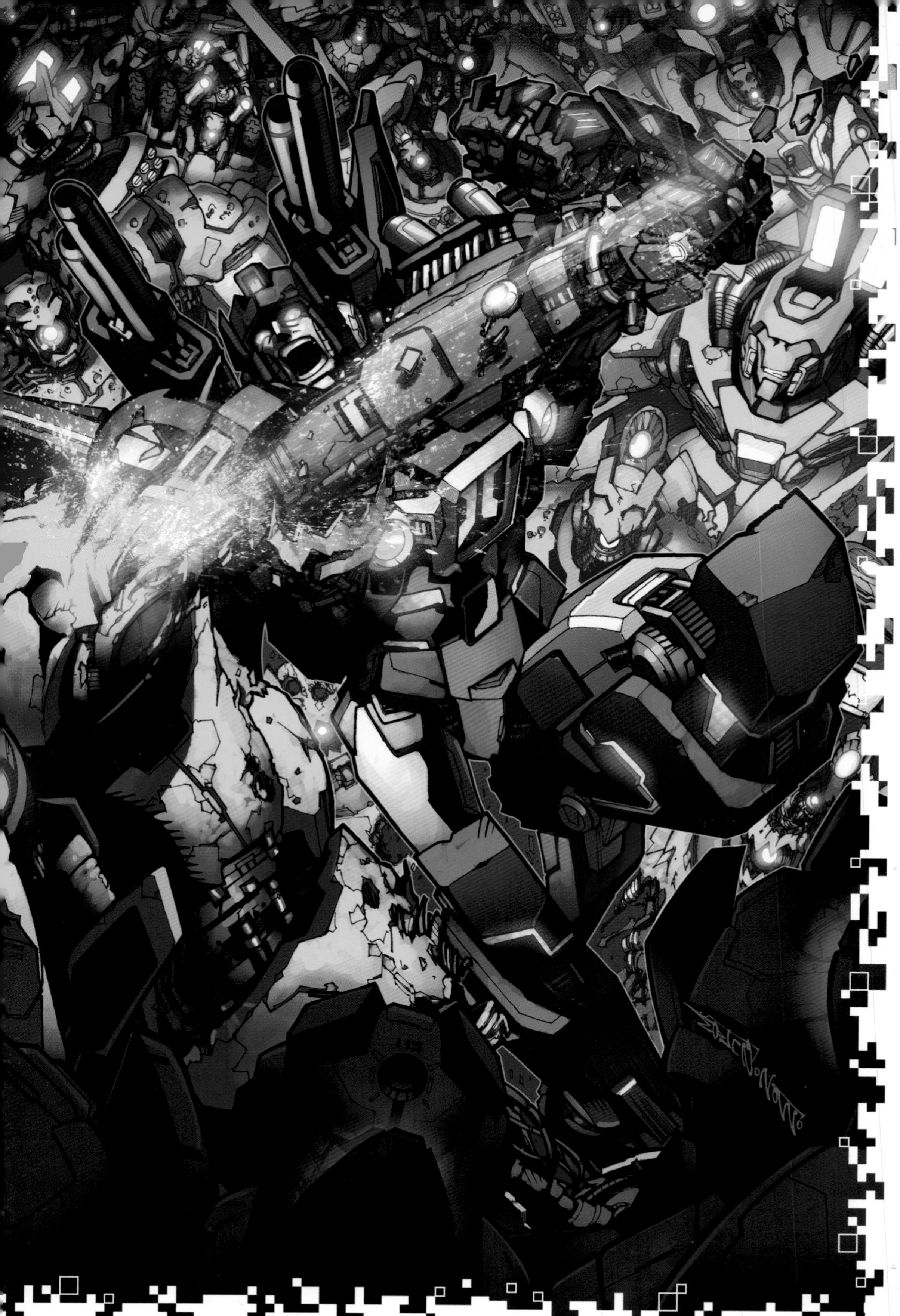

MORE THAN MEETS THE EYE #18 COVER A

by **ALEX MILNE** Colors by **JOSH PEREZ**

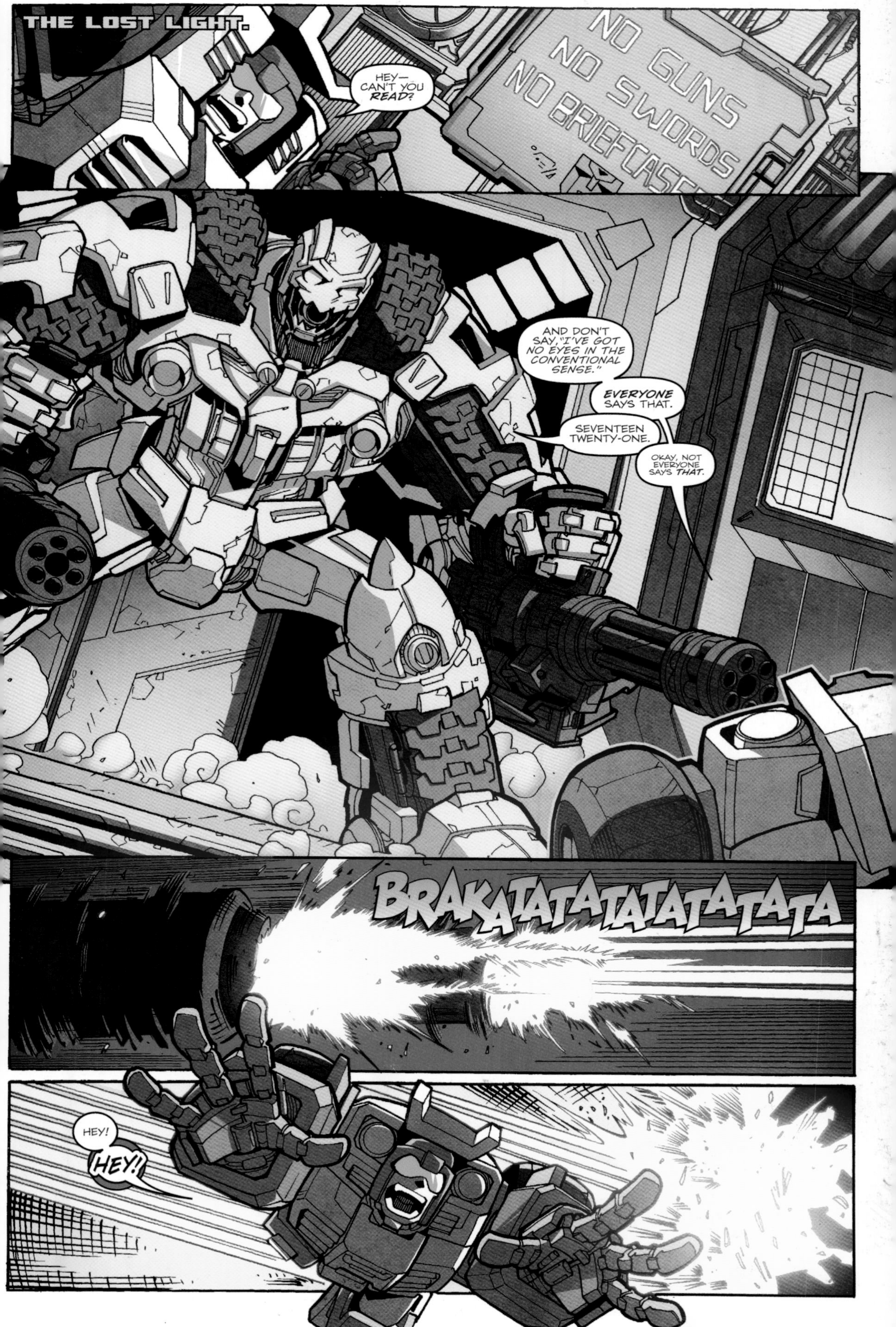
THE LOST LIGHT.
HEY— CAN'T YOU READ?
NO GUNS
NO SWORDS
NO BRIEFCASES
AND DON'T SAY, "I'VE GOT NO EYES IN THE CONVENTIONAL SENSE."
EVERYONE SAYS THAT.
SEVENTEEN TWENTY-ONE.
OKAY, NOT EVERYONE SAYS THAT.
BRAKATATATATATATATATA
HEY!
HEY!

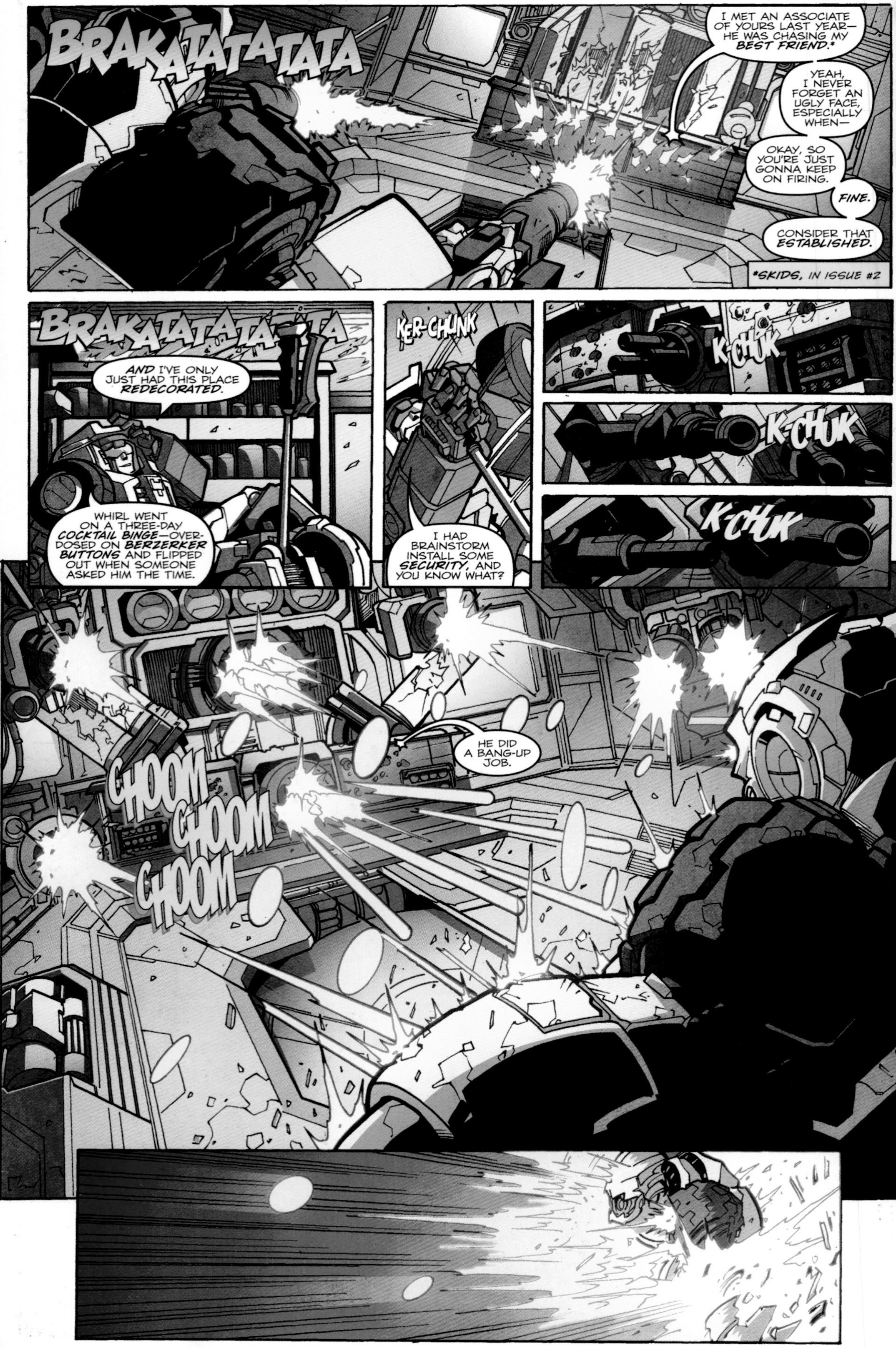
BRAKATATATATA
I MET AN ASSOCIATE OF YOURS LAST YEAR—HE WAS CHASING MY BEST FRIEND.*
YEAH, I NEVER FORGET AN UGLY FACE, ESPECIALLY WHEN—
OKAY, SO YOU'RE JUST GONNA KEEP ON FIRING.
FINE.
CONSIDER THAT ESTABLISHED.
*SKIDS, IN ISSUE #2
BRAKATATATATATA
AND I'VE ONLY JUST HAD THIS PLACE REDECORATED.
WHIRL WENT ON A THREE-DAY COCKTAIL BINGE—OVERDOSED ON BERZERKER BUTTONS AND FLIPPED OUT WHEN SOMEONE ASKED HIM THE TIME.
KER-CHUNK
I HAD BRAINSTORM INSTALL SOME SECURITY, AND YOU KNOW WHAT?
K-CHUK
K-CHUK
K-CHUK
HE DID A BANG-UP JOB.
CHOOM
CHOOM
CHOOM

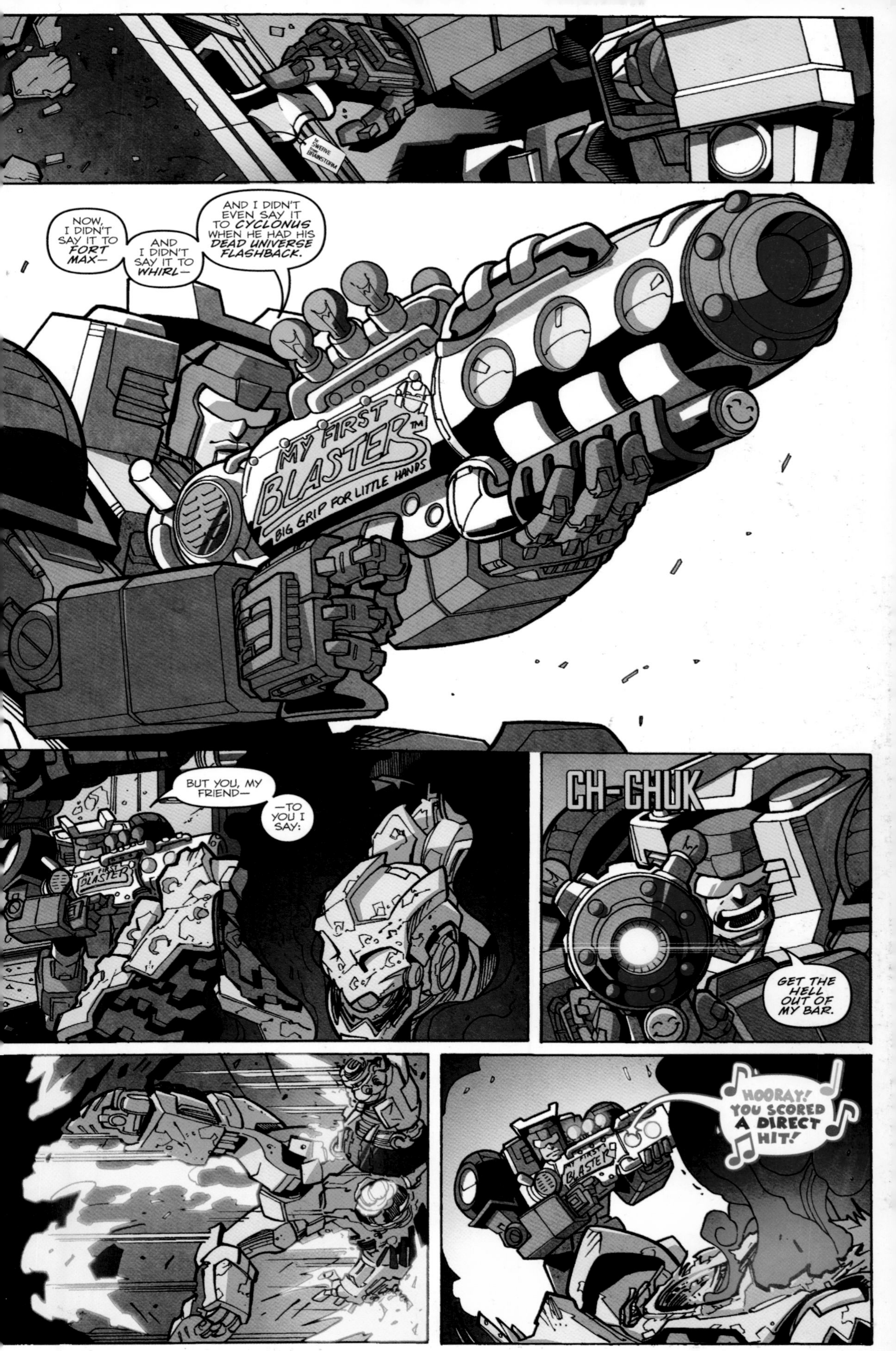

to: SWERVE from: BRAINSTORM
NOW, I DIDN'T SAY IT TO *FORT MAX*—
AND I DIDN'T SAY IT TO *WHIRL*—
AND I DIDN'T EVEN SAY IT TO *CYCLONUS* WHEN HE HAD HIS *DEAD UNIVERSE FLASHBACK*.
MY FIRST BLASTER™
BIG GRIP FOR LITTLE HANDS
BUT YOU, MY FRIEND—
—TO YOU I SAY:
CH-CHUK
GET THE HELL OUT OF MY BAR.
MY FIRST BLASTER
HOORAY! YOU SCORED A DIRECT HIT!

REMAIN IN LIGHT 2 of 5: HOUSE OF AMBUS

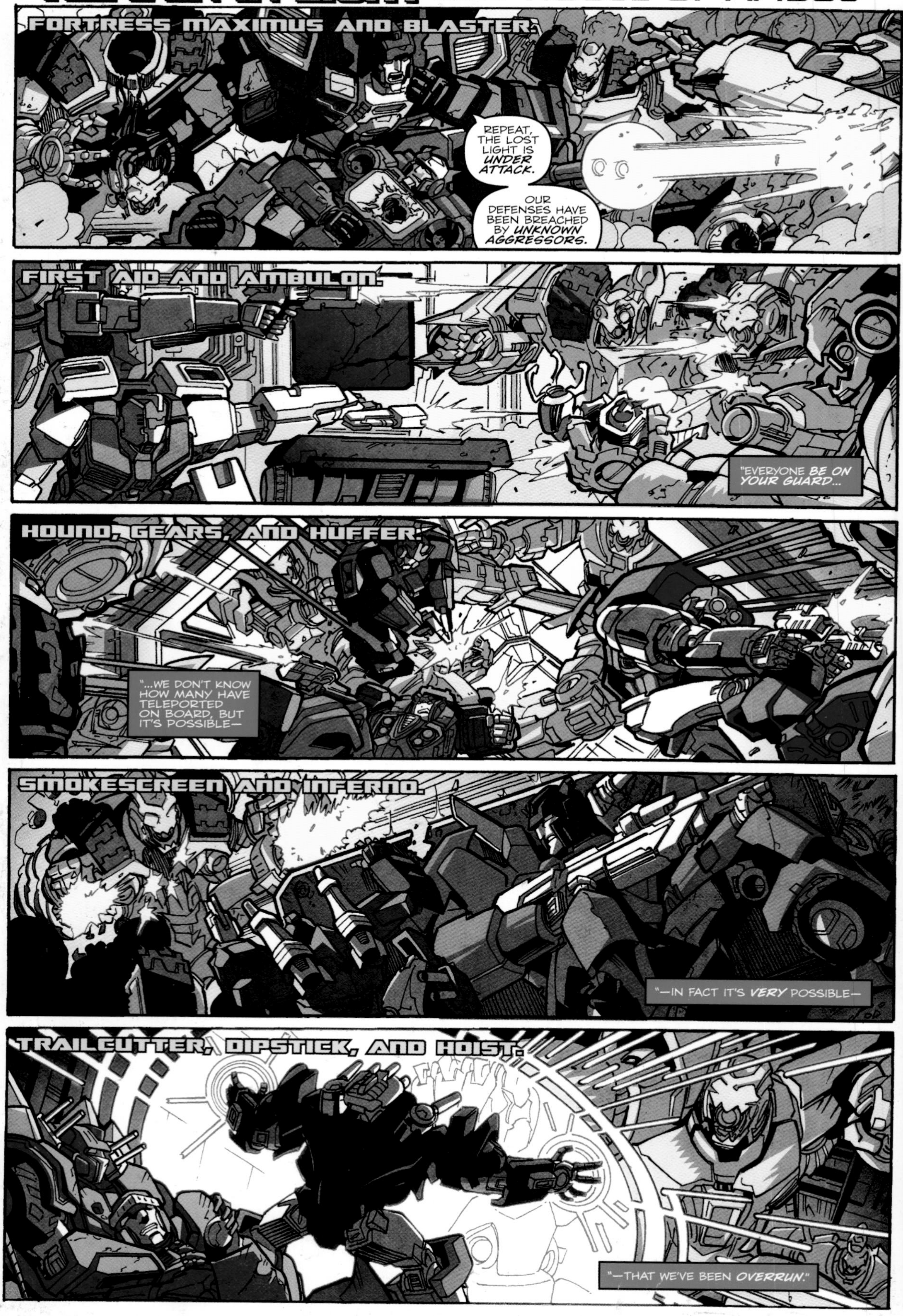
FORTRESS MAXIMUS AND BLASTER.
REPEAT, THE LOST LIGHT IS UNDER ATTACK.
OUR DEFENSES HAVE BEEN BREACHED BY UNKNOWN AGGRESSORS.
FIRST AID AND AMBULON.
"EVERYONE BE ON YOUR GUARD...
HOUND, GEARS, AND HUFFER.
"...WE DON'T KNOW HOW MANY HAVE TELEPORTED ON BOARD, BUT IT'S POSSIBLE—
SMOKESCREEN AND INFERNO.
"—IN FACT IT'S VERY POSSIBLE—
TRAILCUTTER, DIPSTICK, AND HOIST.
"—THAT WE'VE BEEN OVERRUN."

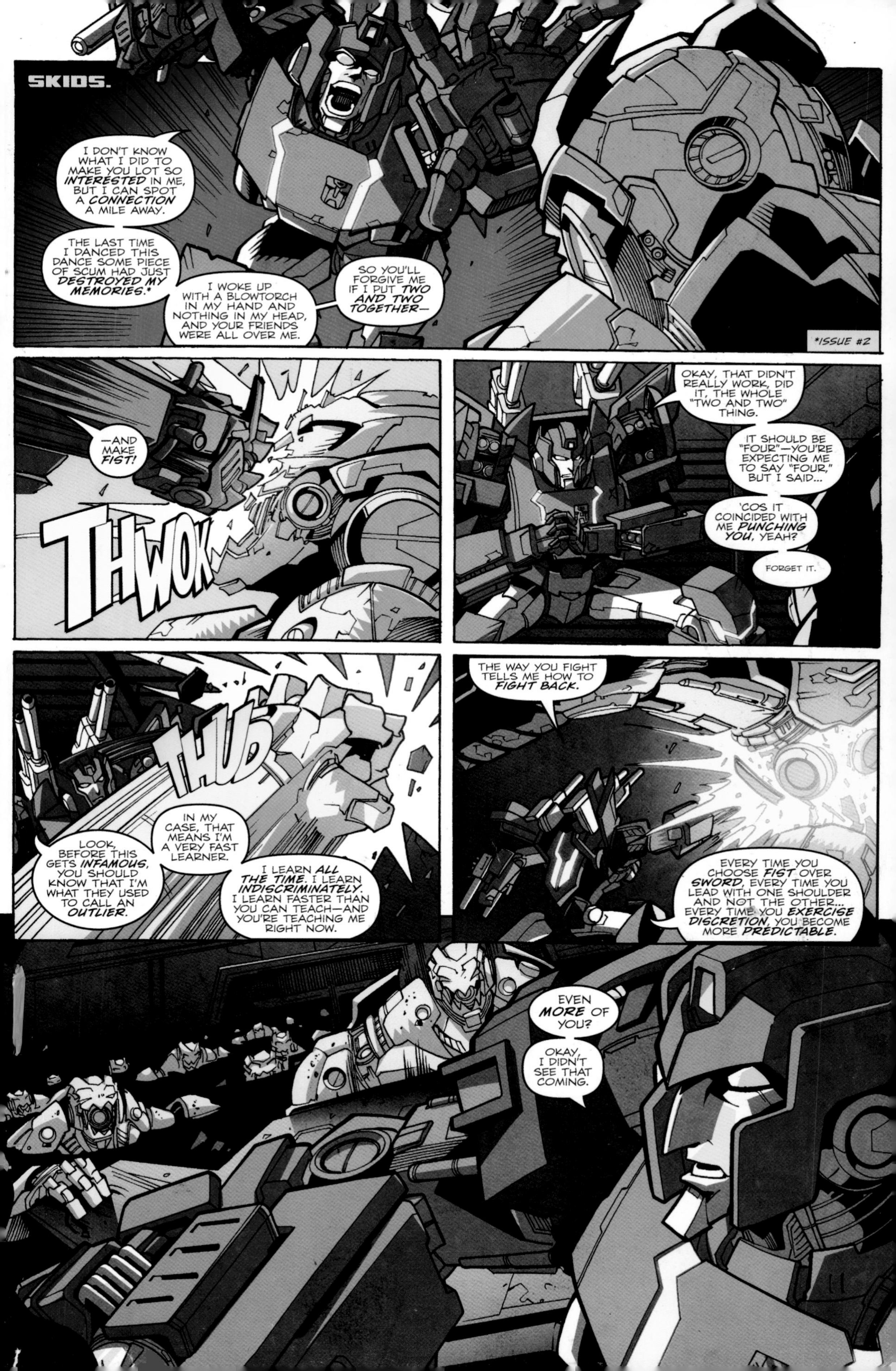
SKIDS.
I DON'T KNOW WHAT I DID TO MAKE YOU LOT SO INTERESTED IN ME, BUT I CAN SPOT A CONNECTION A MILE AWAY.
THE LAST TIME I DANCED THIS DANCE SOME PIECE OF SCUM HAD JUST DESTROYED MY MEMORIES.*
I WOKE UP WITH A BLOWTORCH IN MY HAND AND NOTHING IN MY HEAD, AND YOUR FRIENDS WERE ALL OVER ME.
SO YOU'LL FORGIVE ME IF I PUT TWO AND TWO TOGETHER—
*ISSUE #2
—AND MAKE FIST!
THWOK
OKAY, THAT DIDN'T REALLY WORK, DID IT, THE WHOLE "TWO AND TWO" THING.
IT SHOULD BE "FOUR"—YOU'RE EXPECTING ME TO SAY "FOUR," BUT I SAID...
'COS IT COINCIDED WITH ME PUNCHING YOU, YEAH?
FORGET IT.
THUD
LOOK, BEFORE THIS GETS INFAMOUS, YOU SHOULD KNOW THAT I'M WHAT THEY USED TO CALL AN OUTLIER.
IN MY CASE, THAT MEANS I'M A VERY FAST LEARNER.
I LEARN ALL THE TIME. I LEARN INDISCRIMINATELY. I LEARN FASTER THAN YOU CAN TEACH—AND YOU'RE TEACHING ME RIGHT NOW.
THE WAY YOU FIGHT TELLS ME HOW TO FIGHT BACK.
EVERY TIME YOU CHOOSE FIST OVER SWORD, EVERY TIME YOU LEAD WITH ONE SHOULDER AND NOT THE OTHER... EVERY TIME YOU EXERCISE DISCRETION, YOU BECOME MORE PREDICTABLE.
EVEN MORE OF YOU?
OKAY, I DIDN'T SEE THAT COMING.

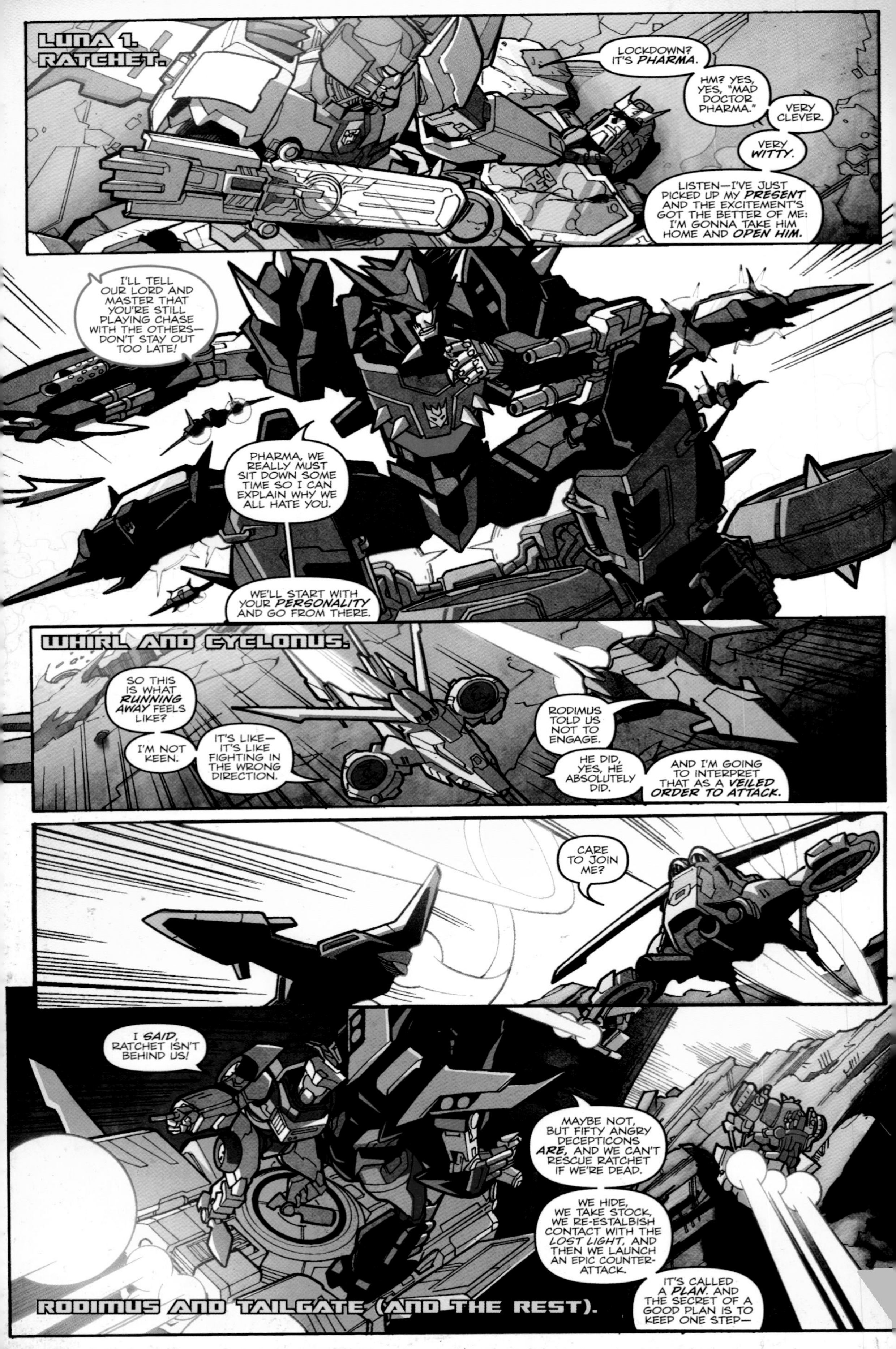
LUNA 1. RATCHET.
LOCKDOWN? IT'S PHARMA.
HM? YES, YES, "MAD DOCTOR PHARMA."
VERY CLEVER.
VERY WITTY.
LISTEN—I'VE JUST PICKED UP MY PRESENT AND THE EXCITEMENT'S GOT THE BETTER OF ME: I'M GONNA TAKE HIM HOME AND OPEN HIM.
I'LL TELL OUR LORD AND MASTER THAT YOU'RE STILL PLAYING CHASE WITH THE OTHERS—DON'T STAY OUT TOO LATE!
PHARMA, WE REALLY MUST SIT DOWN SOME TIME SO I CAN EXPLAIN WHY WE ALL HATE YOU.
WE'LL START WITH YOUR PERSONALITY AND GO FROM THERE.
WHIRL AND CYCLONUS.
SO THIS IS WHAT RUNNING AWAY FEELS LIKE?
I'M NOT KEEN.
IT'S LIKE—IT'S LIKE FIGHTING IN THE WRONG DIRECTION.
RODIMUS TOLD US NOT TO ENGAGE.
HE DID, YES, HE ABSOLUTELY DID.
AND I'M GOING TO INTERPRET THAT AS A VEILED ORDER TO ATTACK.
CARE TO JOIN ME?
I SAID, RATCHET ISN'T BEHIND US!
MAYBE NOT, BUT FIFTY ANGRY DECEPTICONS ARE, AND WE CAN'T RESCUE RATCHET IF WE'RE DEAD.
WE HIDE, WE TAKE STOCK, WE RE-ESTALBISH CONTACT WITH THE LOST LIGHT, AND THEN WE LAUNCH AN EPIC COUNTER-ATTACK.
IT'S CALLED A PLAN. AND THE SECRET OF A GOOD PLAN IS TO KEEP ONE STEP—
RODIMUS AND TAILGATE (AND THE REST).

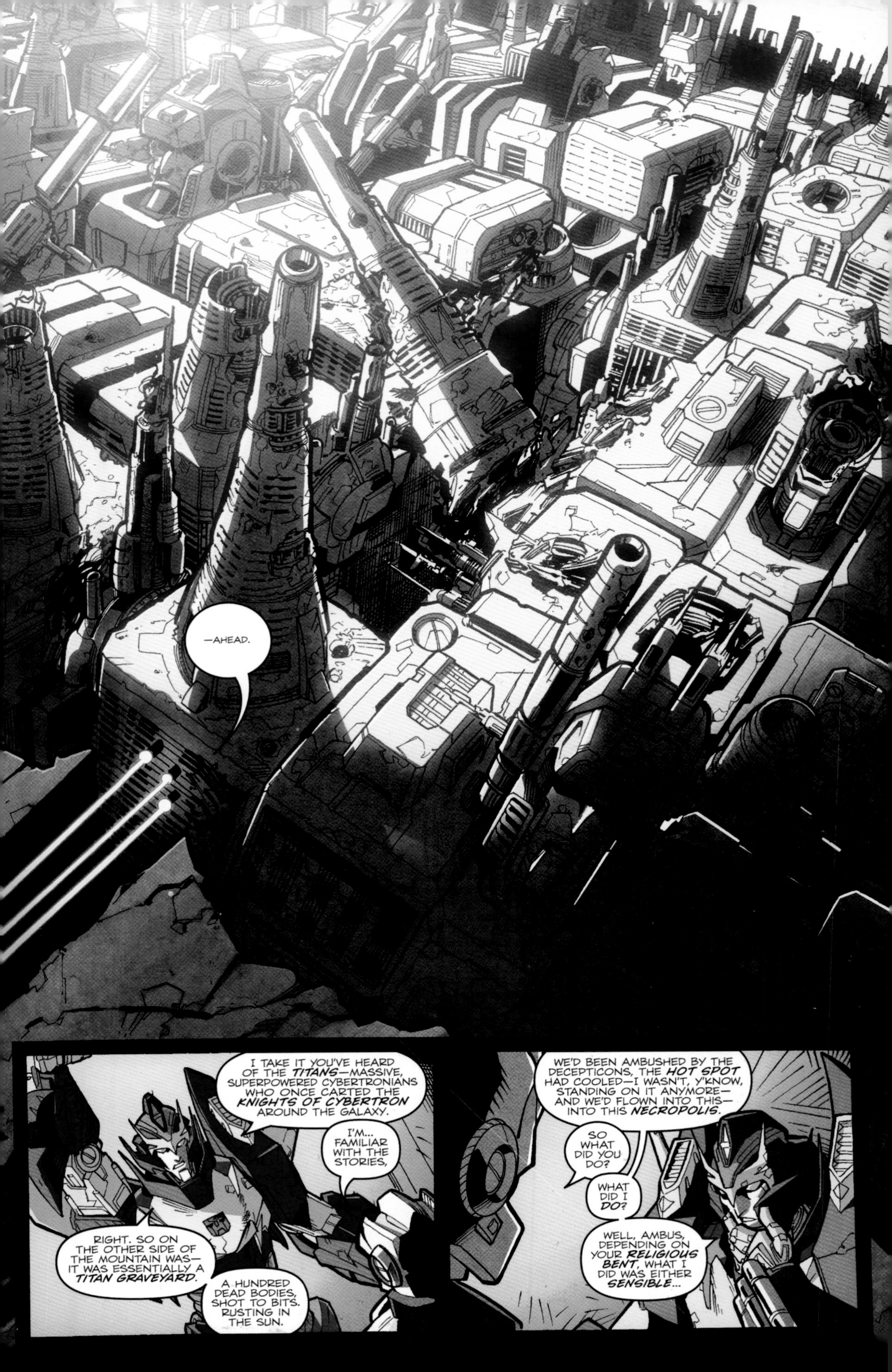
—AHEAD.
I TAKE IT YOU'VE HEARD OF THE TITANS—MASSIVE, SUPERPOWERED CYBERTRONIANS WHO ONCE CARTED THE KNIGHTS OF CYBERTRON AROUND THE GALAXY.
I'M... FAMILIAR WITH THE STORIES.
RIGHT. SO ON THE OTHER SIDE OF THE MOUNTAIN WAS— IT WAS ESSENTIALLY A TITAN GRAVEYARD.
A HUNDRED DEAD BODIES, SHOT TO BITS. RUSTING IN THE SUN.
WE'D BEEN AMBUSHED BY THE DECEPTICONS, THE HOT SPOT HAD COOLED—I WASN'T, Y'KNOW, STANDING ON IT ANYMORE— AND WE'D FLOWN INTO THIS— INTO THIS NECROPOLIS.
SO WHAT DID YOU DO?
WHAT DID I DO?
WELL, AMBUS, DEPENDING ON YOUR RELIGIOUS BENT, WHAT I DID WAS EITHER SENSIBLE...

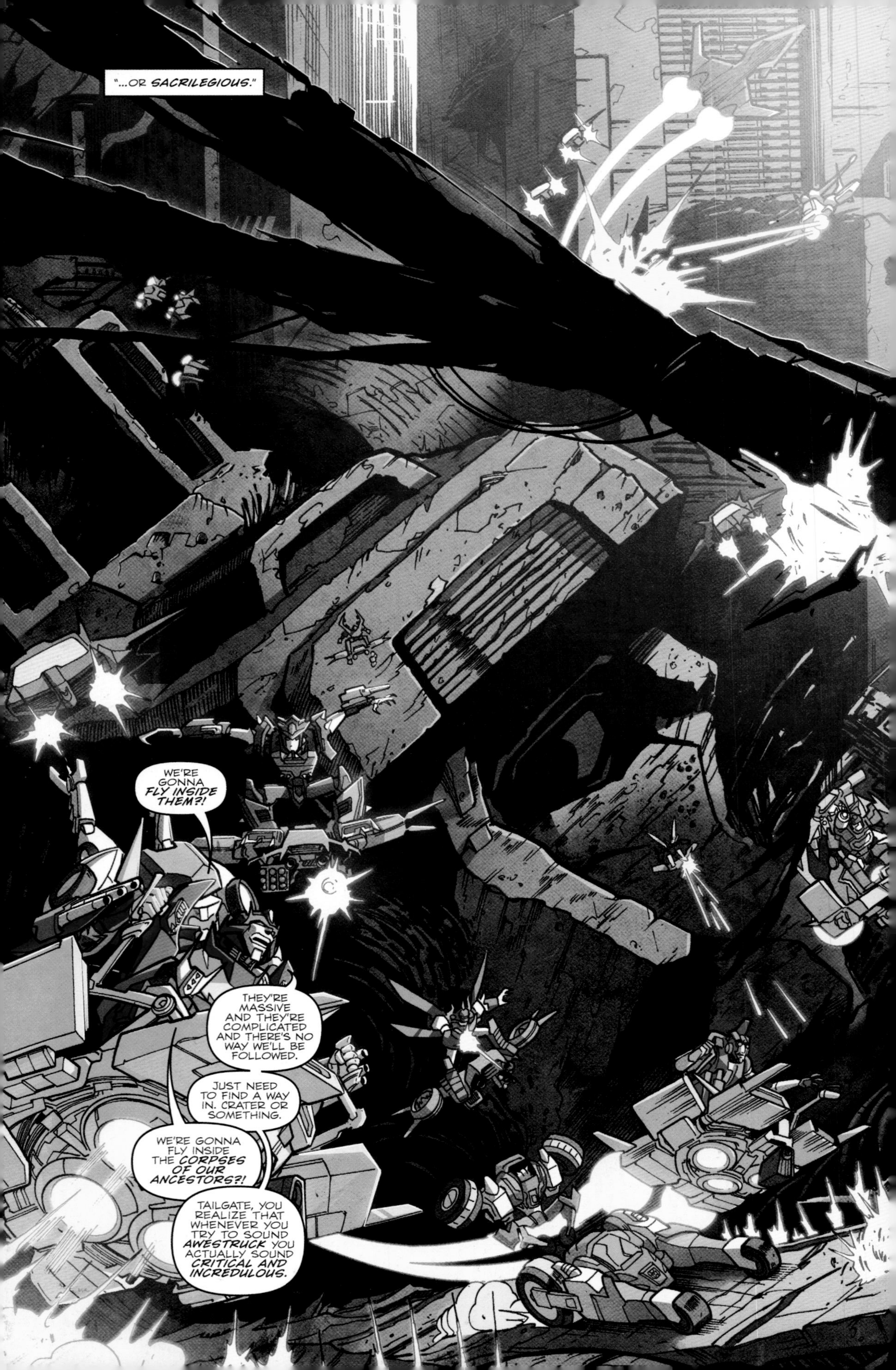
"...OR SACRILEGIOUS."
WE'RE GONNA FLY INSIDE THEM?!
THEY'RE MASSIVE AND THEY'RE COMPLICATED AND THERE'S NO WAY WE'LL BE FOLLOWED.
JUST NEED TO FIND A WAY IN. CRATER OR SOMETHING.
WE'RE GONNA FLY INSIDE THE CORPSES OF OUR ANCESTORS?!
TAILGATE, YOU REALIZE THAT WHENEVER YOU TRY TO SOUND AWESTRUCK YOU ACTUALLY SOUND CRITICAL AND INCREDULOUS.

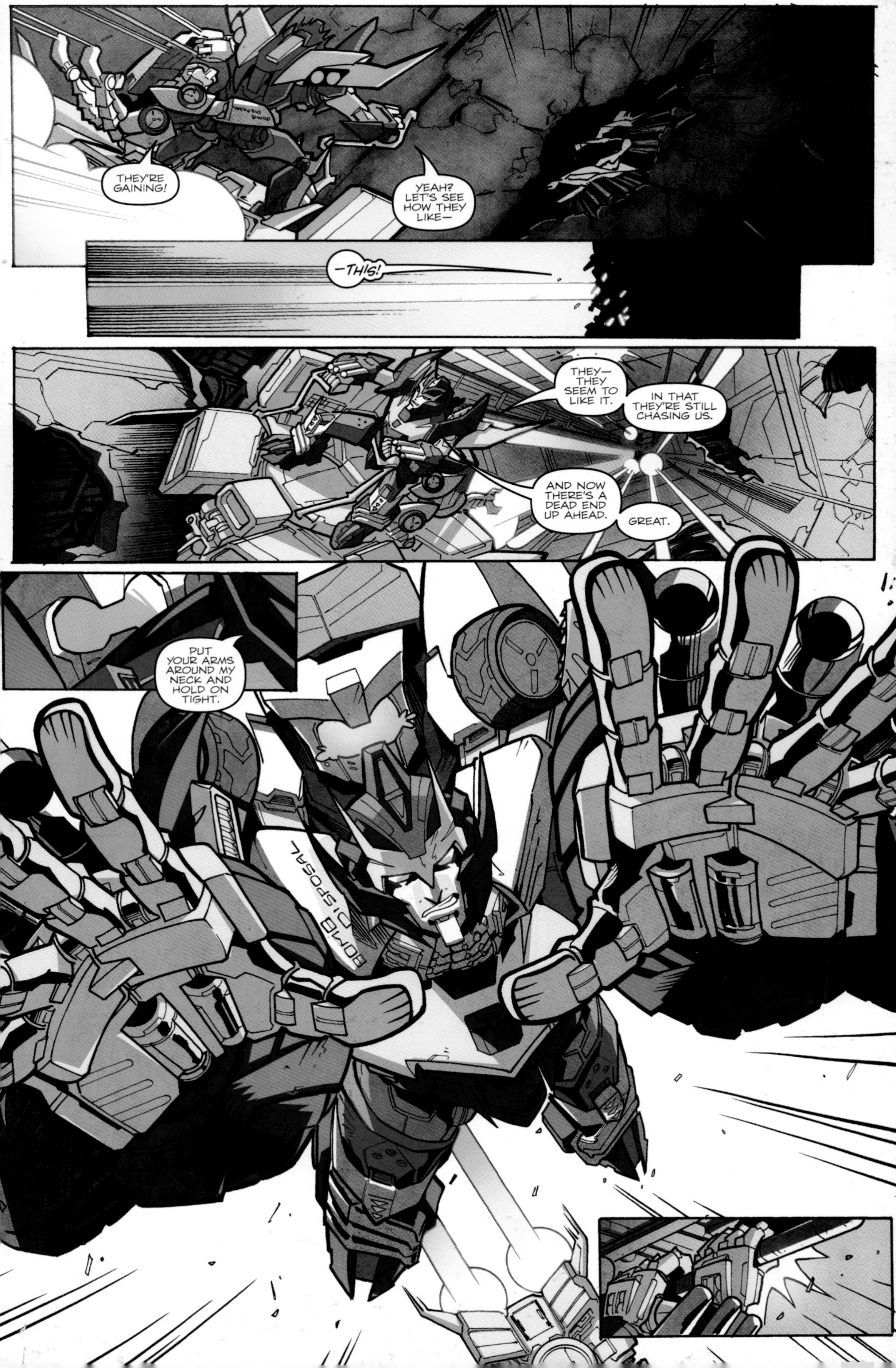
THEY'RE GAINING!
YEAH? LET'S SEE HOW THEY LIKE—
—THIS!
THEY— THEY SEEM TO LIKE IT.
IN THAT THEY'RE STILL CHASING US.
AND NOW THERE'S A DEAD END UP AHEAD.
GREAT.
PUT YOUR ARMS AROUND MY NECK AND HOLD ON TIGHT.
BOMB DISPOSAL

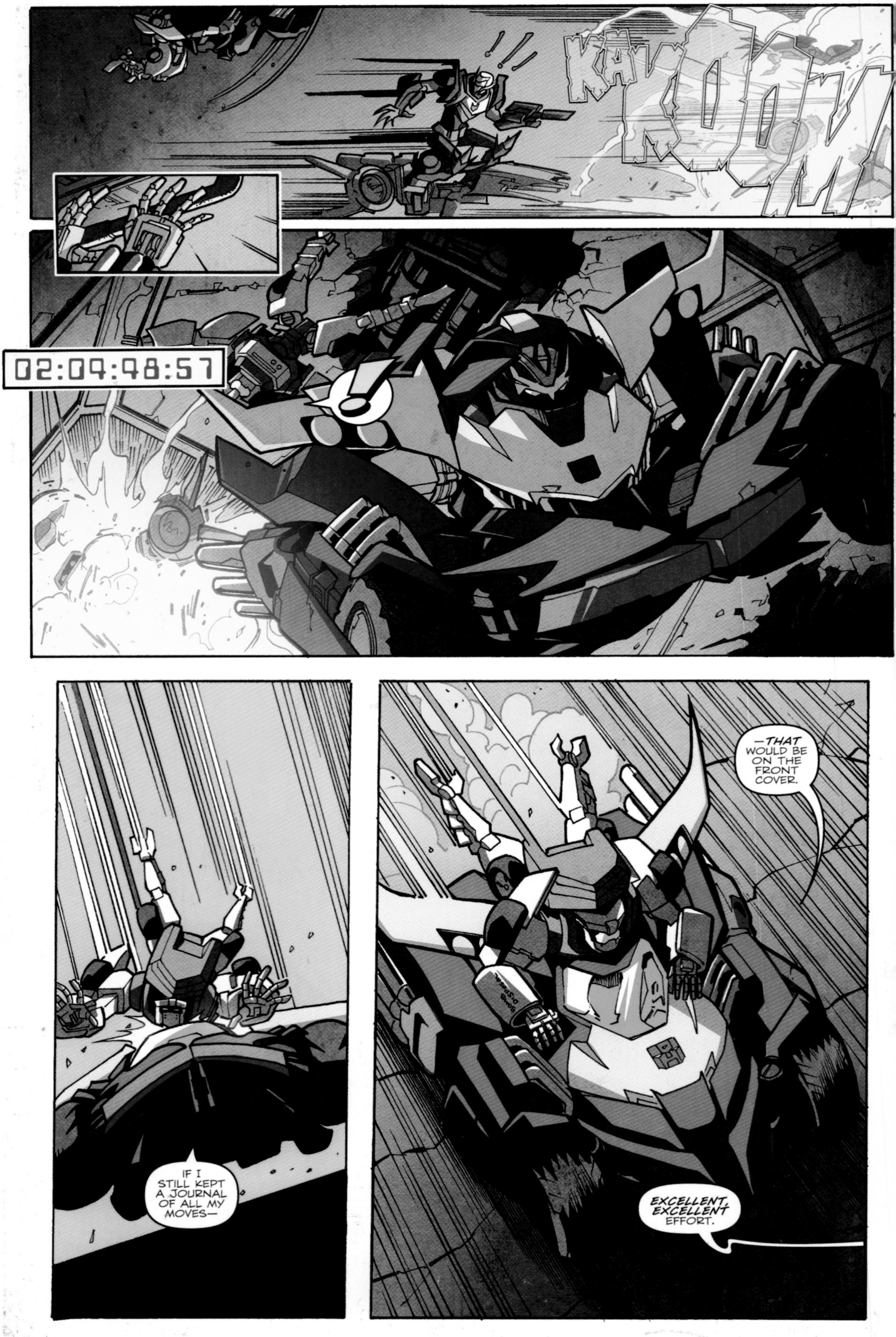
!!
02:09:48:57
IF I STILL KEPT A JOURNAL OF ALL MY MOVES—
—*THAT* WOULD BE ON THE FRONT COVER.
EXCELLENT, EXCELLENT EFFORT.

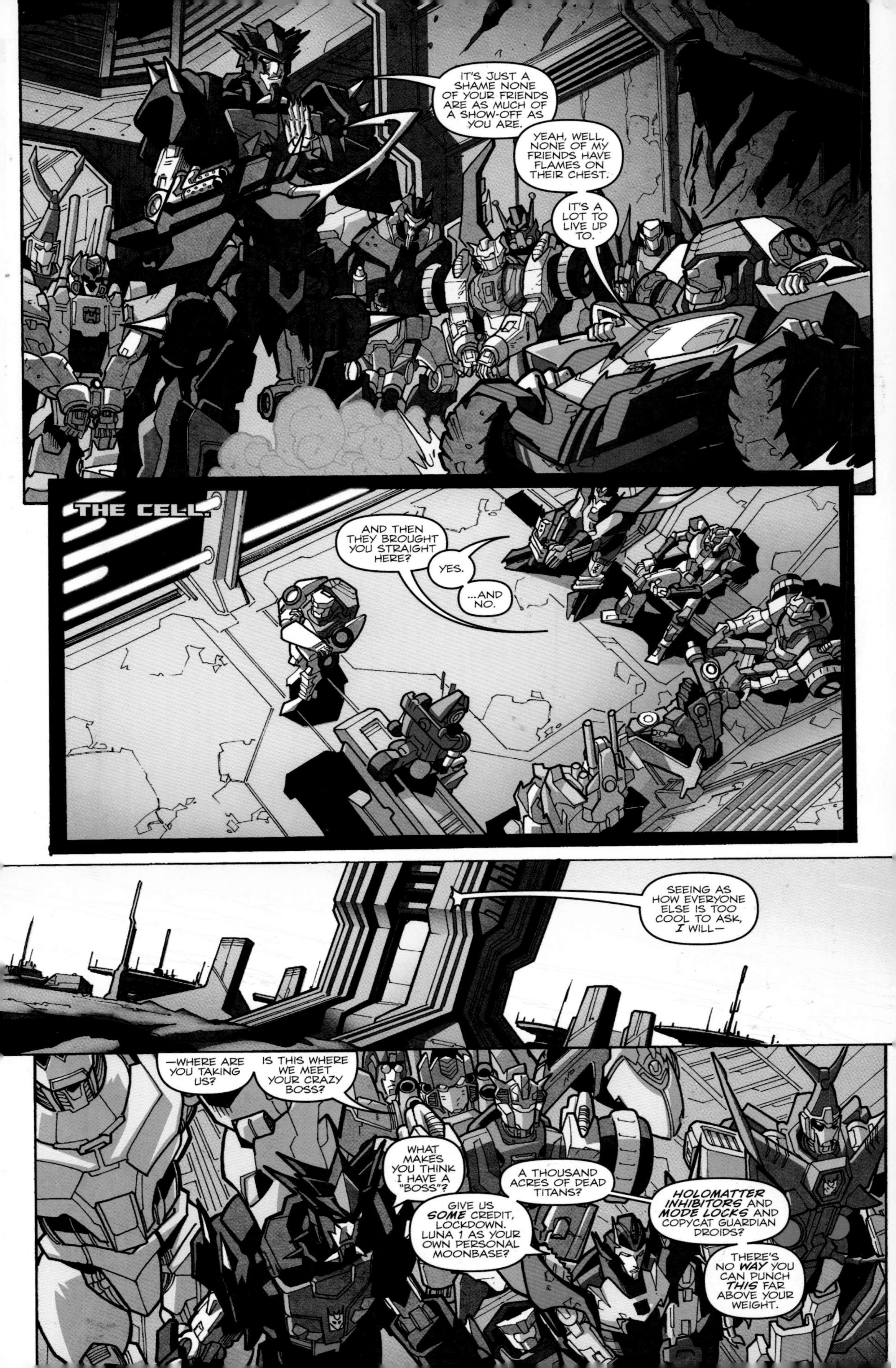

IT'S JUST A SHAME NONE OF YOUR FRIENDS ARE AS MUCH OF A SHOW-OFF AS YOU ARE.
YEAH, WELL, NONE OF MY FRIENDS HAVE FLAMES ON THEIR CHEST.
IT'S A LOT TO LIVE UP TO.
THE CELL.
AND THEN THEY BROUGHT YOU STRAIGHT HERE?
YES.
...AND NO.
SEEING AS HOW EVERYONE ELSE IS TOO COOL TO ASK, *I* WILL—
—WHERE ARE YOU TAKING US?
IS THIS WHERE WE MEET YOUR CRAZY BOSS?
WHAT MAKES YOU THINK I HAVE A "BOSS"?
GIVE US *SOME* CREDIT, LOCKDOWN. LUNA 1 AS YOUR OWN PERSONAL MOONBASE?
A THOUSAND ACRES OF DEAD TITANS?
HOLOMATTER INHIBITORS AND *MODE LOCKS* AND COPYCAT GUARDIAN DROIDS?
THERE'S NO *WAY* YOU CAN PUNCH *THIS* FAR ABOVE YOUR WEIGHT.

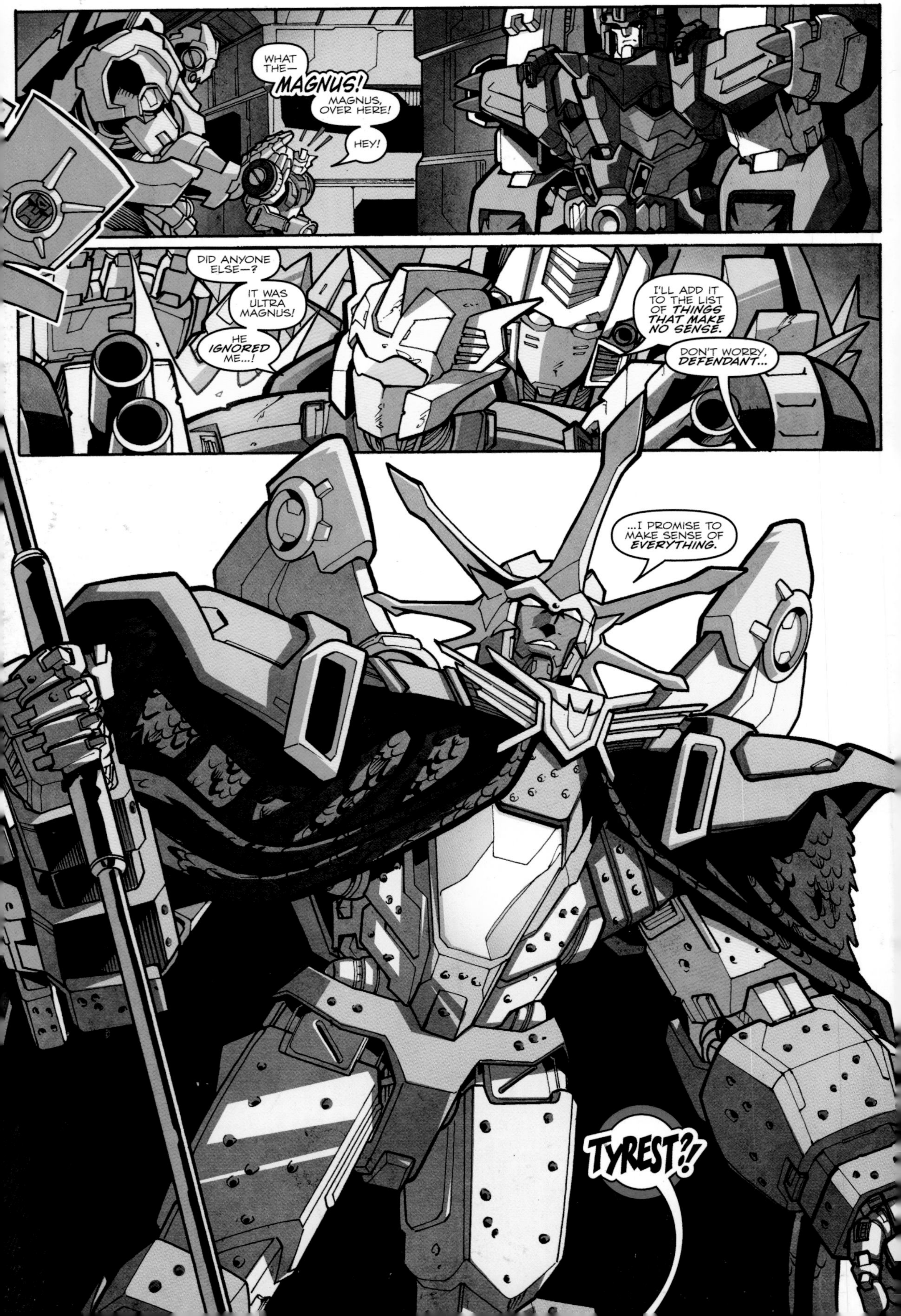
WHAT THE—
MAGNUS!
MAGNUS, OVER HERE!
HEY!
DID ANYONE ELSE—?
IT WAS ULTRA MAGNUS!
HE IGNORED ME...!
I'LL ADD IT TO THE LIST OF THINGS THAT MAKE NO SENSE.
DON'T WORRY, DEFENDANT...
...I PROMISE TO MAKE SENSE OF EVERYTHING.
TYREST?!

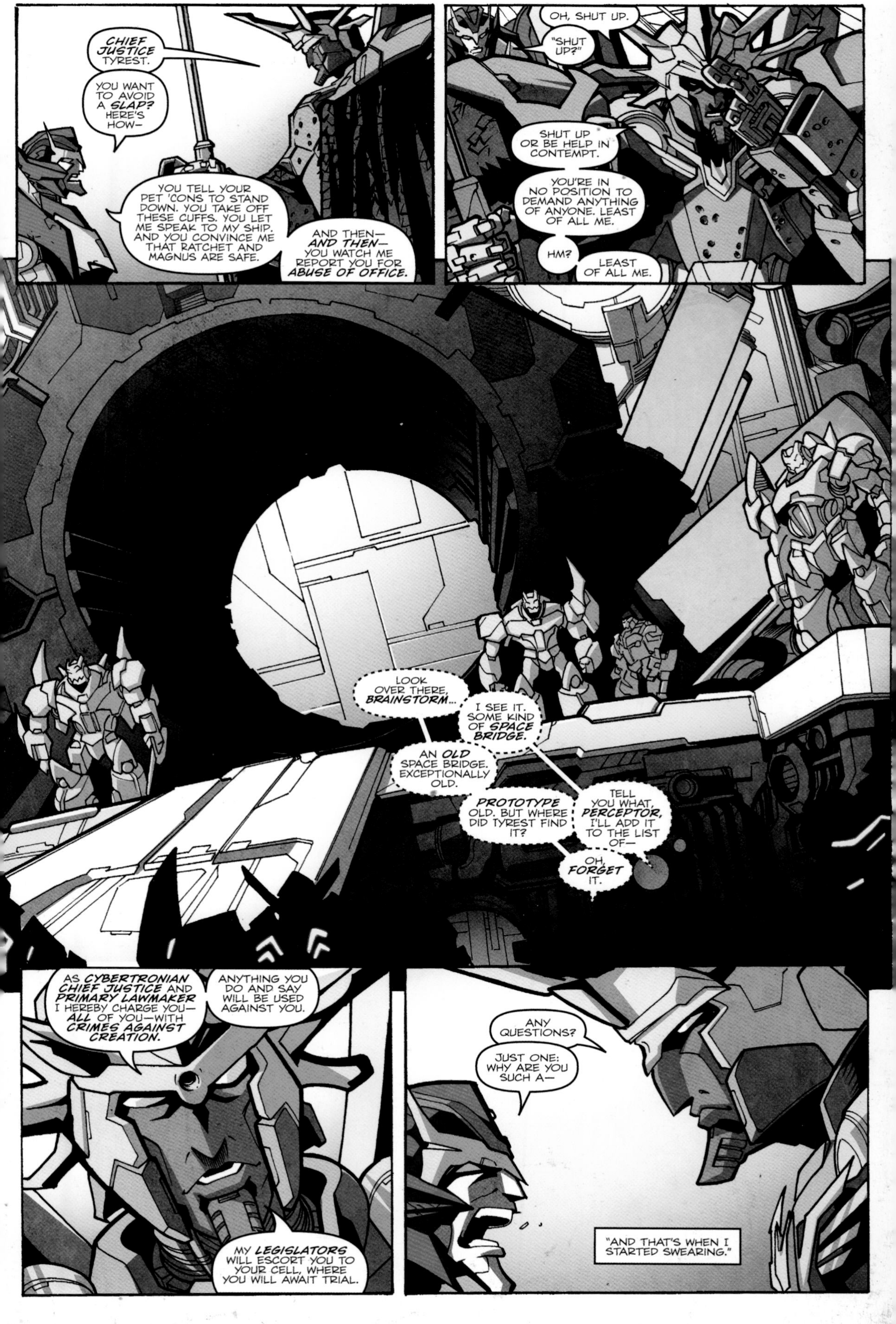
CHIEF JUSTICE TYREST.
YOU WANT TO AVOID A SLAP? HERE'S HOW—
YOU TELL YOUR PET 'CONS TO STAND DOWN. YOU TAKE OFF THESE CUFFS. YOU LET ME SPEAK TO MY SHIP. AND YOU CONVINCE ME THAT RATCHET AND MAGNUS ARE SAFE.
AND THEN— AND THEN— YOU WATCH ME REPORT YOU FOR ABUSE OF OFFICE.
OH, SHUT UP.
"SHUT UP?"
SHUT UP OR BE HELP IN CONTEMPT.
YOU'RE IN NO POSITION TO DEMAND ANYTHING OF ANYONE. LEAST OF ALL ME.
HM?
LEAST OF ALL ME.
LOOK OVER THERE, BRAINSTORM...
I SEE IT. SOME KIND OF SPACE BRIDGE.
AN OLD SPACE BRIDGE. EXCEPTIONALLY OLD.
PROTOTYPE OLD. BUT WHERE DID TYREST FIND IT?
TELL YOU WHAT, PERCEPTOR, I'LL ADD IT TO THE LIST OF—
OH, FORGET IT.
AS CYBERTRONIAN CHIEF JUSTICE AND PRIMARY LAWMAKER I HEREBY CHARGE YOU—ALL OF YOU—WITH CRIMES AGAINST CREATION.
ANYTHING YOU DO AND SAY WILL BE USED AGAINST YOU.
MY LEGISLATORS WILL ESCORT YOU TO YOUR CELL, WHERE YOU WILL AWAIT TRIAL.
ANY QUESTIONS?
JUST ONE: WHY ARE YOU SUCH A—
"AND THAT'S WHEN I STARTED SWEARING."

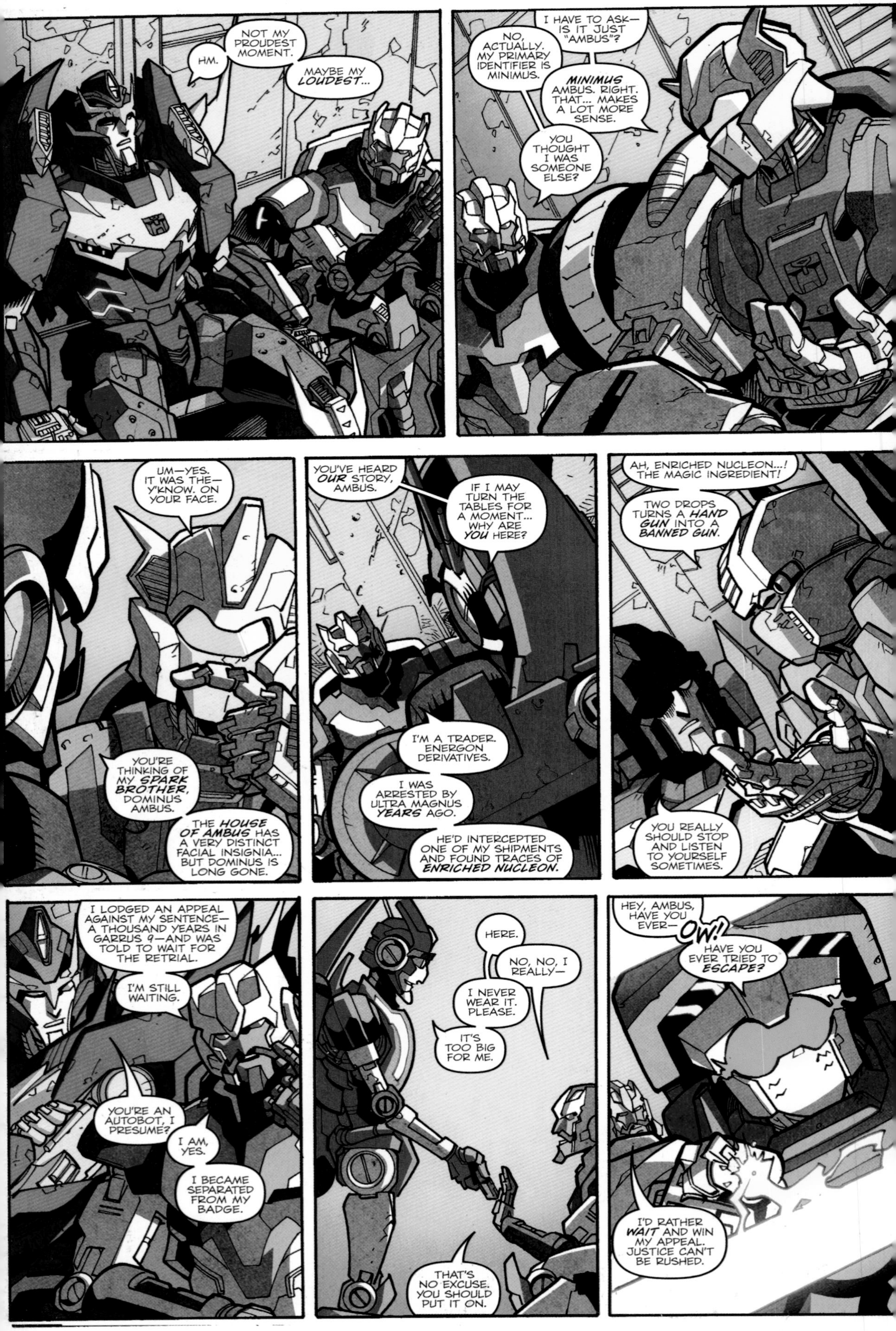
HM.
NOT MY PROUDEST MOMENT.
MAYBE MY *LOUDEST*...
I HAVE TO ASK—IS IT JUST "AMBUS"?
NO, ACTUALLY. MY PRIMARY IDENTIFIER IS MINIMUS.
MINIMUS AMBUS. RIGHT. THAT... MAKES A LOT MORE SENSE.
YOU THOUGHT I WAS SOMEONE ELSE?
UM—YES. IT WAS THE—Y'KNOW. ON YOUR FACE.
YOU'RE THINKING OF MY *SPARK BROTHER*, DOMINUS AMBUS.
THE *HOUSE OF AMBUS* HAS A VERY DISTINCT FACIAL INSIGNIA... BUT DOMINUS IS LONG GONE.
YOU'VE HEARD *OUR* STORY, AMBUS.
IF I MAY TURN THE TABLES FOR A MOMENT... WHY ARE *YOU* HERE?
I'M A TRADER. ENERGON DERIVATIVES.
I WAS ARRESTED BY ULTRA MAGNUS *YEARS* AGO.
HE'D INTERCEPTED ONE OF MY SHIPMENTS AND FOUND TRACES OF *ENRICHED NUCLEON*.
AH, ENRICHED NUCLEON...! THE MAGIC INGREDIENT!
TWO DROPS TURNS A *HAND GUN* INTO A *BANNED GUN*.
YOU REALLY SHOULD STOP AND LISTEN TO YOURSELF SOMETIMES.
I LODGED AN APPEAL AGAINST MY SENTENCE—A THOUSAND YEARS IN GARRUS 9—AND WAS TOLD TO WAIT FOR THE RETRIAL.
I'M STILL WAITING.
YOU'RE AN AUTOBOT, I PRESUME?
I AM, YES.
I BECAME SEPARATED FROM MY BADGE.
HERE.
NO, NO, I REALLY—
I NEVER WEAR IT. PLEASE.
IT'S TOO BIG FOR ME.
THAT'S NO EXCUSE. YOU SHOULD PUT IT ON.
HEY, AMBUS, HAVE YOU EVER—
OW!!
HAVE YOU EVER TRIED TO *ESCAPE?*
I'D RATHER *WAIT* AND WIN MY APPEAL. JUSTICE CAN'T BE RUSHED.

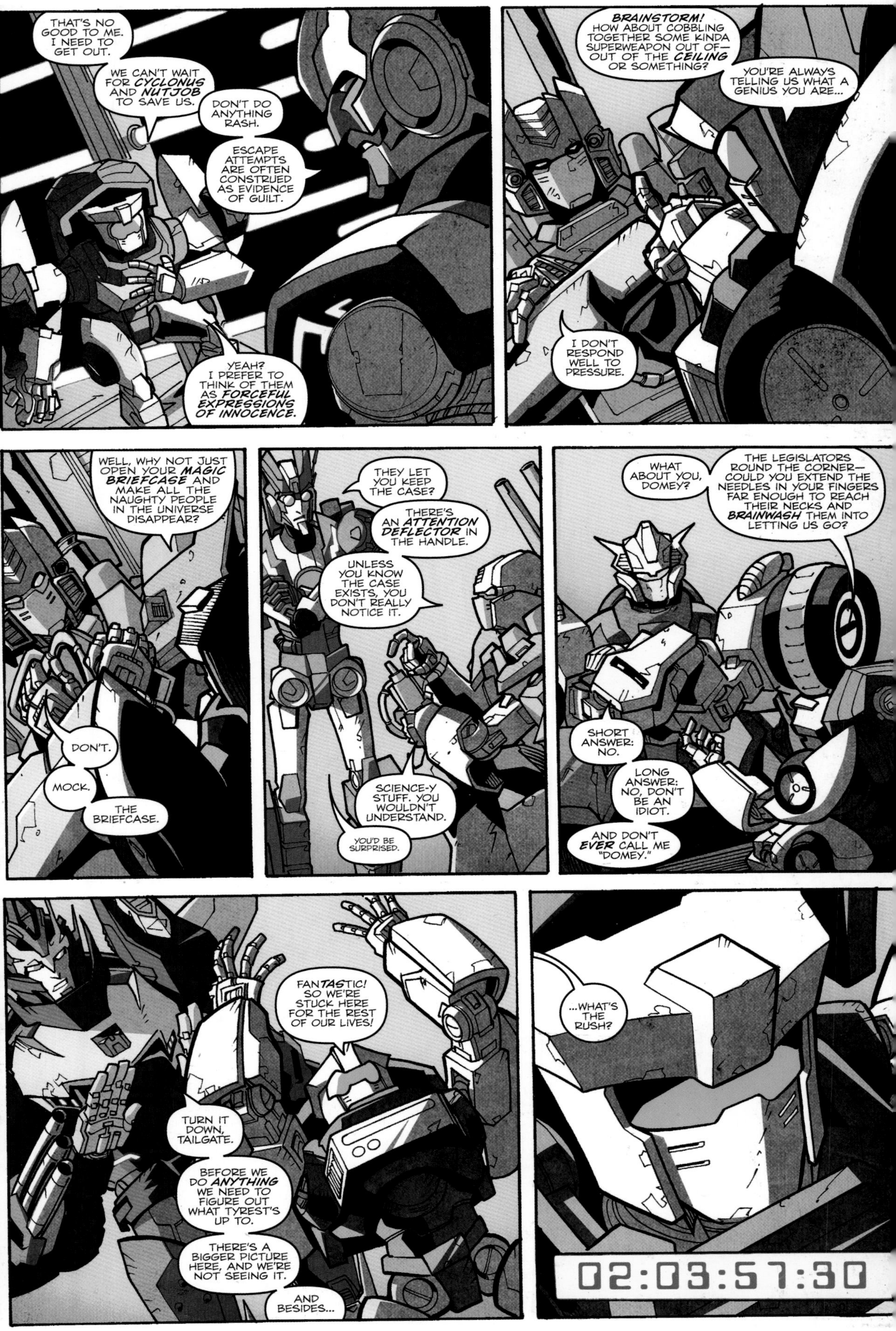
THAT'S NO GOOD TO ME. I NEED TO GET OUT.
WE CAN'T WAIT FOR CYCLONUS AND NUTJOB TO SAVE US.
DON'T DO ANYTHING RASH.
ESCAPE ATTEMPTS ARE OFTEN CONSTRUED AS EVIDENCE OF GUILT.
YEAH? I PREFER TO THINK OF THEM AS FORCEFUL EXPRESSIONS OF INNOCENCE.
BRAINSTORM! HOW ABOUT COBBLING TOGETHER SOME KINDA SUPERWEAPON OUT OF— OUT OF THE CEILING OR SOMETHING?
YOU'RE ALWAYS TELLING US WHAT A GENIUS YOU ARE...
I DON'T RESPOND WELL TO PRESSURE.
WELL, WHY NOT JUST OPEN YOUR MAGIC BRIEFCASE AND MAKE ALL THE NAUGHTY PEOPLE IN THE UNIVERSE DISAPPEAR?
DON'T.
MOCK.
THE BRIEFCASE.
THEY LET YOU KEEP THE CASE?
THERE'S AN ATTENTION DEFLECTOR IN THE HANDLE.
UNLESS YOU KNOW THE CASE EXISTS, YOU DON'T REALLY NOTICE IT.
SCIENCE-Y STUFF. YOU WOULDN'T UNDERSTAND.
YOU'D BE SURPRISED.
WHAT ABOUT YOU, DOMEY?
THE LEGISLATORS ROUND THE CORNER— COULD YOU EXTEND THE NEEDLES IN YOUR FINGERS FAR ENOUGH TO REACH THEIR NECKS AND BRAINWASH THEM INTO LETTING US GO?
SHORT ANSWER: NO.
LONG ANSWER: NO, DON'T BE AN IDIOT.
AND DON'T EVER CALL ME "DOMEY."
FANTASTIC! SO WE'RE STUCK HERE FOR THE REST OF OUR LIVES!
TURN IT DOWN, TAILGATE.
BEFORE WE DO ANYTHING WE NEED TO FIGURE OUT WHAT TYREST'S UP TO.
THERE'S A BIGGER PICTURE HERE, AND WE'RE NOT SEEING IT.
AND BESIDES...
...WHAT'S THE RUSH?
02:03:57:30

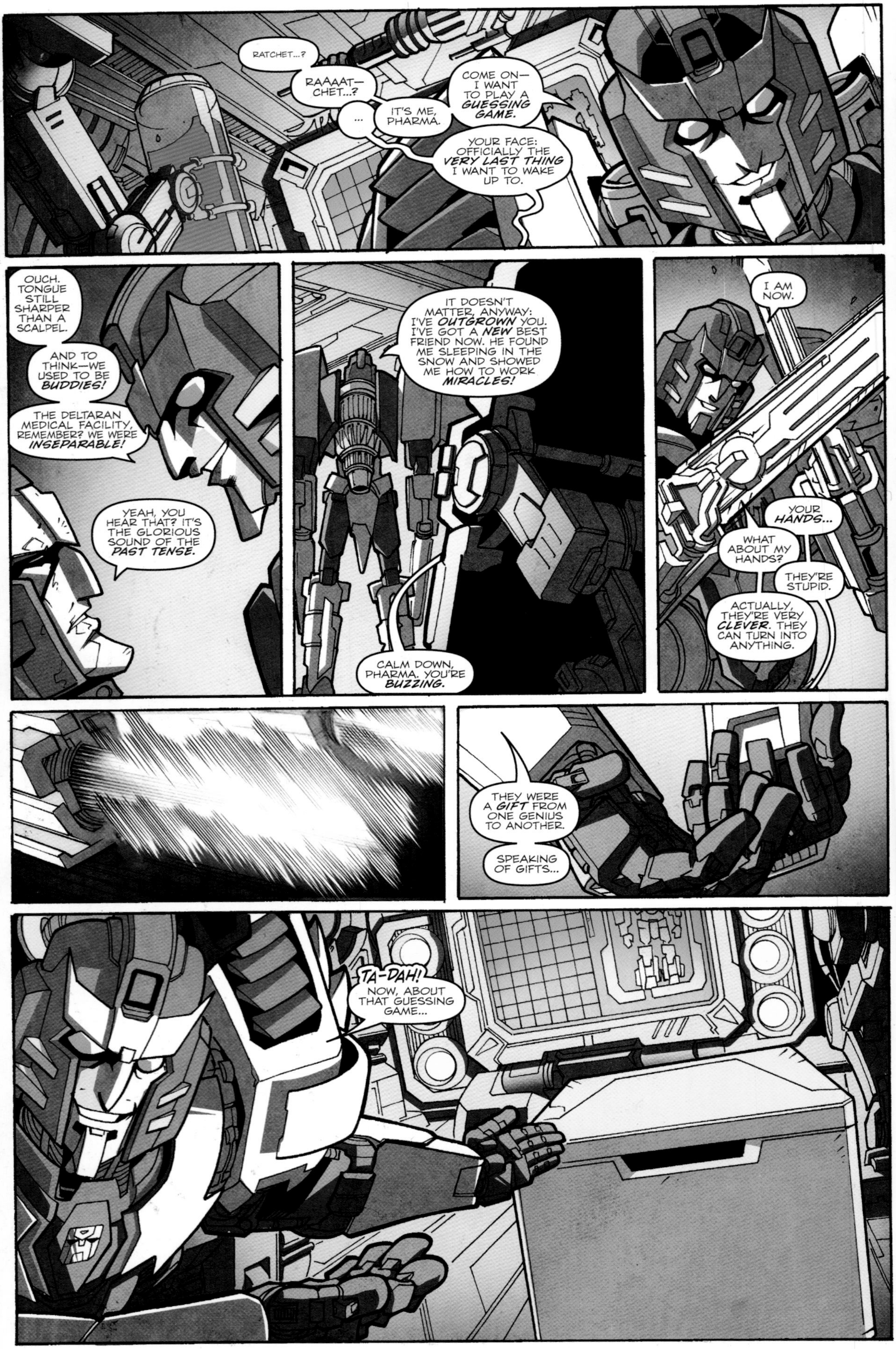
RATCHET...?
RAAAAT—CHET...?
...
IT'S ME, PHARMA.
COME ON—I WANT TO PLAY A GUESSING GAME.
YOUR FACE: OFFICIALLY THE VERY LAST THING I WANT TO WAKE UP TO.
OUCH. TONGUE STILL SHARPER THAN A SCALPEL.
AND TO THINK—WE USED TO BE BUDDIES!
THE DELTARAN MEDICAL FACILITY, REMEMBER? WE WERE INSEPARABLE!
YEAH, YOU HEAR THAT? IT'S THE GLORIOUS SOUND OF THE PAST TENSE.
IT DOESN'T MATTER, ANYWAY: I'VE OUTGROWN YOU. I'VE GOT A NEW BEST FRIEND NOW. HE FOUND ME SLEEPING IN THE SNOW AND SHOWED ME HOW TO WORK MIRACLES!
CALM DOWN, PHARMA. YOU'RE BUZZING.
I AM NOW.
YOUR HANDS...
WHAT ABOUT MY HANDS?
THEY'RE STUPID.
ACTUALLY, THEY'RE VERY CLEVER. THEY CAN TURN INTO ANYTHING.
THEY WERE A GIFT FROM ONE GENIUS TO ANOTHER.
SPEAKING OF GIFTS...
TA-DAH!
NOW, ABOUT THAT GUESSING GAME...

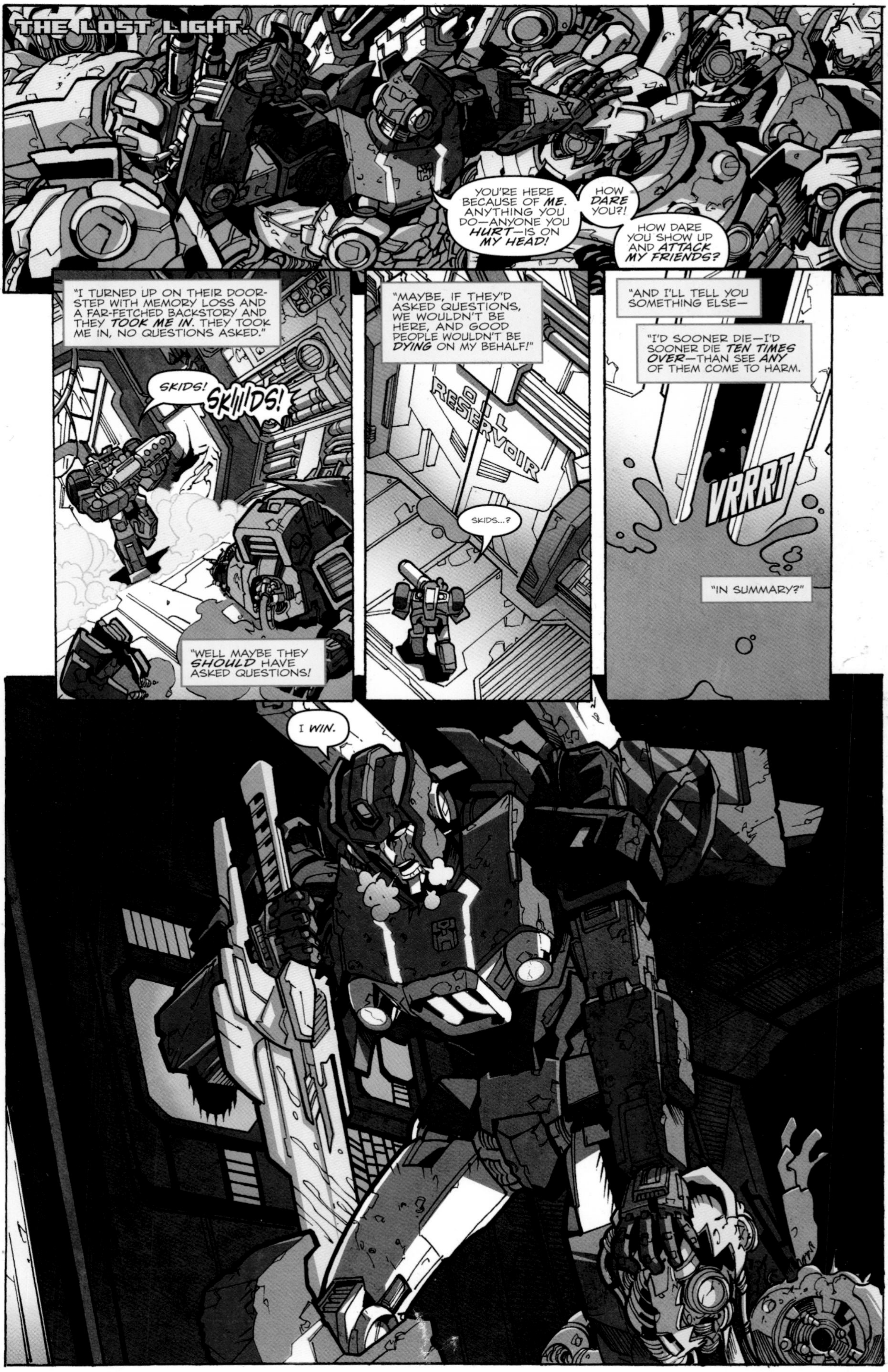
THE LOST LIGHT.
YOU'RE HERE BECAUSE OF ME. ANYTHING YOU DO—ANYONE YOU HURT—IS ON MY HEAD!
HOW DARE YOU?!
HOW DARE YOU SHOW UP AND ATTACK MY FRIENDS?
"I TURNED UP ON THEIR DOORSTEP WITH MEMORY LOSS AND A FAR-FETCHED BACKSTORY AND THEY TOOK ME IN. THEY TOOK ME IN, NO QUESTIONS ASKED."
SKIDS!
SKIIIDS!
"WELL MAYBE THEY SHOULD HAVE ASKED QUESTIONS!
"MAYBE, IF THEY'D ASKED QUESTIONS, WE WOULDN'T BE HERE, AND GOOD PEOPLE WOULDN'T BE DYING ON MY BEHALF!"
OIL RESERVOIR
SKIDS...?
"AND I'LL TELL YOU SOMETHING ELSE—
"I'D SOONER DIE—I'D SOONER DIE TEN TIMES OVER—THAN SEE ANY OF THEM COME TO HARM.
VRRRT
"IN SUMMARY?"
I WIN.

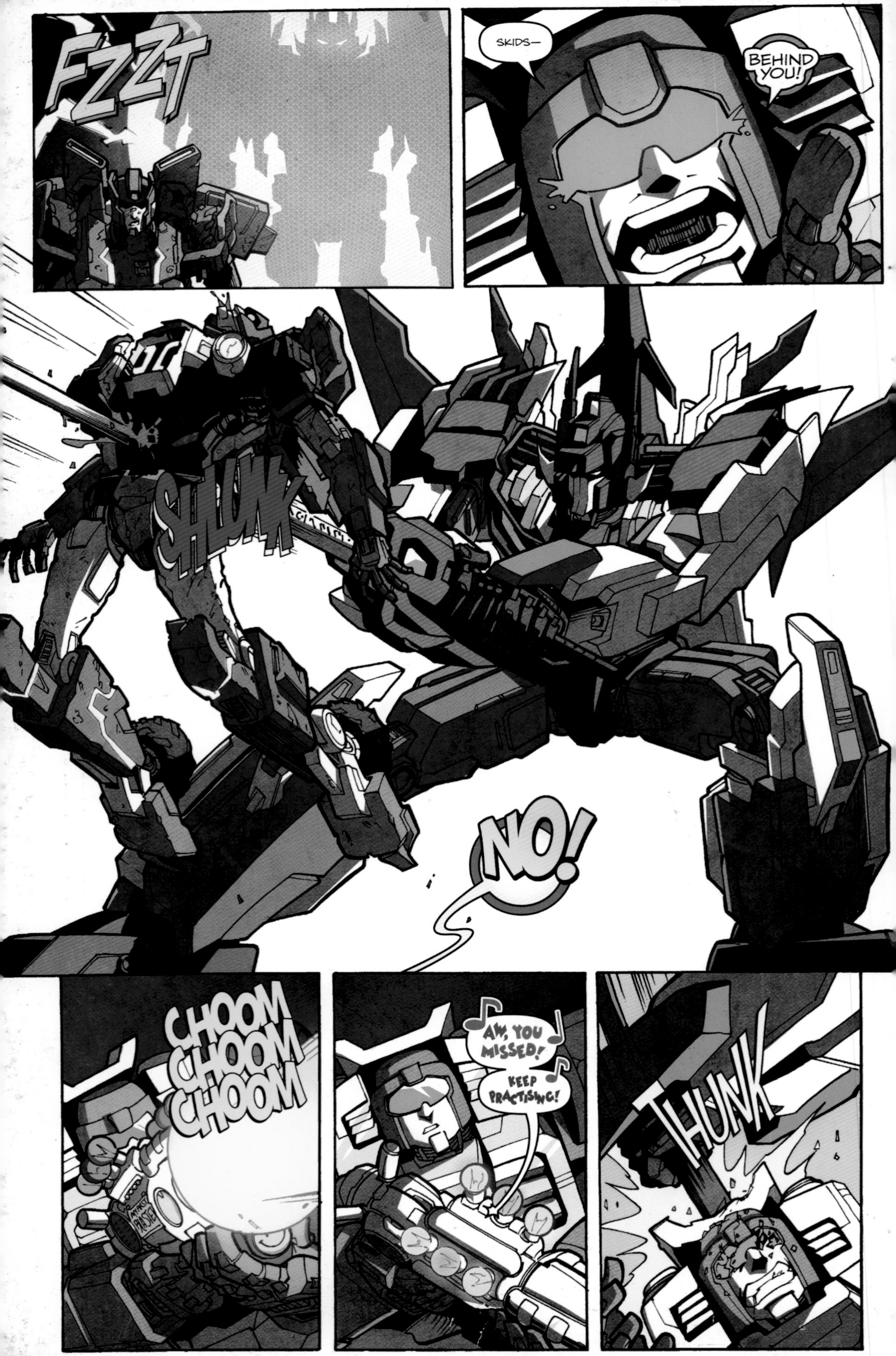
FZZZT
SKIDS—
BEHIND YOU!
SHLUNK
NO!
CHOOM CHOOM CHOOM
AW, YOU MISSED!
KEEP PRACTISING!
THUNK

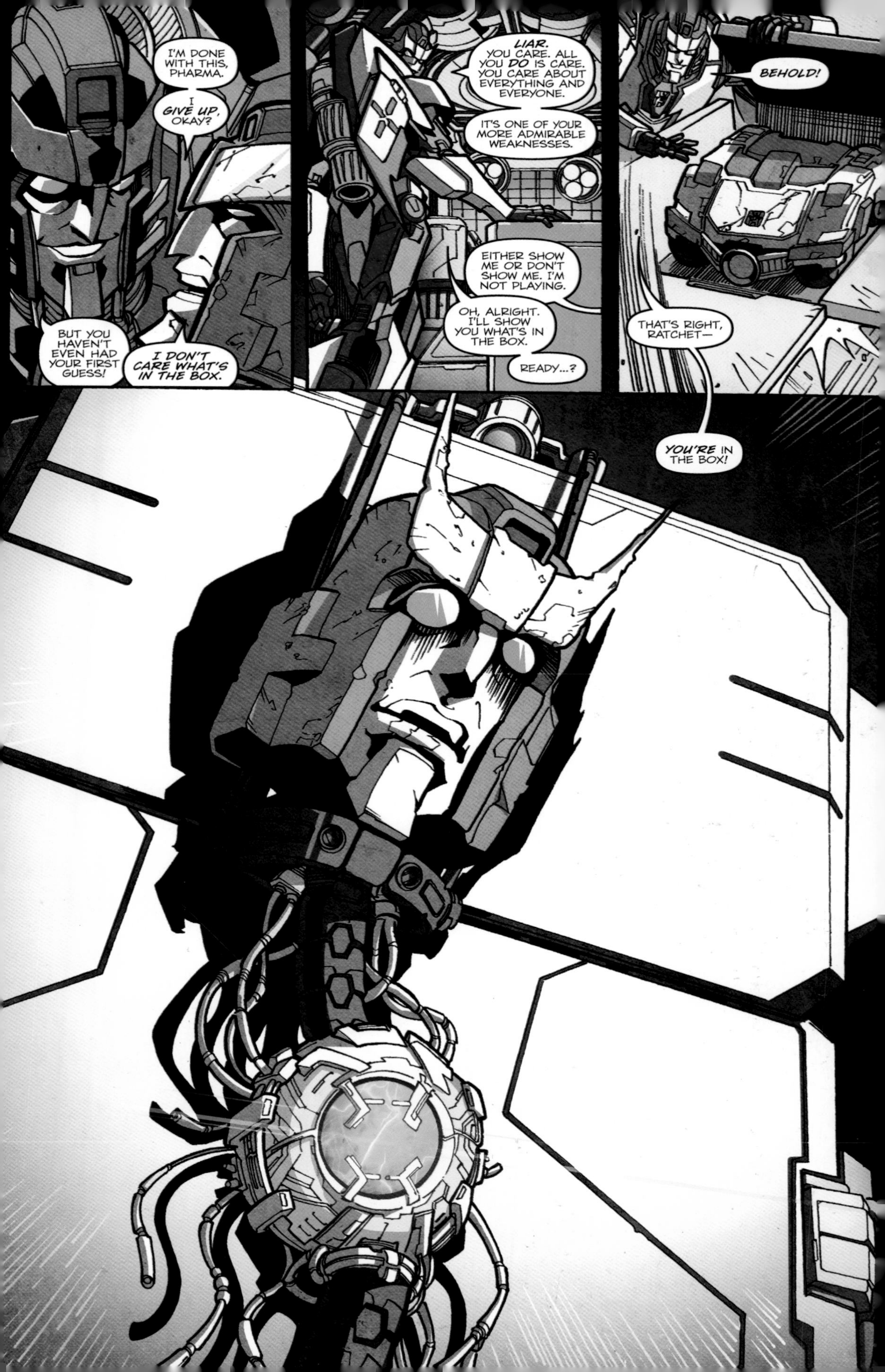
I'M DONE WITH THIS, PHARMA.
I GIVE UP, OKAY?
BUT YOU HAVEN'T EVEN HAD YOUR FIRST GUESS!
I DON'T CARE WHAT'S IN THE BOX.
LIAR. YOU CARE. ALL YOU DO IS CARE. YOU CARE ABOUT EVERYTHING AND EVERYONE.
IT'S ONE OF YOUR MORE ADMIRABLE WEAKNESSES.
EITHER SHOW ME OR DON'T SHOW ME. I'M NOT PLAYING.
OH, ALRIGHT. I'LL SHOW YOU WHAT'S IN THE BOX.
READY...?
BEHOLD!
THAT'S RIGHT, RATCHET—
YOU'RE IN THE BOX!

ENERGON STICK?

MIGHT HELP YOU RELAX.

THANKS, RUNG.

HOW'D YOU SMUGGLE THESE IN?

I'M 90% SECRET COMPARTMENTS.

I THINK THERE WAS A TYREST BACK IN MY DAY— ONE OF *NOVA'S* COTERIE.

CHIEF ENGINEERING OFFICER...?

IT'S THE SAME TYREST.

HE DIDN'T REALLY MAKE A NAME FOR HIMSELF UNTIL THE WAR, WHEN HE ORGANIZED THE *EXODUS*... HE AND *DAI ATLAS* MUST'VE HELPED TEN, TWENTY MILLION NEUTRALS LEAVE THE PLANET.

AND WHAT, HE STAYED BEHIND TO FIGHT?

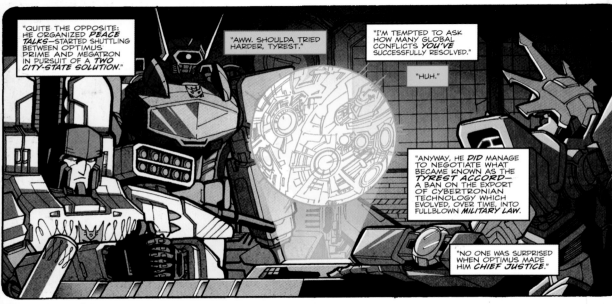

"QUITE THE OPPOSITE: HE ORGANIZED *PEACE TALKS*—STARTED SHUTTLING BETWEEN OPTIMUS PRIME AND MEGATRON IN PURSUIT OF A *TWO CITY-STATE SOLUTION*."

"AWW. SHOULDA TRIED HARDER, TYREST."

"I'M TEMPTED TO ASK HOW MANY GLOBAL CONFLICTS *YOU'VE* SUCCESSFULLY RESOLVED."

"HUH."

"ANYWAY, HE *DID* MANAGE TO NEGOTIATE WHAT BECAME KNOWN AS THE *TYREST ACCORD*— A BAN ON THE EXPORT OF CYBERTRONIAN TECHNOLOGY WHICH EVOLVED, OVER TIME, INTO FULLBLOWN *MILITARY LAW*.

"NO ONE WAS SURPRISED WHEN OPTIMUS MADE HIM *CHIEF JUSTICE*."

THESE ARE GOOD.

HAVE SOME MORE.

SO HANG ON— HOW DID TYREST END UP ON LUNA 1?

WHO KNOWS?

HE'S BEEN OFF THE RADAR SINCE THE *AEQUITAS* TRIALS.

ER, JUST— MAYBE JUST BE A LITTLE CAREFUL.

THOSE TRIALS ARE *TOP SECRET*...

I AGREE. IT'S NOT MY PLACE, BUT I'D STRONGLY ADVISE YOU AGAINST DISCLOSING ANYTHING CONFIDENTIAL.

YOU'RE RIGHT—IT'S NOT YOUR PLACE.

BESIDES, I'M ONLY GONNA GIVE THE *NUTSHELL* VERSION.

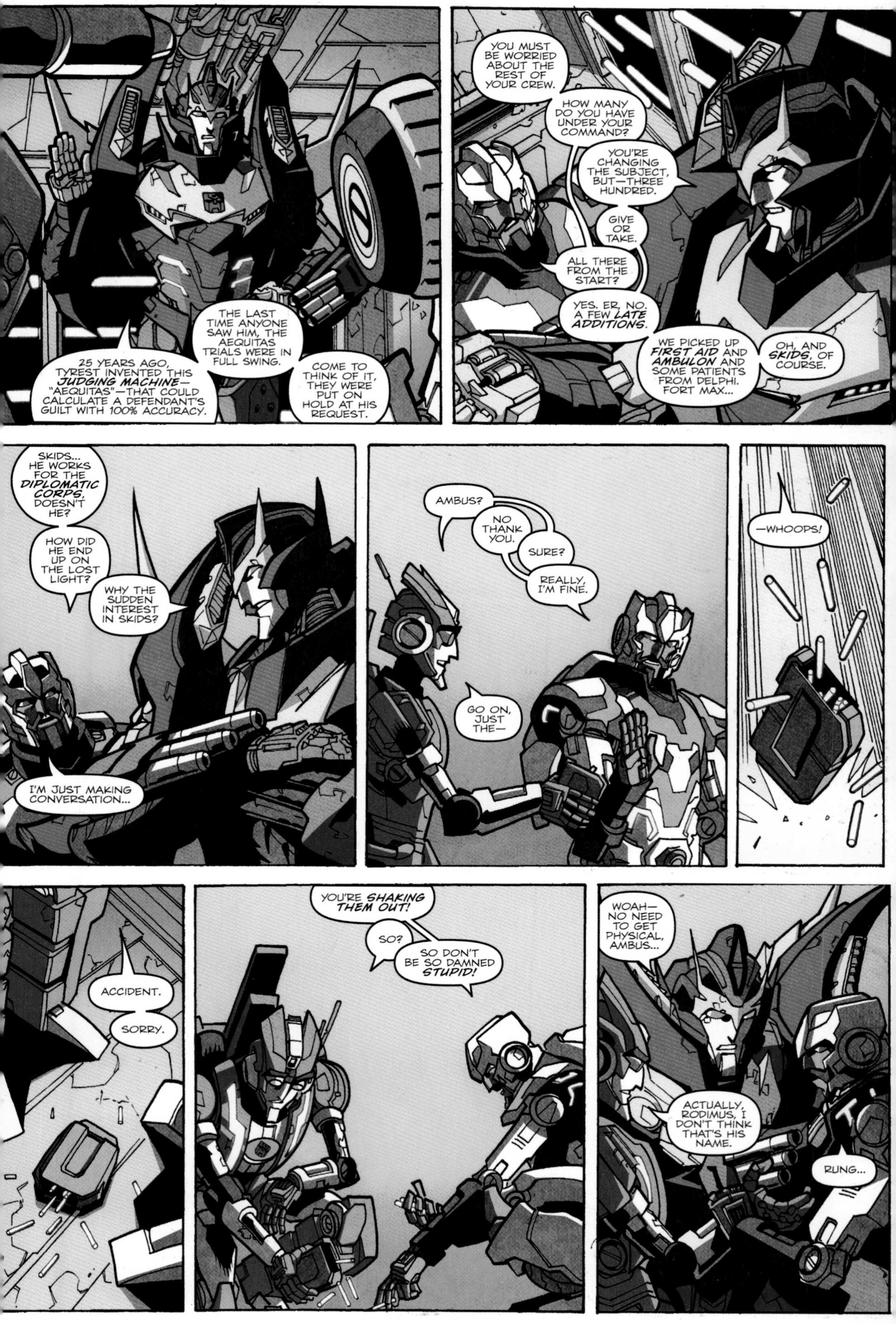

25 YEARS AGO, TYREST INVENTED THIS JUDGING MACHINE—"AEQUITAS"—THAT COULD CALCULATE A DEFENDANT'S GUILT WITH 100% ACCURACY.
THE LAST TIME ANYONE SAW HIM, THE AEQUITAS TRIALS WERE IN FULL SWING.
COME TO THINK OF IT, THEY WERE PUT ON HOLD AT HIS REQUEST.
YOU MUST BE WORRIED ABOUT THE REST OF YOUR CREW.
HOW MANY DO YOU HAVE UNDER YOUR COMMAND?
YOU'RE CHANGING THE SUBJECT, BUT—THREE HUNDRED.
GIVE OR TAKE.
ALL THERE FROM THE START?
YES. ER, NO. A FEW LATE ADDITIONS.
WE PICKED UP FIRST AID AND AMBULON AND SOME PATIENTS FROM DELPHI. FORT MAX...
OH, AND SKIDS, OF COURSE.
SKIDS... HE WORKS FOR THE DIPLOMATIC CORPS, DOESN'T HE?
HOW DID HE END UP ON THE LOST LIGHT?
WHY THE SUDDEN INTEREST IN SKIDS?
I'M JUST MAKING CONVERSATION...
AMBUS?
NO THANK YOU.
SURE?
REALLY, I'M FINE.
GO ON, JUST THE—
—WHOOPS!
ACCIDENT.
SORRY.
YOU'RE SHAKING THEM OUT!
SO?
SO DON'T BE SO DAMNED STUPID!
WOAH—NO NEED TO GET PHYSICAL, AMBUS...
ACTUALLY, RODIMUS, I DON'T THINK THAT'S HIS NAME.
RUNG...

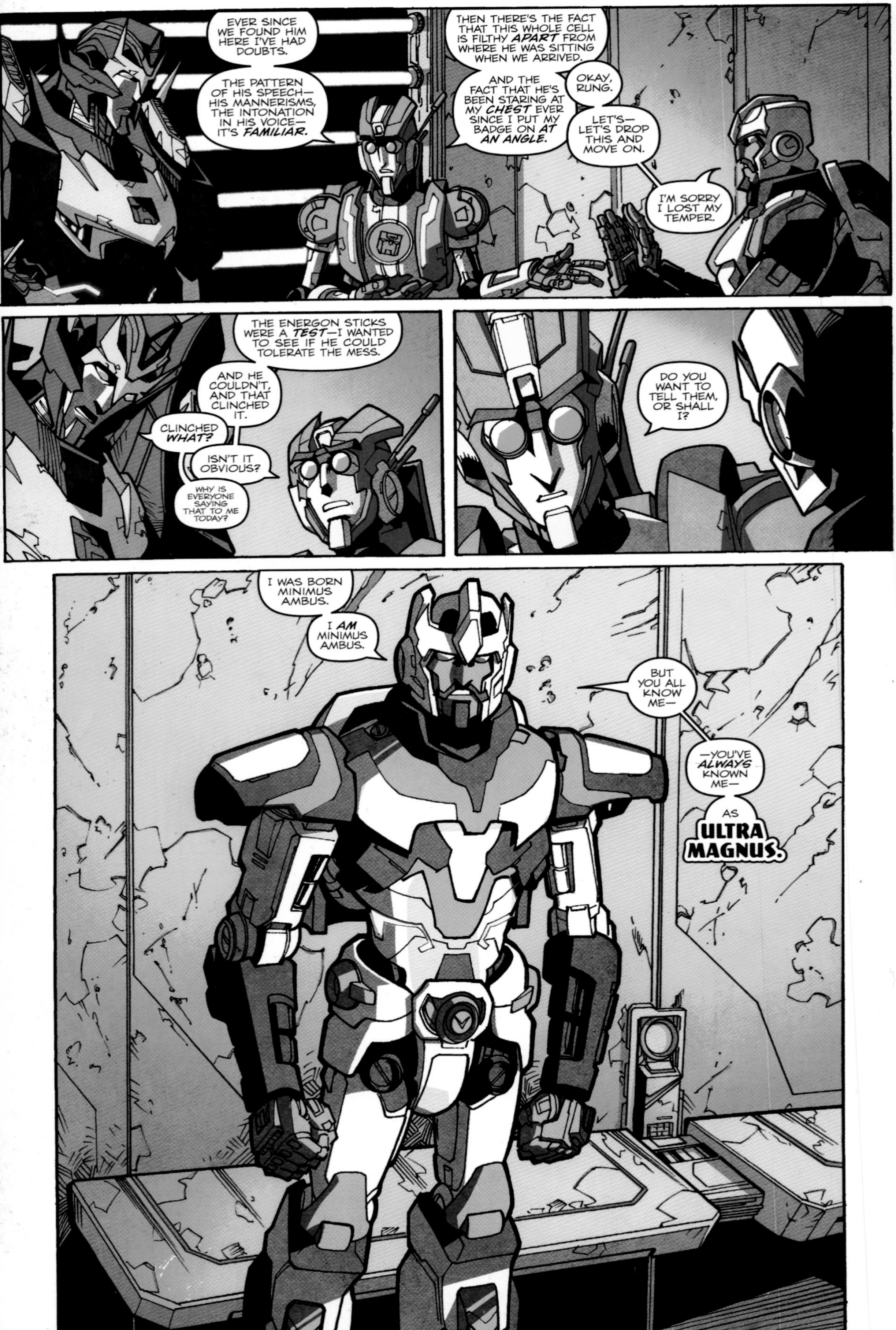
EVER SINCE WE FOUND HIM HERE I'VE HAD DOUBTS.
THE PATTERN OF HIS SPEECH—HIS MANNERISMS, THE INTONATION IN HIS VOICE—IT'S *FAMILIAR*.
THEN THERE'S THE FACT THAT THIS WHOLE CELL IS FILTHY *APART* FROM WHERE HE WAS SITTING WHEN WE ARRIVED.
AND THE FACT THAT HE'S BEEN STARING AT MY *CHEST* EVER SINCE I PUT MY BADGE ON *AT AN ANGLE*.
OKAY, RUNG.
LET'S—LET'S DROP THIS AND MOVE ON.
I'M SORRY I LOST MY TEMPER.
THE ENERGON STICKS WERE A *TEST*—I WANTED TO SEE IF HE COULD TOLERATE THE MESS.
AND HE COULDN'T, AND THAT CLINCHED IT.
CLINCHED *WHAT?*
ISN'T IT OBVIOUS?
WHY IS EVERYONE SAYING THAT TO ME TODAY?
DO YOU WANT TO TELL THEM, OR SHALL I?
I WAS BORN MINIMUS AMBUS.
I *AM* MINIMUS AMBUS.
BUT YOU ALL KNOW ME—
—YOU'VE *ALWAYS* KNOWN ME—
AS
ULTRA MAGNUS.

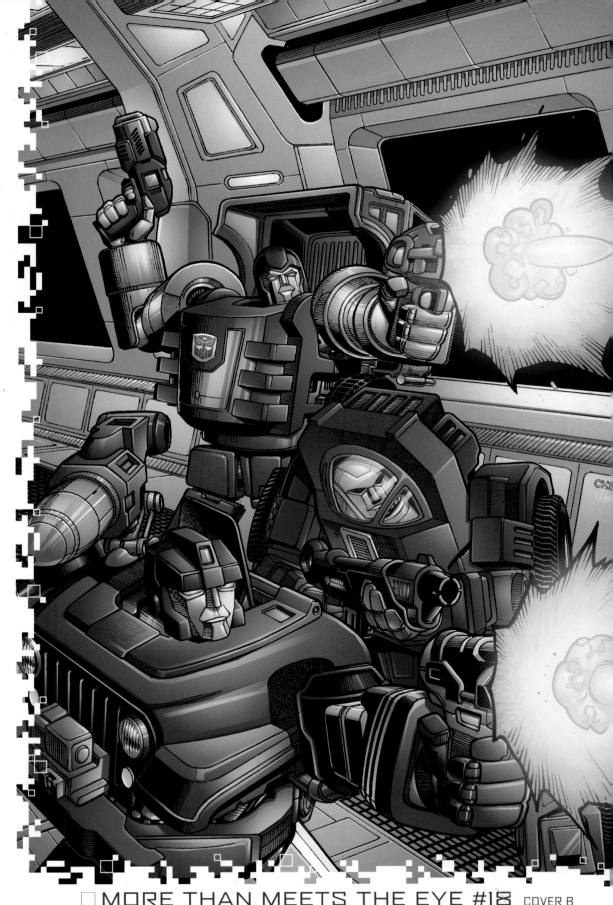

MORE THAN MEETS THE EYE #18 COVER B
by SEAN CHEN Colors by TOM CHU

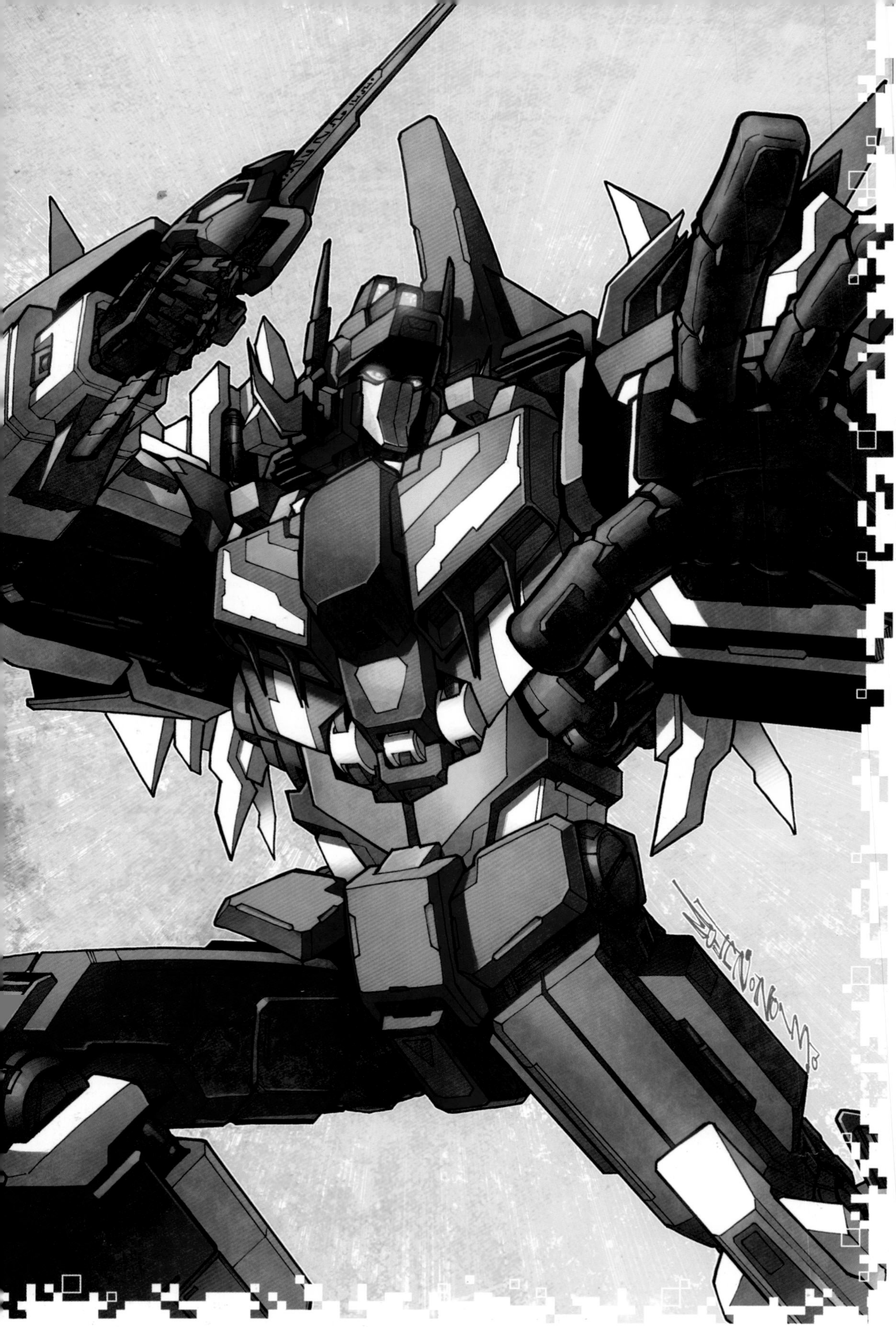

MORE THAN MEETS THE EYE #19 COVER A

by **ALEX MILNE** Colors by **JOSH PEREZ**

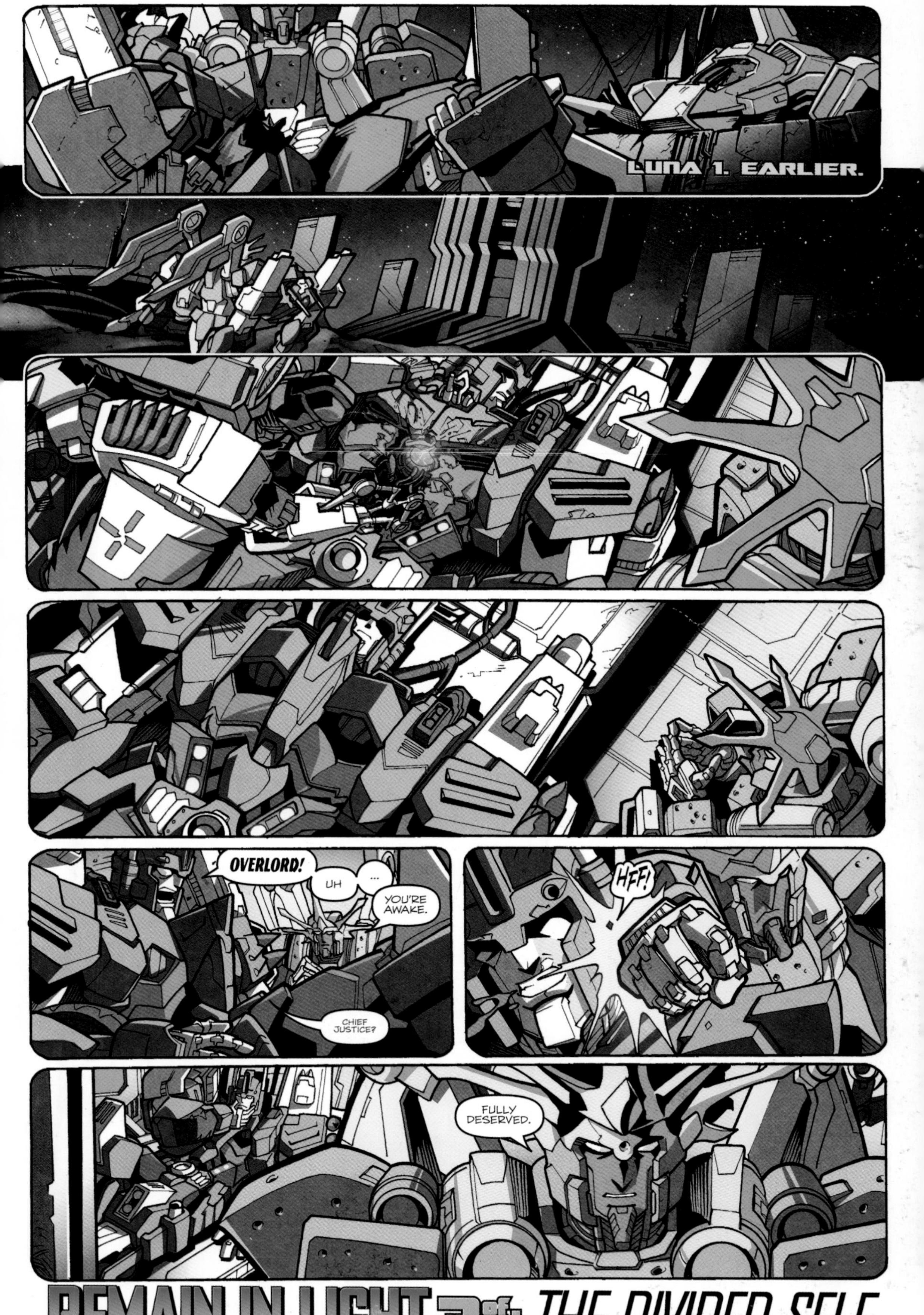
LUNA 1. EARLIER.
OVERLORD!
UH
...
YOU'RE AWAKE.
CHIEF JUSTICE?
HFF!
FULLY DESERVED.

REMAIN IN LIGHT 3 of 5: THE DIVIDED SELF

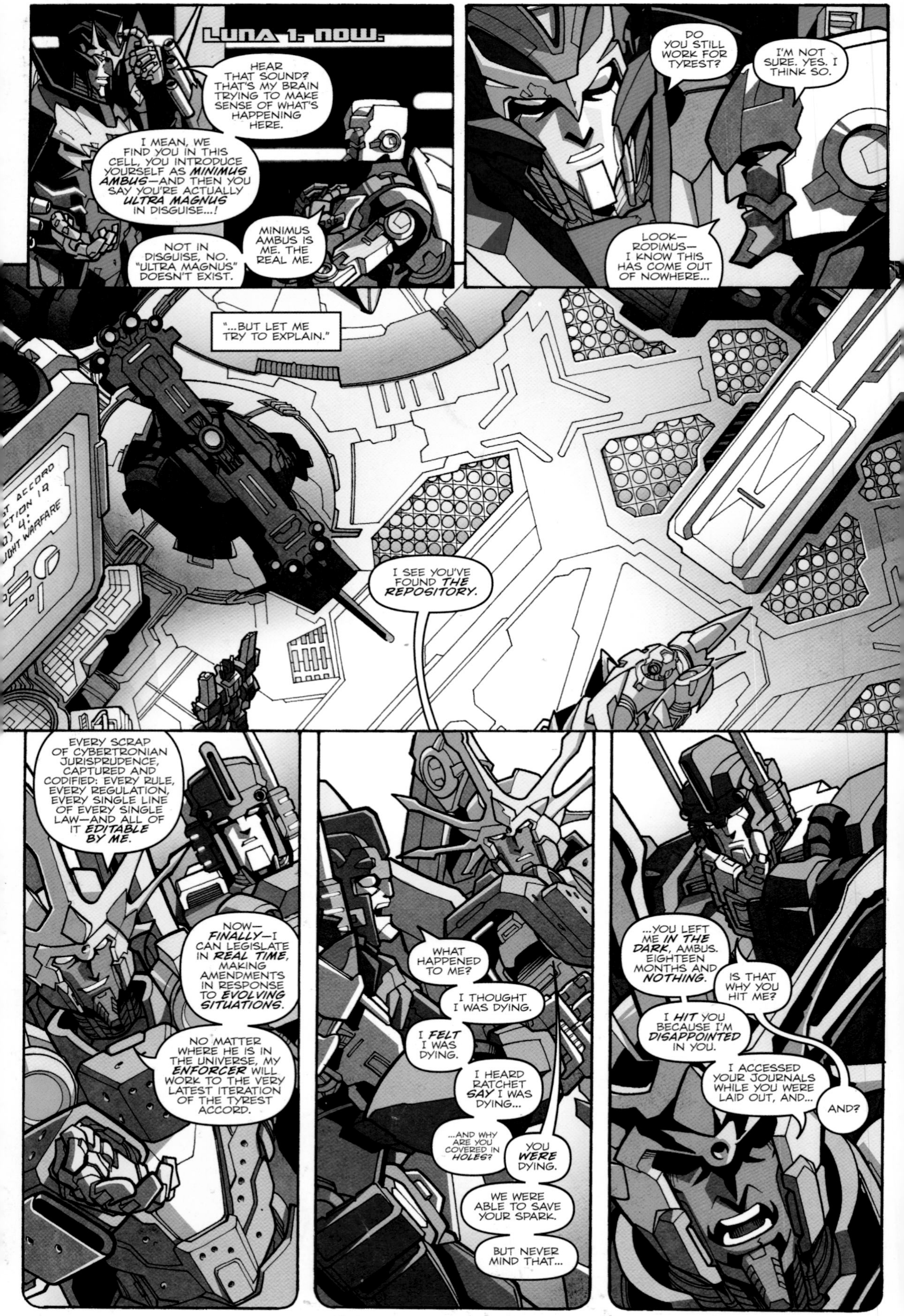
LUNA 1. NOW.
HEAR THAT SOUND? THAT'S MY BRAIN TRYING TO MAKE SENSE OF WHAT'S HAPPENING HERE.
I MEAN, WE FIND YOU IN THIS CELL, YOU INTRODUCE YOURSELF AS MINIMUS AMBUS—AND THEN YOU SAY YOU'RE ACTUALLY ULTRA MAGNUS IN DISGUISE...!
NOT IN DISGUISE, NO. "ULTRA MAGNUS" DOESN'T EXIST.
MINIMUS AMBUS IS ME. THE REAL ME.
DO YOU STILL WORK FOR TYREST?
I'M NOT SURE. YES. I THINK SO.
LOOK— RODIMUS— I KNOW THIS HAS COME OUT OF NOWHERE...
"...BUT LET ME TRY TO EXPLAIN."
I SEE YOU'VE FOUND THE REPOSITORY.
EVERY SCRAP OF CYBERTRONIAN JURISPRUDENCE, CAPTURED AND CODIFIED: EVERY RULE, EVERY REGULATION, EVERY SINGLE LINE OF EVERY SINGLE LAW—AND ALL OF IT EDITABLE BY ME.
NOW— FINALLY—I CAN LEGISLATE IN REAL TIME, MAKING AMENDMENTS IN RESPONSE TO EVOLVING SITUATIONS.
NO MATTER WHERE HE IS IN THE UNIVERSE, MY ENFORCER WILL WORK TO THE VERY LATEST ITERATION OF THE TYREST ACCORD.
WHAT HAPPENED TO ME?
I THOUGHT I WAS DYING.
I FELT I WAS DYING.
I HEARD RATCHET SAY I WAS DYING...
...AND WHY ARE YOU COVERED IN HOLES?
YOU WERE DYING.
WE WERE ABLE TO SAVE YOUR SPARK.
BUT NEVER MIND THAT...
...YOU LEFT ME IN THE DARK, AMBUS. EIGHTEEN MONTHS AND NOTHING.
IS THAT WHY YOU HIT ME?
I HIT YOU BECAUSE I'M DISAPPOINTED IN YOU.
I ACCESSED YOUR JOURNALS WHILE YOU WERE LAID OUT, AND...
AND?

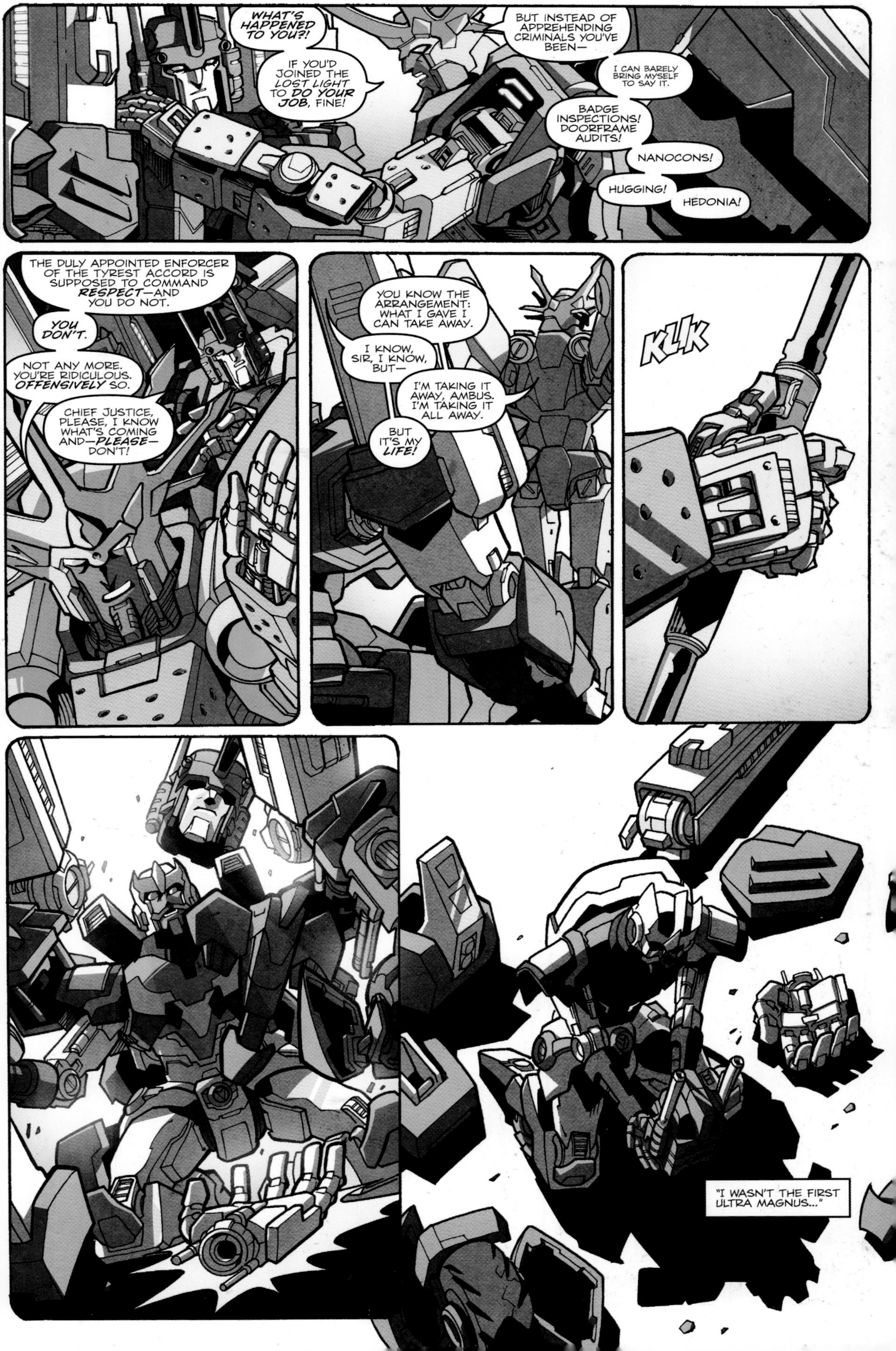
WHAT'S HAPPENED TO YOU?!
IF YOU'D JOINED THE LOST LIGHT TO DO YOUR JOB, FINE!
BUT INSTEAD OF APPREHENDING CRIMINALS YOU'VE BEEN—
I CAN BARELY BRING MYSELF TO SAY IT.
BADGE INSPECTIONS! DOORFRAME AUDITS!
NANOCONS!
HUGGING!
HEDONIA!
THE DULY APPOINTED ENFORCER OF THE TYREST ACCORD IS SUPPOSED TO COMMAND RESPECT—AND YOU DO NOT.
YOU DON'T.
NOT ANY MORE. YOU'RE RIDICULOUS. OFFENSIVELY SO.
CHIEF JUSTICE, PLEASE, I KNOW WHAT'S COMING AND—PLEASE—DON'T!
YOU KNOW THE ARRANGEMENT: WHAT I GAVE I CAN TAKE AWAY.
I KNOW, SIR, I KNOW, BUT—
I'M TAKING IT AWAY, AMBUS. I'M TAKING IT ALL AWAY.
BUT IT'S MY LIFE!
KLIK
"I WASN'T THE FIRST ULTRA MAGNUS..."

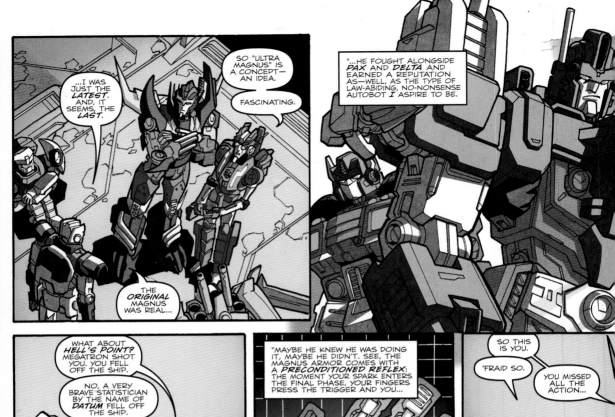

...I WAS JUST THE *LATEST.* AND, IT SEEMS, THE *LAST.*

SO "ULTRA MAGNUS" IS A CONCEPT— AN IDEA.

FASCINATING.

THE *ORIGINAL* MAGNUS WAS REAL...

"...HE FOUGHT ALONGSIDE *PAX* AND *DELTA* AND EARNED A REPUTATION AS—WELL, AS THE TYPE OF LAW-ABIDING, NO-NONSENSE AUTOBOT *I* ASPIRE TO BE.

WHAT ABOUT *HELL'S POINT?* MEGATRON SHOT YOU. YOU FELL OFF THE SHIP.

NO, A VERY BRAVE STATISTICIAN BY THE NAME OF *DATUM* FELL OFF THE SHIP.

AS HE FELL HE'D HAVE PRESSED THE *RECALL TRIGGER* IN THE PALM OF THE MAGNUS ARMOR.

"MAYBE HE KNEW HE WAS DOING IT, MAYBE HE DIDN'T. SEE, THE MAGNUS ARMOR COMES WITH A *PRECONDITIONED REFLEX:* THE MOMENT YOUR SPARK ENTERS THE FINAL PHASE, YOUR FINGERS PRESS THE TRIGGER AND YOU..."

"WELL, LET'S JUST SAY YOU FIND YOUR WAY BACK TO TYREST, WHEREVER HE MAY BE AT THE TIME, SO HE CAN GIVE THE ARMOR TO SOMEONE ELSE".

SO THIS IS YOU.

'FRAID SO.

YOU MISSED ALL THE ACTION...

OVERLORD. I'VE BEEN DESPERATE TO ASK.

I WASN'T BUILT AT ALL, I WAS *FORGED.*

THAT'S NOT WHAT I—

NO, NO, I KNOW, BUT IT'S RELEVANT.

I'M A *POINT ONE PERCENTER.* NOT *HEAVYWEIGHT CLASS* LIKE GRIMLOCK OR ROLLER, BUT STILL—YOU KNOW— SPECIAL.

TECHNICALLY, I'M A *LOAD-BEARER.*

"LOAD-BEARER?" ANYONE? DO I HAVE TO PUT MY HAND UP?

'COS THAT— NNG!—MIGHT BE ASKING A LOT OF ME RIGHT NOW.

IT MEANS MY BODY LENDS ITSELF TO *AUGMENTATION.*

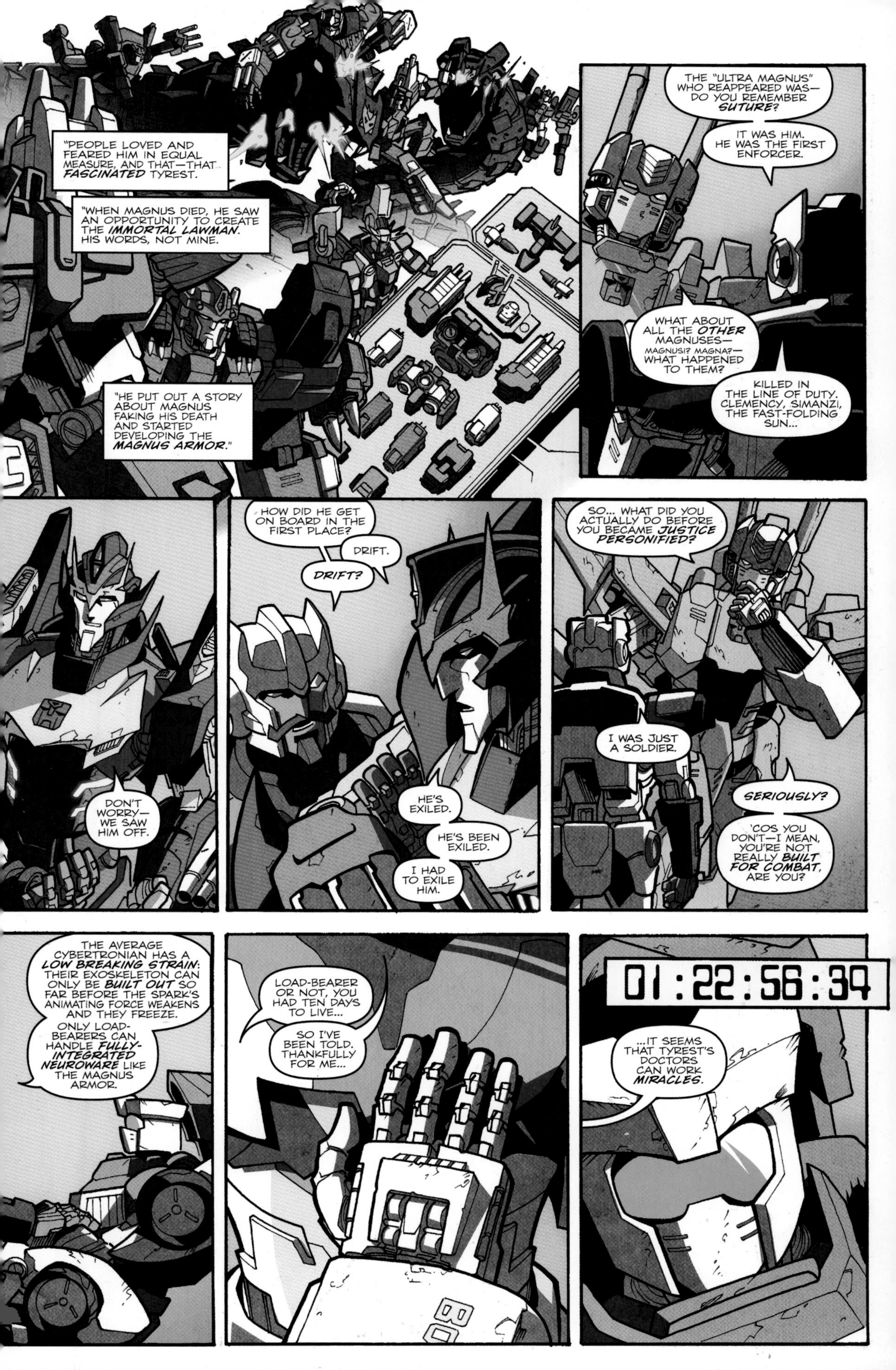
"PEOPLE LOVED AND FEARED HIM IN EQUAL MEASURE, AND THAT—THAT FASCINATED TYREST.
"WHEN MAGNUS DIED, HE SAW AN OPPORTUNITY TO CREATE THE IMMORTAL LAWMAN. HIS WORDS, NOT MINE.
"HE PUT OUT A STORY ABOUT MAGNUS FAKING HIS DEATH AND STARTED DEVELOPING THE MAGNUS ARMOR."
THE "ULTRA MAGNUS" WHO REAPPEARED WAS—DO YOU REMEMBER SUTURE?
IT WAS HIM. HE WAS THE FIRST ENFORCER.
WHAT ABOUT ALL THE OTHER MAGNUSES—MAGNUSI? MAGNA?—WHAT HAPPENED TO THEM?
KILLED IN THE LINE OF DUTY. CLEMENCY, SIMANZI, THE FAST-FOLDING SUN...
DON'T WORRY—WE SAW HIM OFF.
HOW DID HE GET ON BOARD IN THE FIRST PLACE?
DRIFT.
DRIFT?
HE'S EXILED.
HE'S BEEN EXILED.
I HAD TO EXILE HIM.
SO... WHAT DID YOU ACTUALLY DO BEFORE YOU BECAME JUSTICE PERSONIFIED?
I WAS JUST A SOLDIER.
SERIOUSLY?
'COS YOU DON'T—I MEAN, YOU'RE NOT REALLY BUILT FOR COMBAT, ARE YOU?
THE AVERAGE CYBERTRONIAN HAS A LOW BREAKING STRAIN: THEIR EXOSKELETON CAN ONLY BE BUILT OUT SO FAR BEFORE THE SPARK'S ANIMATING FORCE WEAKENS AND THEY FREEZE.
ONLY LOAD-BEARERS CAN HANDLE FULLY-INTEGRATED NEUROWARE LIKE THE MAGNUS ARMOR.
LOAD-BEARER OR NOT, YOU HAD TEN DAYS TO LIVE...
SO I'VE BEEN TOLD. THANKFULLY FOR ME...
01:22:56:34
...IT SEEMS THAT TYREST'S DOCTORS CAN WORK MIRACLES.

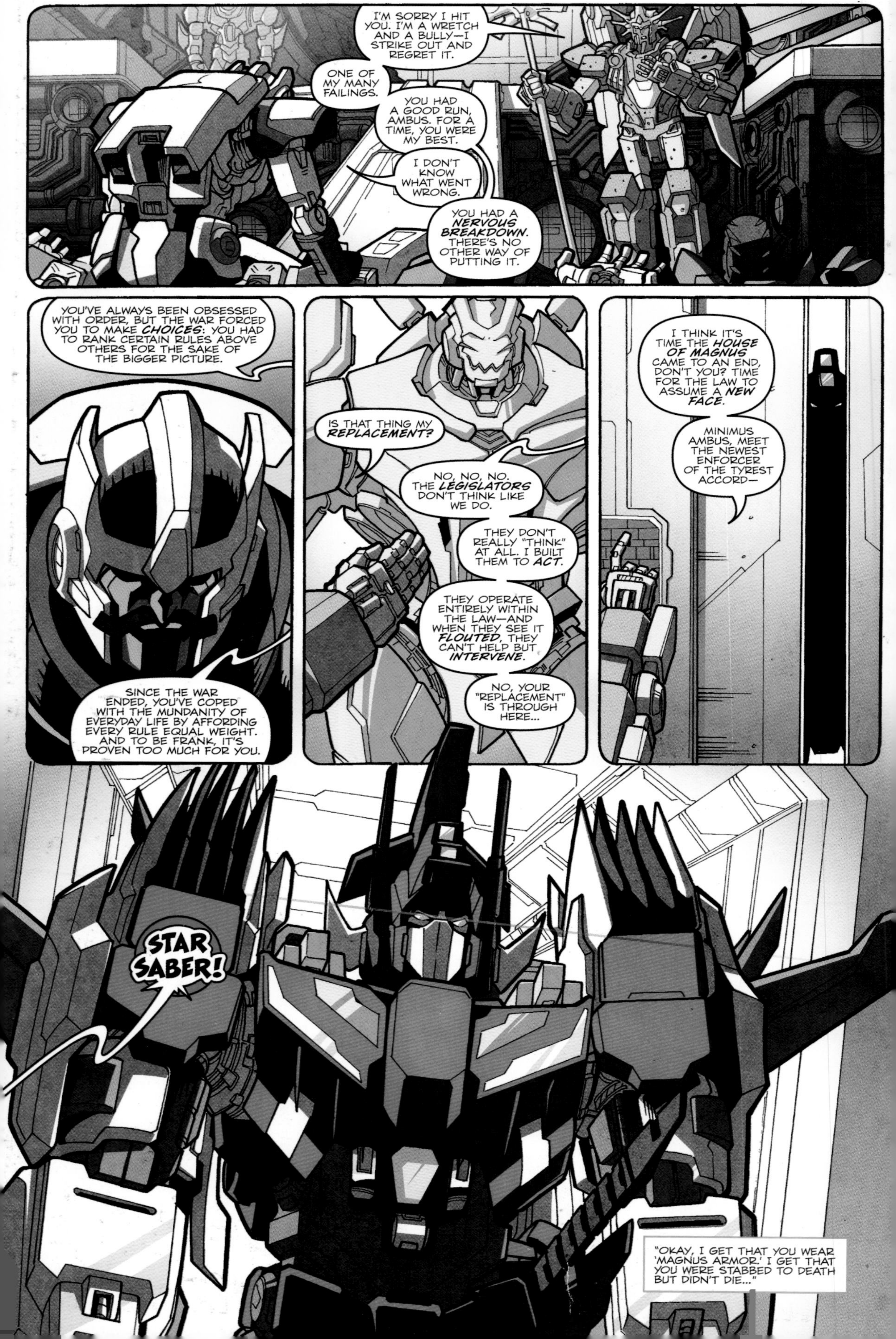

I'M SORRY I HIT YOU. I'M A WRETCH AND A BULLY—I STRIKE OUT AND REGRET IT.
ONE OF MY MANY FAILINGS.
YOU HAD A GOOD RUN, AMBUS. FOR A TIME, YOU WERE MY BEST.
I DON'T KNOW WHAT WENT WRONG.
YOU HAD A NERVOUS BREAKDOWN. THERE'S NO OTHER WAY OF PUTTING IT.
YOU'VE ALWAYS BEEN OBSESSED WITH ORDER, BUT THE WAR FORCED YOU TO MAKE CHOICES: YOU HAD TO RANK CERTAIN RULES ABOVE OTHERS FOR THE SAKE OF THE BIGGER PICTURE.
SINCE THE WAR ENDED, YOU'VE COPED WITH THE MUNDANITY OF EVERYDAY LIFE BY AFFORDING EVERY RULE EQUAL WEIGHT. AND TO BE FRANK, IT'S PROVEN TOO MUCH FOR YOU.
IS THAT THING MY REPLACEMENT?
NO, NO, NO. THE LEGISLATORS DON'T THINK LIKE WE DO.
THEY DON'T REALLY "THINK" AT ALL. I BUILT THEM TO ACT.
THEY OPERATE ENTIRELY WITHIN THE LAW—AND WHEN THEY SEE IT FLOUTED, THEY CAN'T HELP BUT INTERVENE.
NO, YOUR "REPLACEMENT" IS THROUGH HERE...
I THINK IT'S TIME THE HOUSE OF MAGNUS CAME TO AN END, DON'T YOU? TIME FOR THE LAW TO ASSUME A NEW FACE.
MINIMUS AMBUS, MEET THE NEWEST ENFORCER OF THE TYREST ACCORD—
STAR SABER!
"OKAY, I GET THAT YOU WEAR 'MAGNUS ARMOR.' I GET THAT YOU WERE STABBED TO DEATH BUT DIDN'T DIE..."

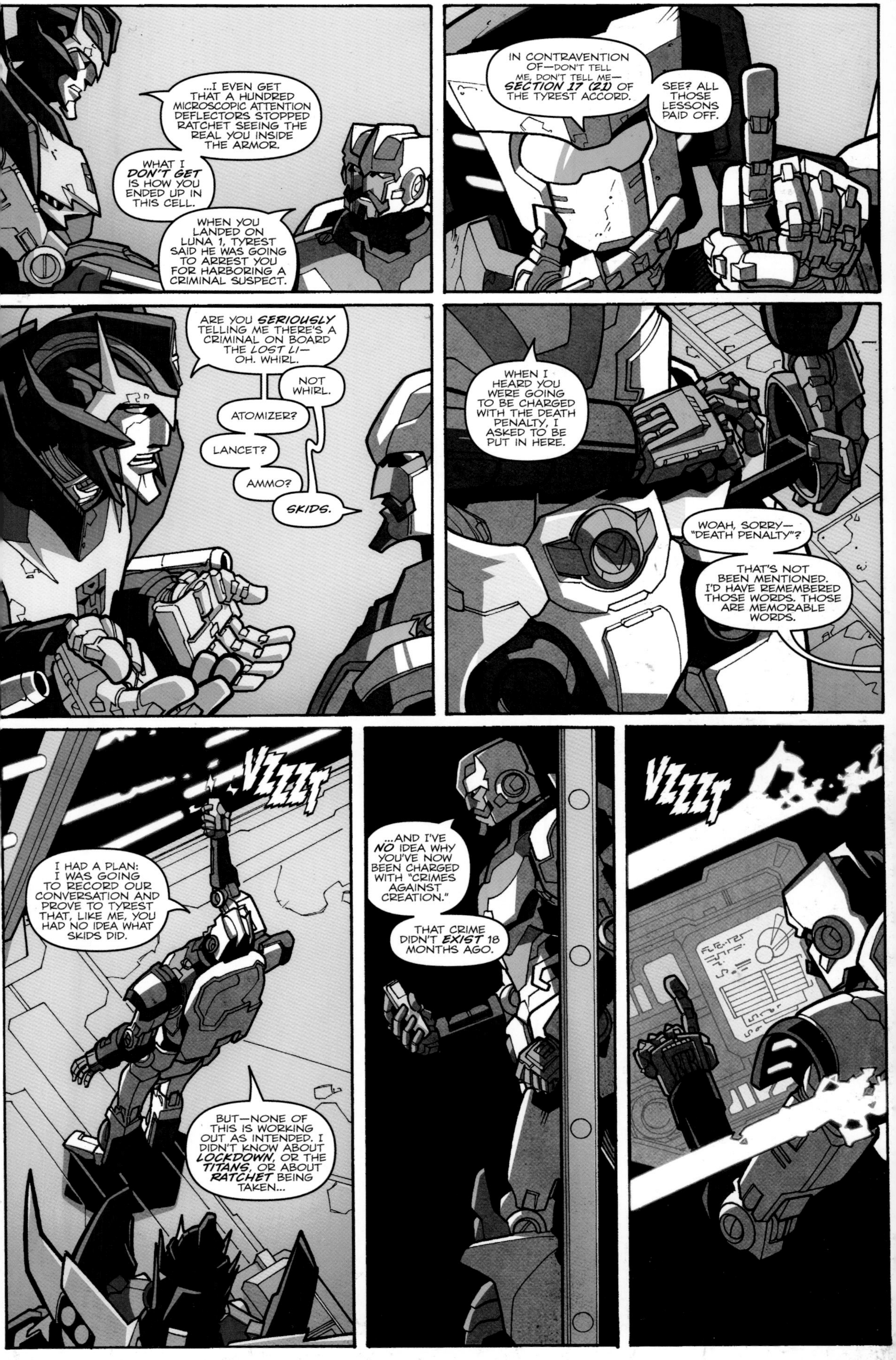
...I EVEN GET THAT A HUNDRED MICROSCOPIC ATTENTION DEFLECTORS STOPPED RATCHET SEEING THE REAL YOU INSIDE THE ARMOR.
WHAT I *DON'T GET* IS HOW YOU ENDED UP IN THIS CELL.
WHEN YOU LANDED ON LUNA 1, TYREST SAID HE WAS GOING TO ARREST YOU FOR HARBORING A CRIMINAL SUSPECT.
IN CONTRAVENTION OF—DON'T TELL ME, DON'T TELL ME—*SECTION 17 (21)* OF THE TYREST ACCORD.
SEE? ALL THOSE LESSONS PAID OFF.
ARE YOU *SERIOUSLY* TELLING ME THERE'S A CRIMINAL ON BOARD THE *LOST LI*— OH. WHIRL.
NOT WHIRL.
ATOMIZER?
LANCET?
AMMO?
SKIDS.
WHEN I HEARD YOU WERE GOING TO BE CHARGED WITH THE DEATH PENALTY, I ASKED TO BE PUT IN HERE.
WOAH, SORRY— "DEATH PENALTY"?
THAT'S NOT BEEN MENTIONED. I'D HAVE REMEMBERED THOSE WORDS. THOSE ARE MEMORABLE WORDS.
VZZZT
I HAD A PLAN: I WAS GOING TO RECORD OUR CONVERSATION AND PROVE TO TYREST THAT, LIKE ME, YOU HAD NO IDEA WHAT SKIDS DID.
BUT—NONE OF THIS IS WORKING OUT AS INTENDED. I DIDN'T KNOW ABOUT *LOCKDOWN*, OR THE *TITANS*, OR ABOUT *RATCHET* BEING TAKEN...
...AND I'VE *NO* IDEA WHY YOU'VE NOW BEEN CHARGED WITH "CRIMES AGAINST CREATION."
THAT CRIME DIDN'T *EXIST* 18 MONTHS AGO.
VZZZT

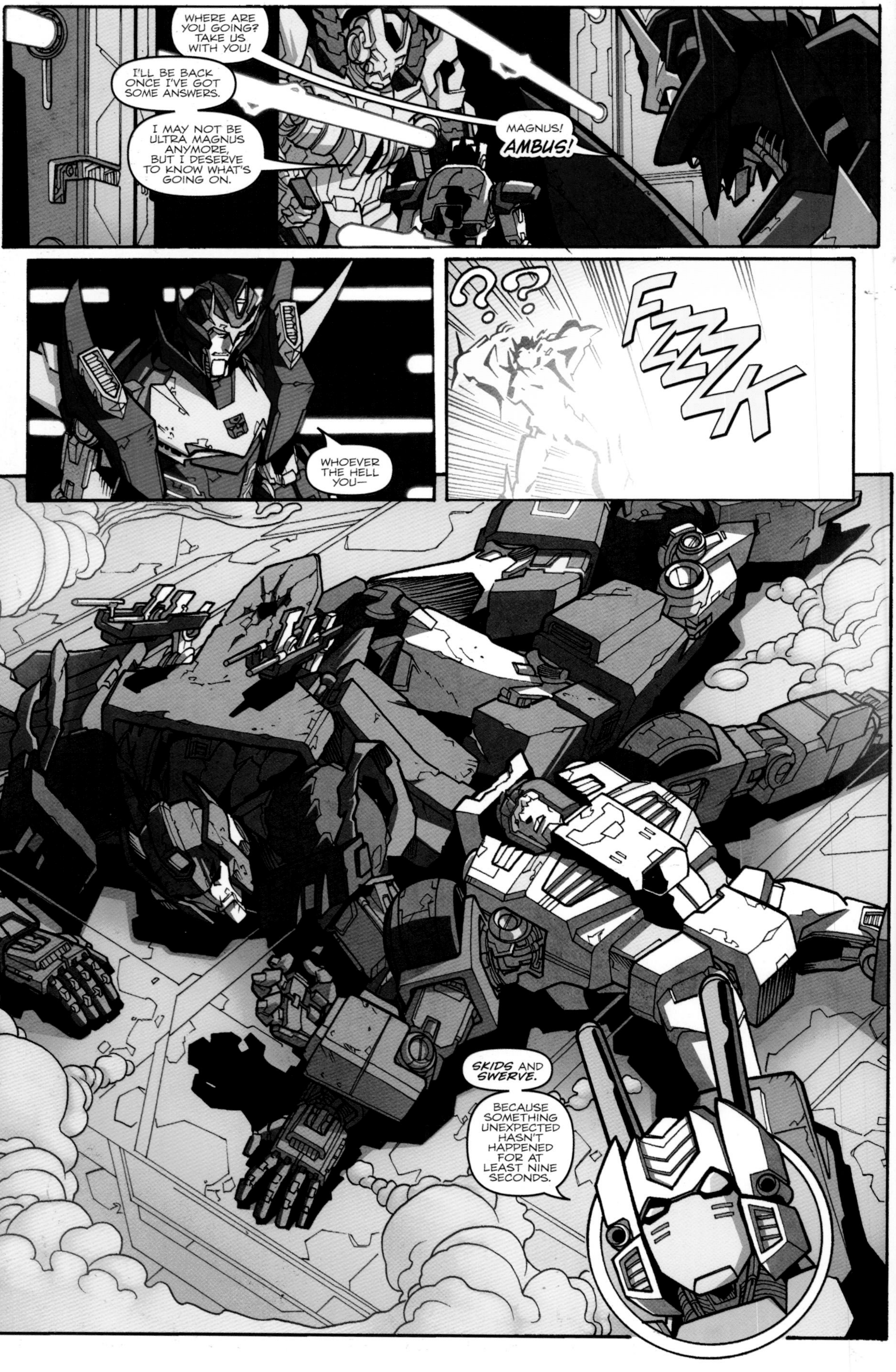

WHERE ARE YOU GOING? TAKE US WITH YOU!
I'LL BE BACK ONCE I'VE GOT SOME ANSWERS.
I MAY NOT BE ULTRA MAGNUS ANYMORE, BUT I DESERVE TO KNOW WHAT'S GOING ON.
MAGNUS! AMBUS!
WHOEVER THE HELL YOU—
? ?
FZZZK
SKIDS AND SWERVE.
BECAUSE SOMETHING UNEXPECTED HASN'T HAPPENED FOR AT LEAST NINE SECONDS.

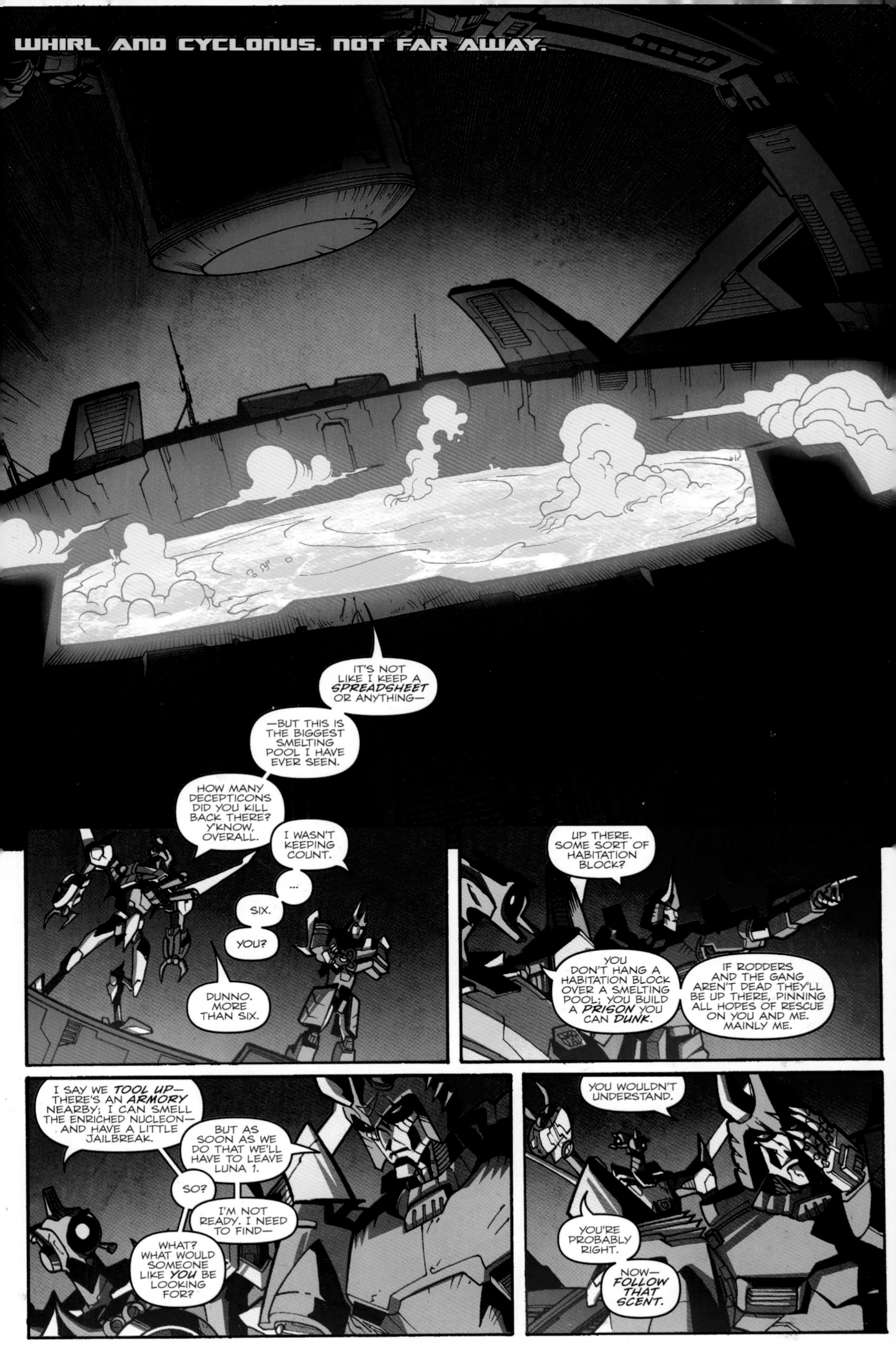
WHIRL AND CYCLONUS. NOT FAR AWAY.
IT'S NOT LIKE I KEEP A SPREADSHEET OR ANYTHING—
—BUT THIS IS THE BIGGEST SMELTING POOL I HAVE EVER SEEN.
HOW MANY DECEPTICONS DID YOU KILL BACK THERE? Y'KNOW, OVERALL.
I WASN'T KEEPING COUNT.
...
SIX.
YOU?
DUNNO. MORE THAN SIX.
UP THERE. SOME SORT OF HABITATION BLOCK?
YOU DON'T HANG A HABITATION BLOCK OVER A SMELTING POOL; YOU BUILD A PRISON YOU CAN DUNK.
IF RODDERS AND THE GANG AREN'T DEAD THEY'LL BE UP THERE, PINNING ALL HOPES OF RESCUE ON YOU AND ME. MAINLY ME.
I SAY WE TOOL UP—THERE'S AN ARMORY NEARBY; I CAN SMELL THE ENRICHED NUCLEON—AND HAVE A LITTLE JAILBREAK.
BUT AS SOON AS WE DO THAT WE'LL HAVE TO LEAVE LUNA 1.
SO?
I'M NOT READY. I NEED TO FIND—
WHAT? WHAT WOULD SOMEONE LIKE YOU BE LOOKING FOR?
YOU WOULDN'T UNDERSTAND.
YOU'RE PROBABLY RIGHT.
NOW—FOLLOW THAT SCENT.

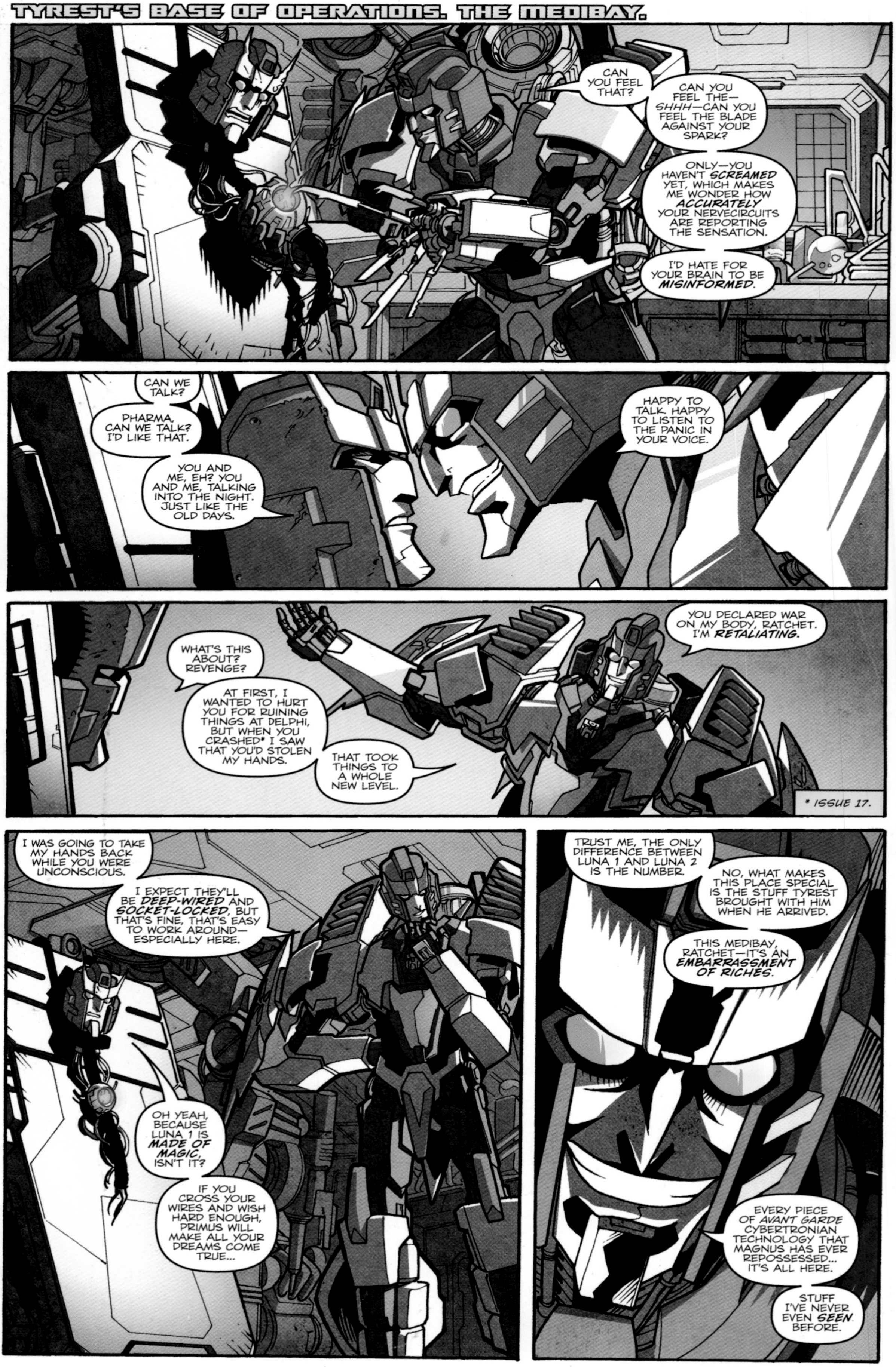
TYREST'S BASE OF OPERATIONS. THE MEDIBAY.
CAN YOU FEEL THAT?
CAN YOU FEEL THE— SHHH—CAN YOU FEEL THE BLADE AGAINST YOUR SPARK?
ONLY—YOU HAVEN'T SCREAMED YET, WHICH MAKES ME WONDER HOW ACCURATELY YOUR NERVECIRCUITS ARE REPORTING THE SENSATION.
I'D HATE FOR YOUR BRAIN TO BE MISINFORMED.
CAN WE TALK?
PHARMA, CAN WE TALK? I'D LIKE THAT.
YOU AND ME, EH? YOU AND ME, TALKING INTO THE NIGHT. JUST LIKE THE OLD DAYS.
HAPPY TO TALK. HAPPY TO LISTEN TO THE PANIC IN YOUR VOICE.
WHAT'S THIS ABOUT? REVENGE?
YOU DECLARED WAR ON MY BODY, RATCHET. I'M RETALIATING.
AT FIRST, I WANTED TO HURT YOU FOR RUINING THINGS AT DELPHI, BUT WHEN YOU CRASHED* I SAW THAT YOU'D STOLEN MY HANDS.
THAT TOOK THINGS TO A WHOLE NEW LEVEL.
* ISSUE 17.
I WAS GOING TO TAKE MY HANDS BACK WHILE YOU WERE UNCONSCIOUS.
I EXPECT THEY'LL BE DEEP-WIRED AND SOCKET-LOCKED, BUT THAT'S FINE, THAT'S EASY TO WORK AROUND— ESPECIALLY HERE.
OH YEAH, BECAUSE LUNA 1 IS MADE OF MAGIC, ISN'T IT?
IF YOU CROSS YOUR WIRES AND WISH HARD ENOUGH, PRIMUS WILL MAKE ALL YOUR DREAMS COME TRUE...
TRUST ME, THE ONLY DIFFERENCE BETWEEN LUNA 1 AND LUNA 2 IS THE NUMBER.
NO, WHAT MAKES THIS PLACE SPECIAL IS THE STUFF TYREST BROUGHT WITH HIM WHEN HE ARRIVED.
THIS MEDIBAY, RATCHET—IT'S AN EMBARRASSMENT OF RICHES.
EVERY PIECE OF AVANT GARDE CYBERTRONIAN TECHNOLOGY THAT MAGNUS HAS EVER REPOSSESSED... IT'S ALL HERE.
STUFF I'VE NEVER EVEN SEEN BEFORE.

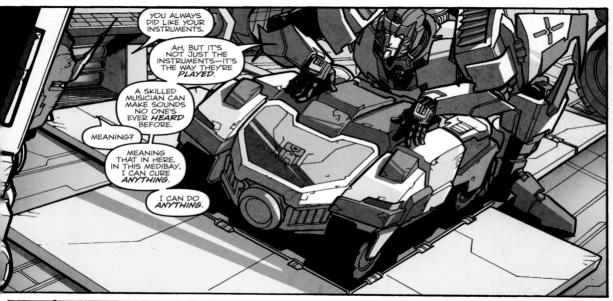

YOU ALWAYS DID LIKE YOUR INSTRUMENTS.

AH, BUT IT'S NOT JUST THE INSTRUMENTS—IT'S THE WAY THEY'RE *PLAYED*.

A SKILLED MUSICIAN CAN MAKE SOUNDS NO ONE'S EVER *HEARD* BEFORE.

MEANING?

MEANING THAT IN HERE, IN THIS MEDIBAY, I CAN CURE *ANYTHING*.

I CAN DO *ANYTHING*.

ANYTHING EXCEPT REMOVE A PAIR OF HANDS.

C'MON, PHARMA— THE TRUTH.

DEEP-WIRED, SOCKET-LOCKED... AND STILL ON MY WRISTS. WHY?

BECAUSE I'M A *DOCTOR*, NOT A *BOMB DISPOSAL EXPERT*.

YOU THINK—

WAIT.

YOU THINK I WIRED *YOUR* HANDS—THE ONES I ATTACHED TO *MY* BODY—YOU THINK I *WIRED THEM TO EXPLODE*?

I... THINK IT'S A POSSIBILITY, YES.

OR MAYBE... MAYBE YOU'RE SCARED OF *FAILURE*.

MAYBE YOU'RE AFRAID YOU WON'T BE ABLE TO PICK THE LOCK OR LOOSEN THE WIRING, SO YOU WANT *HELP*.

I GET IT, PHARMA.

IT TOOK ME A WHILE, BUT—IT MAKES SENSE NOW: *I'M BETTER THAN YOU.*

A BETTER DOCTOR? *PLEASE*. I OVERTOOK YOU YEARS AGO.

I DON'T NEED MY HANDS BACK TO SLAP YOU DOWN.

PROVE IT. PUT ME BACK IN MY BODY AND PROVE IT.

A RACE TO FIX THE SAME INJURY—THE BETTER SURGEON WINS THE HANDS.

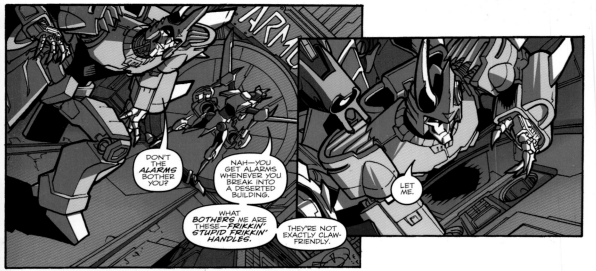

DON'T THE **ALARMS** BOTHER YOU?

NAH—YOU GET ALARMS WHENEVER YOU BREAK INTO A DESERTED BUILDING.

WHAT **BOTHERS** ME ARE THESE—FRIKKIN' STUPID FRIKKIN' HANDLES.

THEY'RE NOT EXACTLY CLAW-FRIENDLY.

LET ME.

I DON'T UNDERSTAND WHY YOU DON'T GET YOURSELF **FIXED**.

IF NOT THE FACE, THEN THE CLAWS.

KLIK

KLIK

YOU WANNA KNOW A **SECRET**, HORN-HEAD?

LIFE'S MESSED UP. **I'M** MESSED UP.

I'VE DONE BAD THINGS AND I **CONTINUE** TO DO BAD THINGS, BECAUSE THE VOICE TELLING ME **NOT TO**...? HE'S NOT SAID MUCH FOR A WHILE.

AND Y'KNOW WHAT KEEPS ME GOING? **ANGER.**

ANGER'S AN **INSULATOR**. STOPS LIFE GETTING **TOO CLOSE**.

IF I GOT MYSELF "FIXED," MAYBE THE ANGER WOULD LEAVE ME—AND THEN I REALLY **WOULD** BE SCREWED.

AND SINCE WE'RE GETTING **PERSONAL**, THOSE MARKS ON YOUR FACE...

NO.

DON'T EVEN—

HRK!

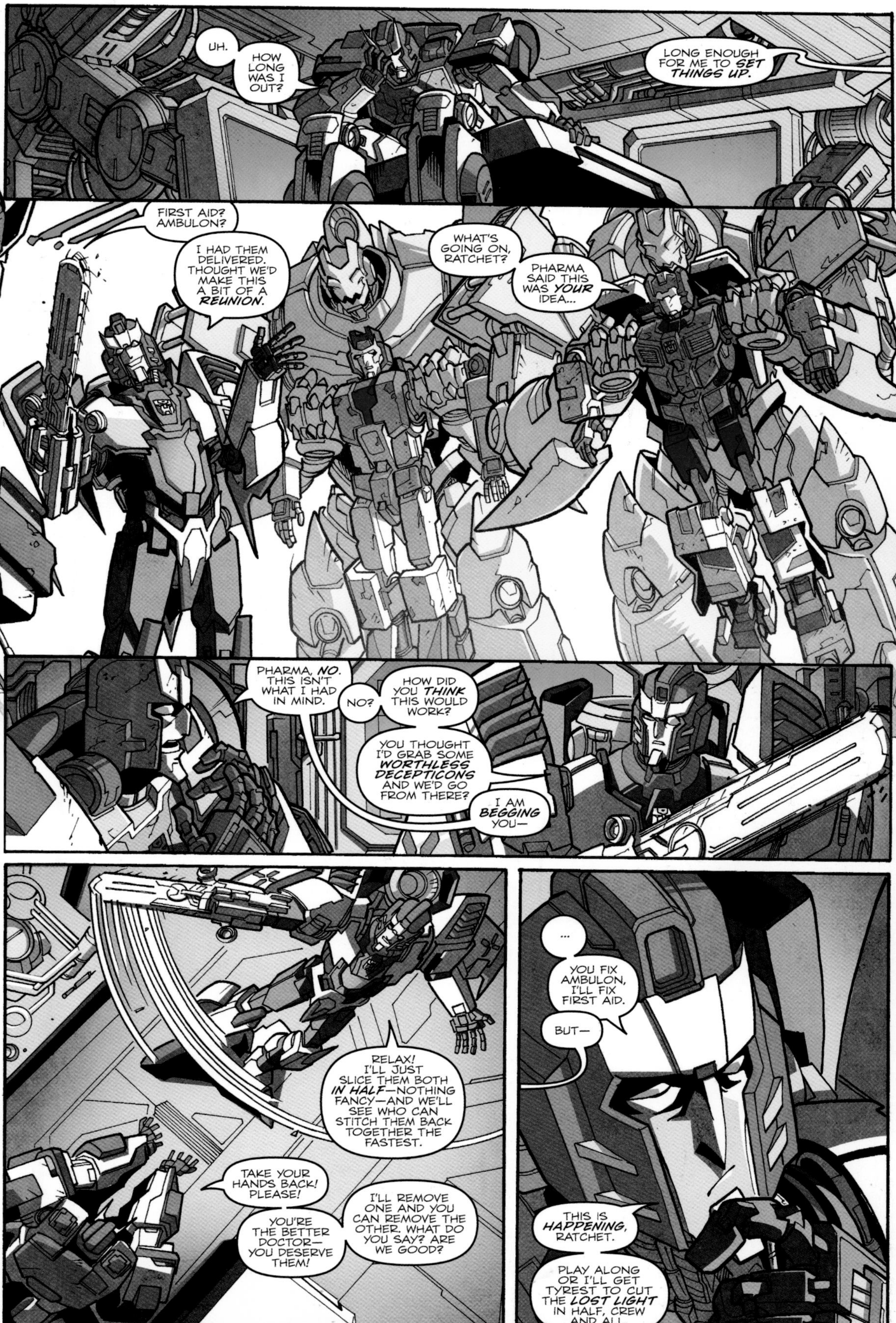
UH.
HOW LONG WAS I OUT?
LONG ENOUGH FOR ME TO SET THINGS UP.
FIRST AID? AMBULON?
I HAD THEM DELIVERED. THOUGHT WE'D MAKE THIS A BIT OF A REUNION.
WHAT'S GOING ON, RATCHET?
PHARMA SAID THIS WAS YOUR IDEA...
PHARMA, NO. THIS ISN'T WHAT I HAD IN MIND.
NO?
HOW DID YOU THINK THIS WOULD WORK?
YOU THOUGHT I'D GRAB SOME WORTHLESS DECEPTICONS AND WE'D GO FROM THERE?
I AM BEGGING YOU—
RELAX! I'LL JUST SLICE THEM BOTH IN HALF—NOTHING FANCY—AND WE'LL SEE WHO CAN STITCH THEM BACK TOGETHER THE FASTEST.
TAKE YOUR HANDS BACK! PLEASE!
YOU'RE THE BETTER DOCTOR—YOU DESERVE THEM!
I'LL REMOVE ONE AND YOU CAN REMOVE THE OTHER. WHAT DO YOU SAY? ARE WE GOOD?
...
YOU FIX AMBULON, I'LL FIX FIRST AID.
BUT—
THIS IS HAPPENING, RATCHET.
PLAY ALONG OR I'LL GET TYREST TO CUT THE LOST LIGHT IN HALF, CREW AND ALL.

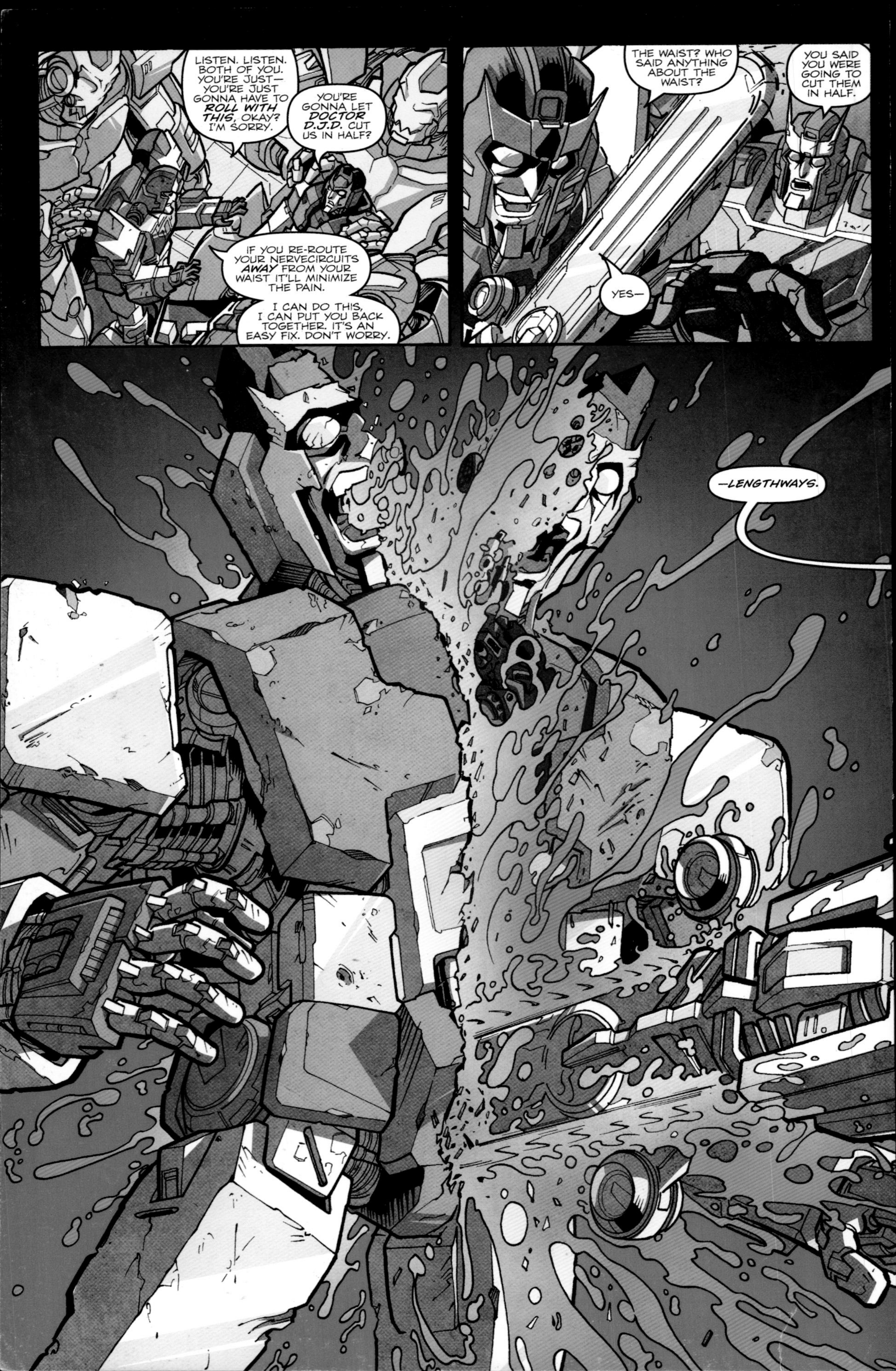
LISTEN. LISTEN. BOTH OF YOU. YOU'RE JUST— YOU'RE JUST GONNA HAVE TO **ROLL WITH THIS**, OKAY? I'M SORRY.
YOU'RE GONNA LET **DOCTOR D.J.D.** CUT US IN HALF?
IF YOU RE-ROUTE YOUR NERVECIRCUITS **AWAY** FROM YOUR WAIST IT'LL MINIMIZE THE PAIN.
I CAN DO THIS, I CAN PUT YOU BACK TOGETHER. IT'S AN EASY FIX. DON'T WORRY.
THE WAIST? WHO SAID ANYTHING ABOUT THE WAIST?
YOU SAID YOU WERE GOING TO CUT THEM IN HALF.
YES—
—*LENGTHWAYS.*

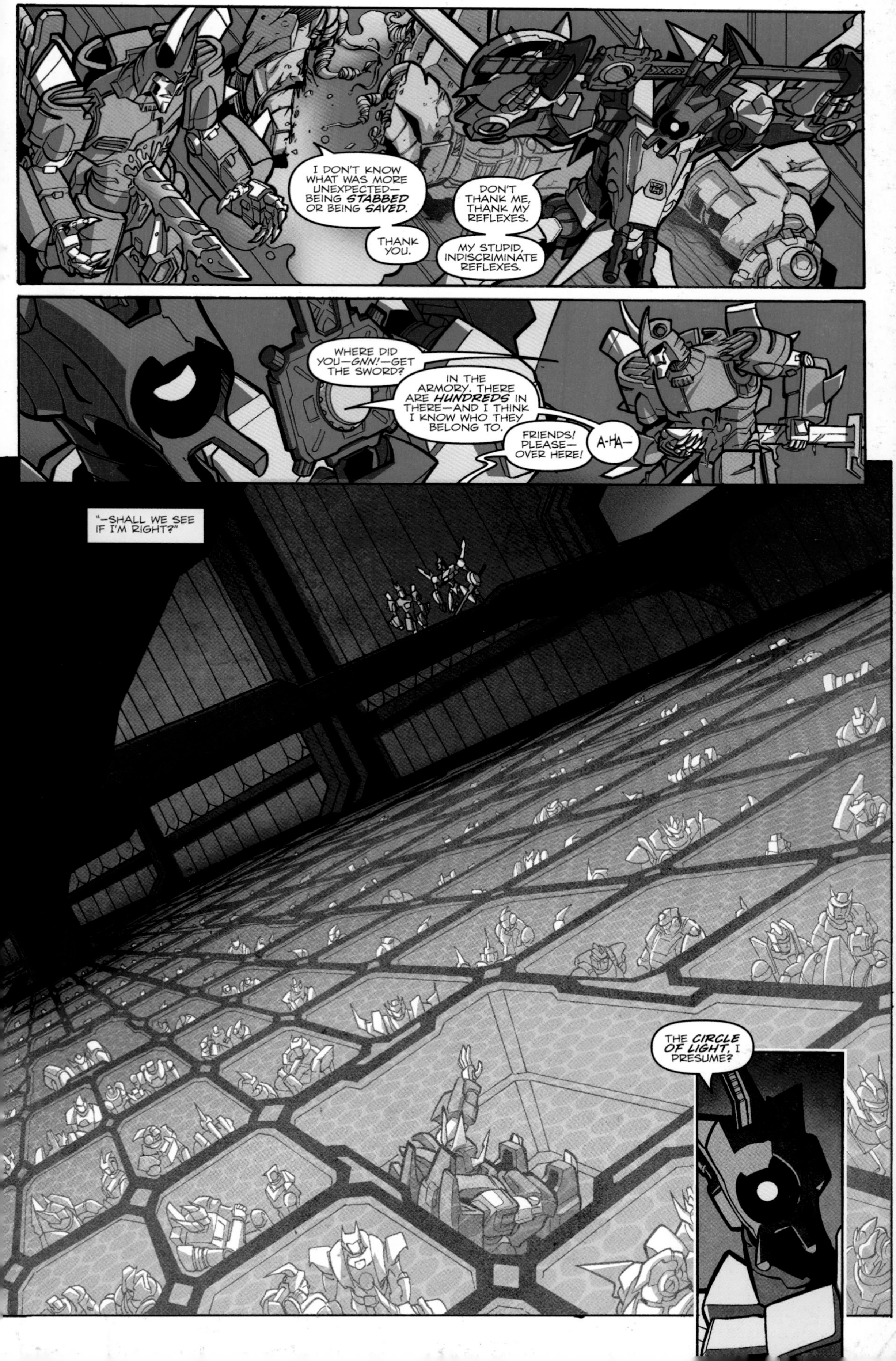
I DON'T KNOW WHAT WAS MORE UNEXPECTED—BEING STABBED OR BEING SAVED.
THANK YOU.
DON'T THANK ME, THANK MY REFLEXES.
MY STUPID, INDISCRIMINATE REFLEXES.
WHERE DID YOU—GNN!—GET THE SWORD?
IN THE ARMORY. THERE ARE HUNDREDS IN THERE—AND I THINK I KNOW WHO THEY BELONG TO.
FRIENDS! PLEASE—OVER HERE!
A-HA—
"—SHALL WE SEE IF I'M RIGHT?"
THE CIRCLE OF LIGHT, I PRESUME?

HOW'S SKIDS?

HE'LL LIVE. IT'S SURPRISING HOW MANY STAB WOUNDS MISS THE SPARK.

I THINK IT WAS *INTENDED* TO INCAPACITATE. TYREST WANTS HIM ALIVE TO STAND TRIAL.

AND YOU'RE SURE IT WAS *STAR SABER* WHO DID THIS?

IT WAS THE GUY FROM THOSE *HOLY WAR* DOCUMENTARIES THAT REWIND SHOWED US.

"THE DARK EVANGELIST." STAR SABER, YEAH.

BUT Y'KNOW THIS ISN'T JUST ABOUT SKIDS, RIGHT?

"THERE WERE THESE GOLDEN ROBOTS, AND THEY WERE ATTACKING THE *WHOLE SHIP.*"

"DUNNO WHETHER ANYONE ELSE IS GONNA BE TELEPORTED DOWN HERE, OR WHETHER THAT PRIVILEGE IS RESERVED FOR *THEORETICIANS AND THEIR FRIENDS.*"

REMEMBER *LAST YEAR*? WE SAW SKIDS GET ATTACKED BY A LEGISLATOR—BY ONE OF THOSE GOLDEN ROBOTS.

BUT DO YOU REMEMBER? HE WAS CARRYING AN *INVISIBLE GUN.* WELL, INVISIBLE TO *HIM.*

SO?

SKIDS MUST'VE STOLEN THE GUN!

THAT'S WHY TYREST WANTS HIM!

SOUNDS PRETTY—⅗KAFF!⅗—PLAUSIBLE TO ME...

SKIDS!

LET'S JUST ASSUME I DID SOMETHING STUPID—SOMETHING REALLY STUPID—AND MOVE STRAIGHT TO THE—⅗KAFF!⅗—APOLOGY.

BECAUSE I JUST WANT TO SAY *SORRY.*

CONTRITION WITHOUT CONFESSION IS MEANINGLESS...

TYREST?

I'M **BUSY**.

A DISTURBANCE NEAR THE SMELTING POOL.

I'M SENDING SOME LEGISLATORS TO INVESTIGATE.

WHAT HAPPENED TO "CHIEF JUSTICE"? HAVE YOU LOST YOUR MANNERS AS WELL AS YOUR ARMOR?

IS THAT WHY YOU'RE KEEPING ME OUT OF THE LOOP?

LUNA 1, THE TITANS OUTSIDE... AND DON'T THINK I HAVEN'T NOTICED THE **SPACE BRIDGE PORTAL** IN THE CORNER.

WHAT'S THIS ABOUT, **TYREST**?

I'VE LOST **EVERYTHING**— AND I'M STARTING TO **LIKE** IT.

FOR THE FIRST TIME SINCE YOU CHOSE ME I FEEL... **UNENCUMBERED**.

UH-HUH.

THIS MAY COME AS A BITTER BLOW, BUT I HAVE PRECISELY NO INTEREST IN WHAT YOU'VE GOT TO SAY.

IN A WORD? **GUILT**.

GUILT IS WHAT MAKES US **DIFFERENT**; IT'S WHAT MAKES US MORE THAN MACHINES.

DO **LEGISLATORS** FEEL GUILT WHEN THEY KILL? DO **SPARKEATERS** FEEL GUILT WHEN THEY FEED?

NO.

ONLY WE HIGHER BEINGS ARE TROUBLED BY OUR CONSCIENCE.

I HAVE SINNED, AMBUS. MY BODY **OVERFLOWS** WITH GUILT.

PLEASE. JUST TELL ME—POINT FOR POINT—WHAT'S GOING ON.

VERY WELL— BUT I WARN YOU. I'LL HAVE TO START AT THE BEGINNING.

"A CYBERTRONIAN IS CREATED IN ONE OF TWO WAYS: WE'RE EITHER **FORGED** OR **CONSTRUCTED COLD**.

"FOR THOSE OF US WHO ARE FORGED, LIFE BEGAN WHEN **PRIMUS**, THROUGH **VECTOR SIGMA**, GENERATED A **PULSEWAVE**.

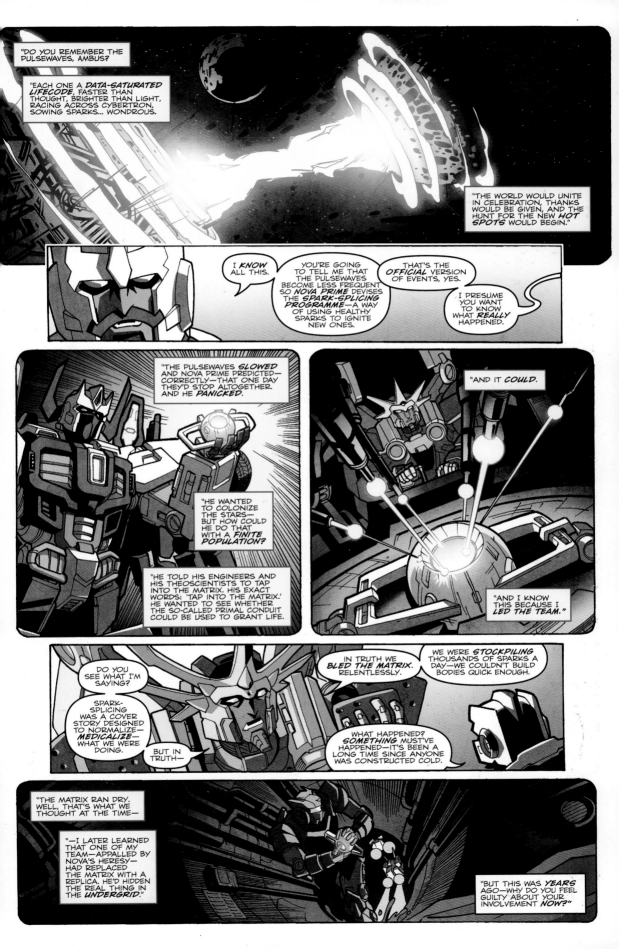

"DO YOU REMEMBER THE PULSEWAVES, AMBUS?

"EACH ONE A *DATA-SATURATED LIFECODE*, FASTER THAN THOUGHT, BRIGHTER THAN LIGHT, RACING ACROSS CYBERTRON, SOWING SPARKS... WONDROUS.

"THE WORLD WOULD UNITE IN CELEBRATION, THANKS WOULD BE GIVEN, AND THE HUNT FOR THE NEW *HOT SPOTS* WOULD BEGIN."

I *KNOW* ALL THIS.

YOU'RE GOING TO TELL ME THAT THE PULSEWAVES BECOME LESS FREQUENT SO *NOVA PRIME* DEVISES THE *SPARK-SPLICING PROGRAMME*—A WAY OF USING HEALTHY SPARKS TO IGNITE NEW ONES.

THAT'S THE *OFFICIAL* VERSION OF EVENTS, YES.

I PRESUME YOU WANT TO KNOW WHAT *REALLY* HAPPENED.

"THE PULSEWAVES *SLOWED* AND NOVA PRIME PREDICTED—CORRECTLY—THAT ONE DAY THEY'D STOP ALTOGETHER. AND HE *PANICKED*.

"HE WANTED TO COLONIZE THE STARS— BUT HOW COULD HE DO THAT WITH A *FINITE POPULATION?*

"HE TOLD HIS ENGINEERS AND HIS THEOSCIENTISTS TO TAP INTO THE MATRIX. HIS EXACT WORDS: 'TAP INTO THE MATRIX.' HE WANTED TO SEE WHETHER THE SO-CALLED PRIMAL CONDUIT COULD BE USED TO GRANT LIFE.

"AND IT *COULD*.

"AND I KNOW THIS BECAUSE I *LED THE TEAM*."

DO YOU SEE WHAT I'M SAYING?

SPARK-SPLICING WAS A COVER STORY DESIGNED TO NORMALIZE— *MEDICALIZE*— WHAT WE WERE DOING.

BUT IN TRUTH—

IN TRUTH WE *BLED THE MATRIX*. RELENTLESSLY.

WE WERE *STOCKPILING* THOUSANDS OF SPARKS A DAY—WE COULDN'T BUILD BODIES QUICK ENOUGH.

WHAT HAPPENED? *SOMETHING* MUST'VE HAPPENED—IT'S BEEN A LONG TIME SINCE ANYONE WAS CONSTRUCTED COLD.

"THE MATRIX RAN DRY. WELL, THAT'S WHAT WE THOUGHT AT THE TIME—

"—I LATER LEARNED THAT ONE OF MY TEAM—APPALLED BY NOVA'S HERESY— HAD REPLACED THE MATRIX WITH A REPLICA. HE'D HIDDEN THE REAL THING IN THE *UNDERGRID*."

"BUT THIS WAS *YEARS* AGO—WHY DO YOU FEEL GUILTY ABOUT YOUR INVOLVEMENT *NOW?*"

I DIDN'T REALIZE THE CIRCLE OF LIGHT WAS SO *POPULAR*, DAI ATLAS.

I MEAN, YOU HEAR *"KNIGHTS OF CYBERTRON CULT"* AND YOU THINK TO YOUR-SELF, *PFFT*, FIFTY PEOPLE? SIXTY?

BUT THERE'S *MASSES* OF YOU!

GUESS SOME PEOPLE WILL DO ANYTHING TO GET A *GREAT SWORD.*

OUR NUMBERS ARE BUT A *TENTH* OF WHAT THEY ONCE WERE.

TYREST USED THE OTHERS AS RAW MATERIAL TO REPLENISH HIS LEGISLATORS.

ALL THE MORE REASON TO FIND TAILGATE AND THE OTHERS *QUICKLY*, BEFORE—

—BEFORE THEY *ARRIVE.*

SO HERE'S THE PLAN: I'LL WATCH YOUR BACK AND YOU WATCH MINE.

AND IF WE MAKE IT OUT OF THIS ALIVE, THEN ALL SCORES ARE *SETTLED*, OKAY?

NO MORE TRYING TO KILL ME. WHAT DO YOU SAY?

I SAY FOCUS ON THE FIGHT.

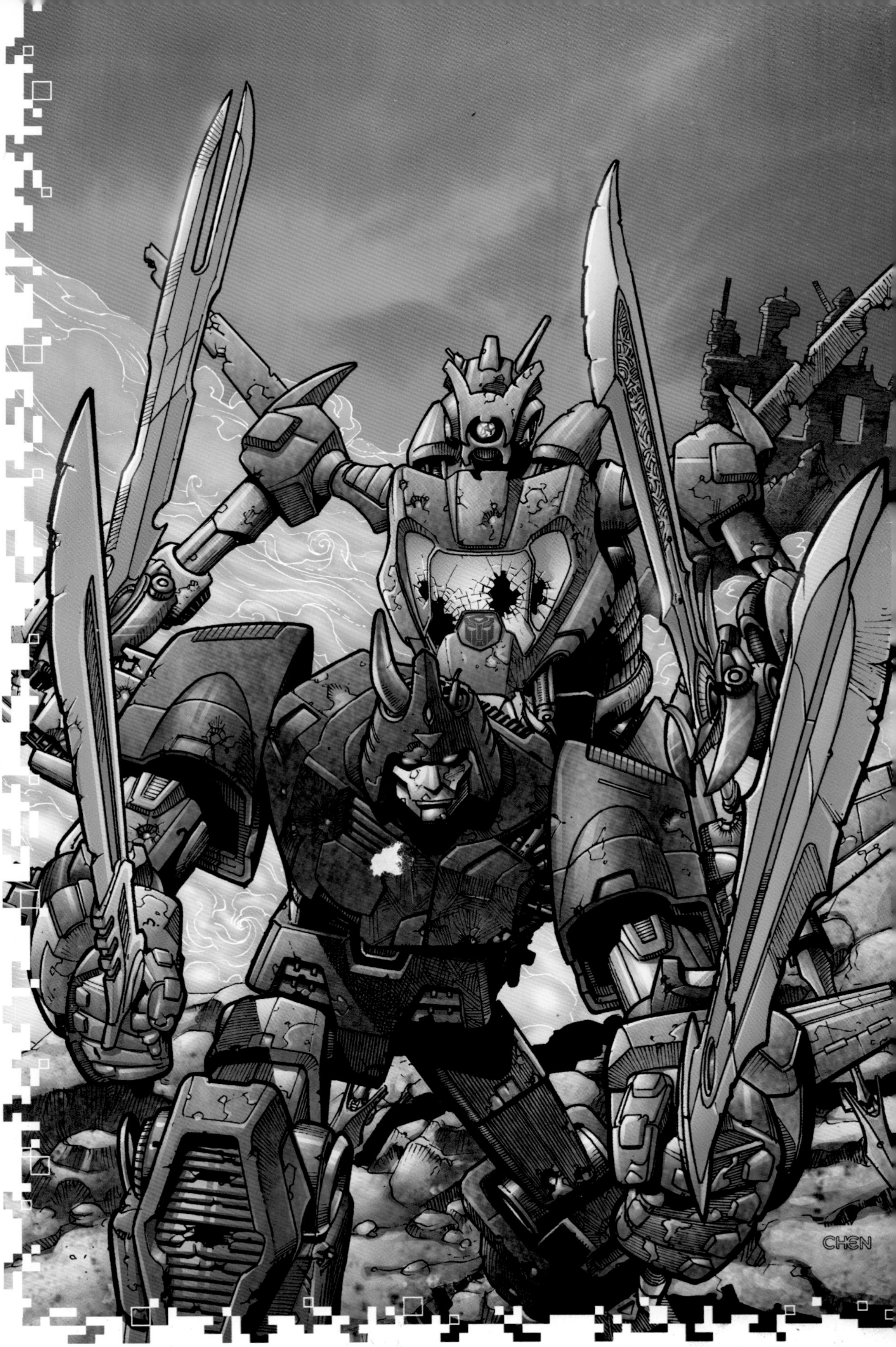
CHEN

MORE THAN MEETS THE EYE #19 COVER B

by SEAN CHEN Colors by TOM CHU

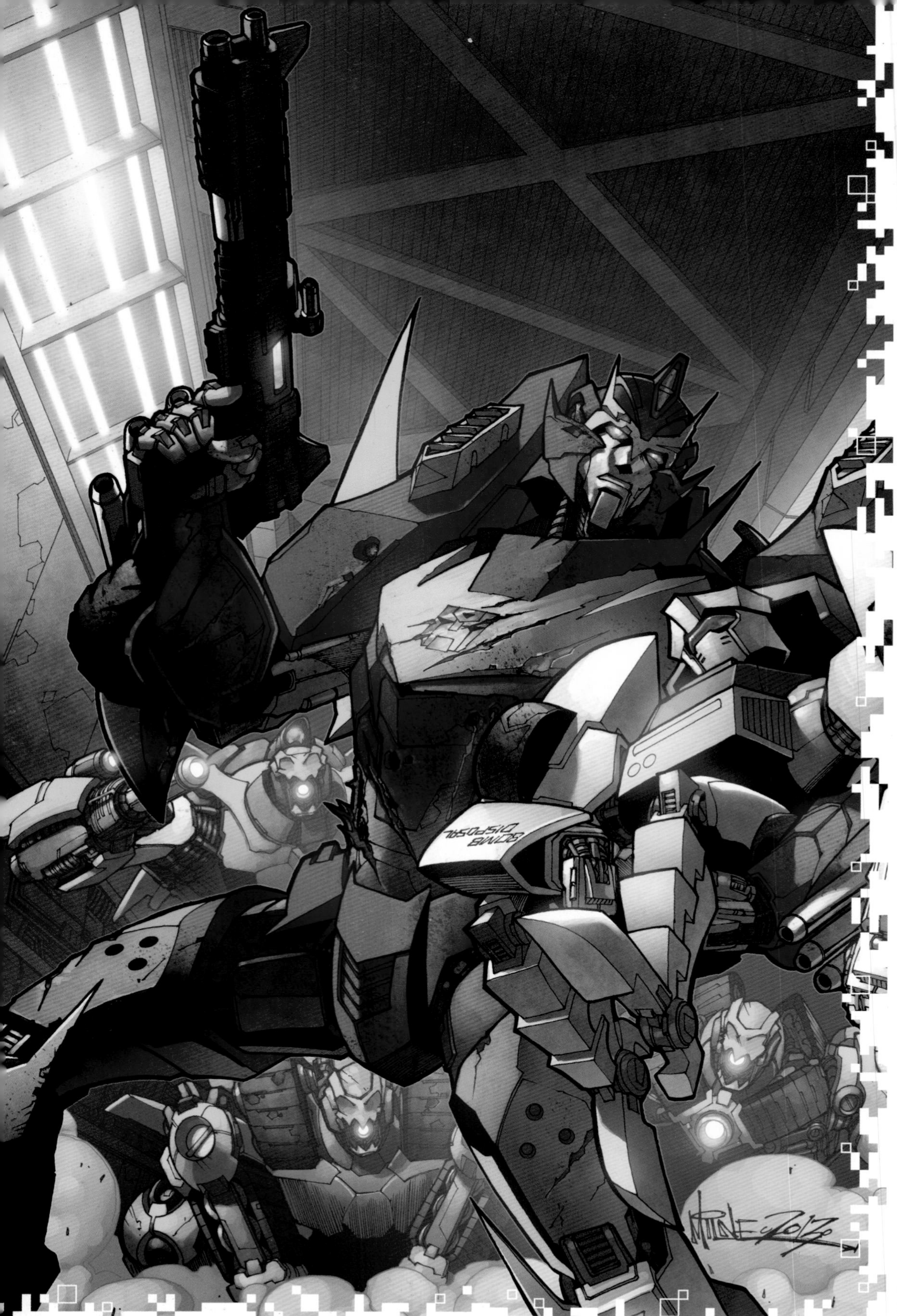

MORE THAN MEETS THE EYE #20 COVER A

by **ALEX MILNE** Colors by **JOSH PEREZ**

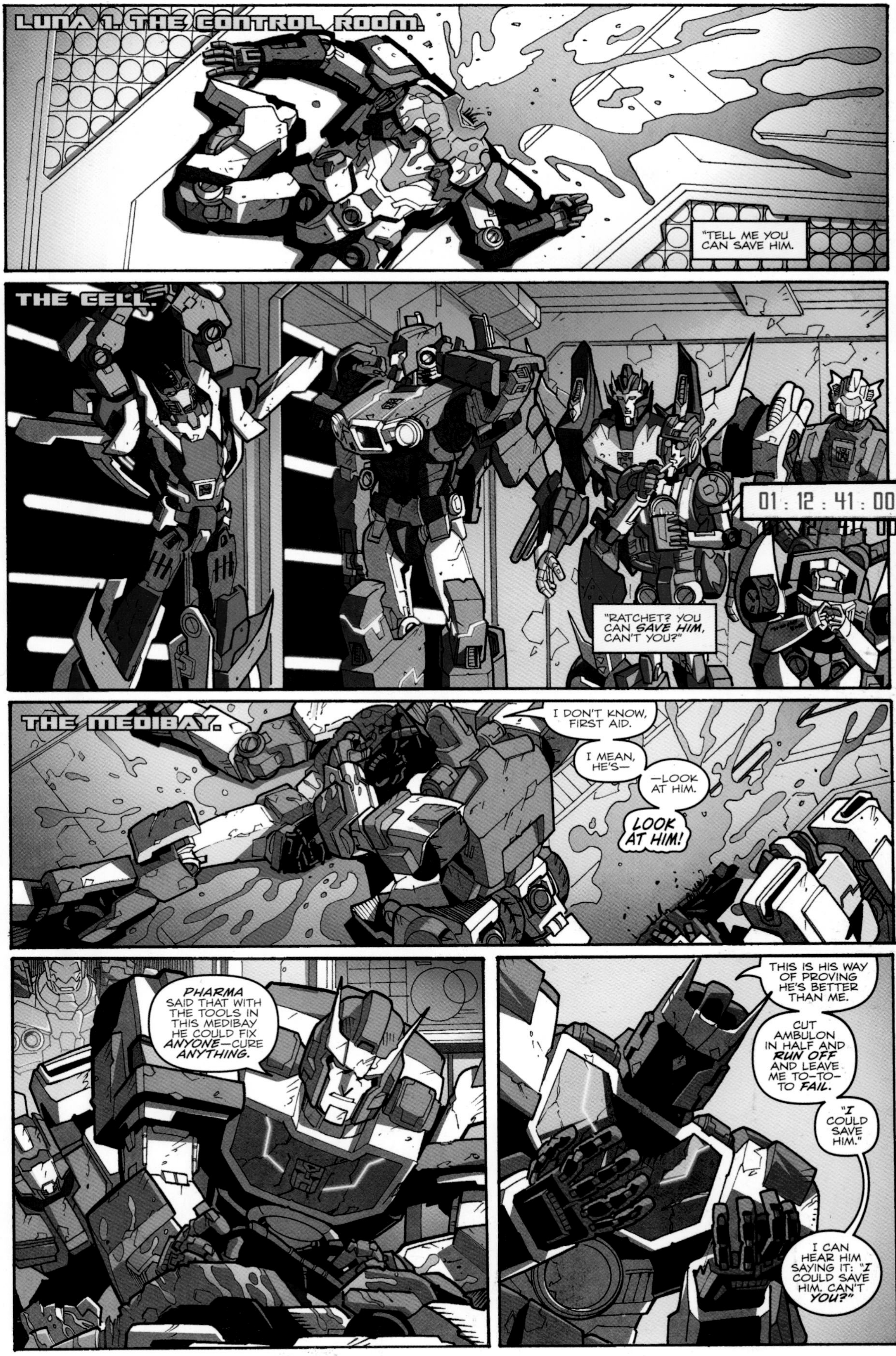
LUNA 1. THE CONTROL ROOM.
"TELL ME YOU CAN SAVE HIM.
THE CELL.
01 : 12 : 41 : 00
"RATCHET? YOU CAN SAVE HIM, CAN'T YOU?"
THE MEDIBAY.
I DON'T KNOW, FIRST AID.
I MEAN, HE'S—
—LOOK AT HIM.
LOOK AT HIM!
PHARMA SAID THAT WITH THE TOOLS IN THIS MEDIBAY HE COULD FIX ANYONE—CURE ANYTHING.
THIS IS HIS WAY OF PROVING HE'S BETTER THAN ME.
CUT AMBULON IN HALF AND RUN OFF AND LEAVE ME TO-TO-TO FAIL.
"I COULD SAVE HIM."
I CAN HEAR HIM SAYING IT: "I COULD SAVE HIM. CAN'T YOU?"

IT'S DRAWING POWER FROM YOUR SPARK TO THE NEXUS IN THE HILT AND THEN *ENERGIZING THE BLADE.*

I HAVE TO SAY, FOR A NOVICE, THAT'S VERY... HM.

DAI ATLAS?

THAT'S A SURPRISINGLY *DEEP* CONNECTION.

YOUR FRIEND IS CLEARLY *DEVOUT.*

SORRY, MY *WHAT?*

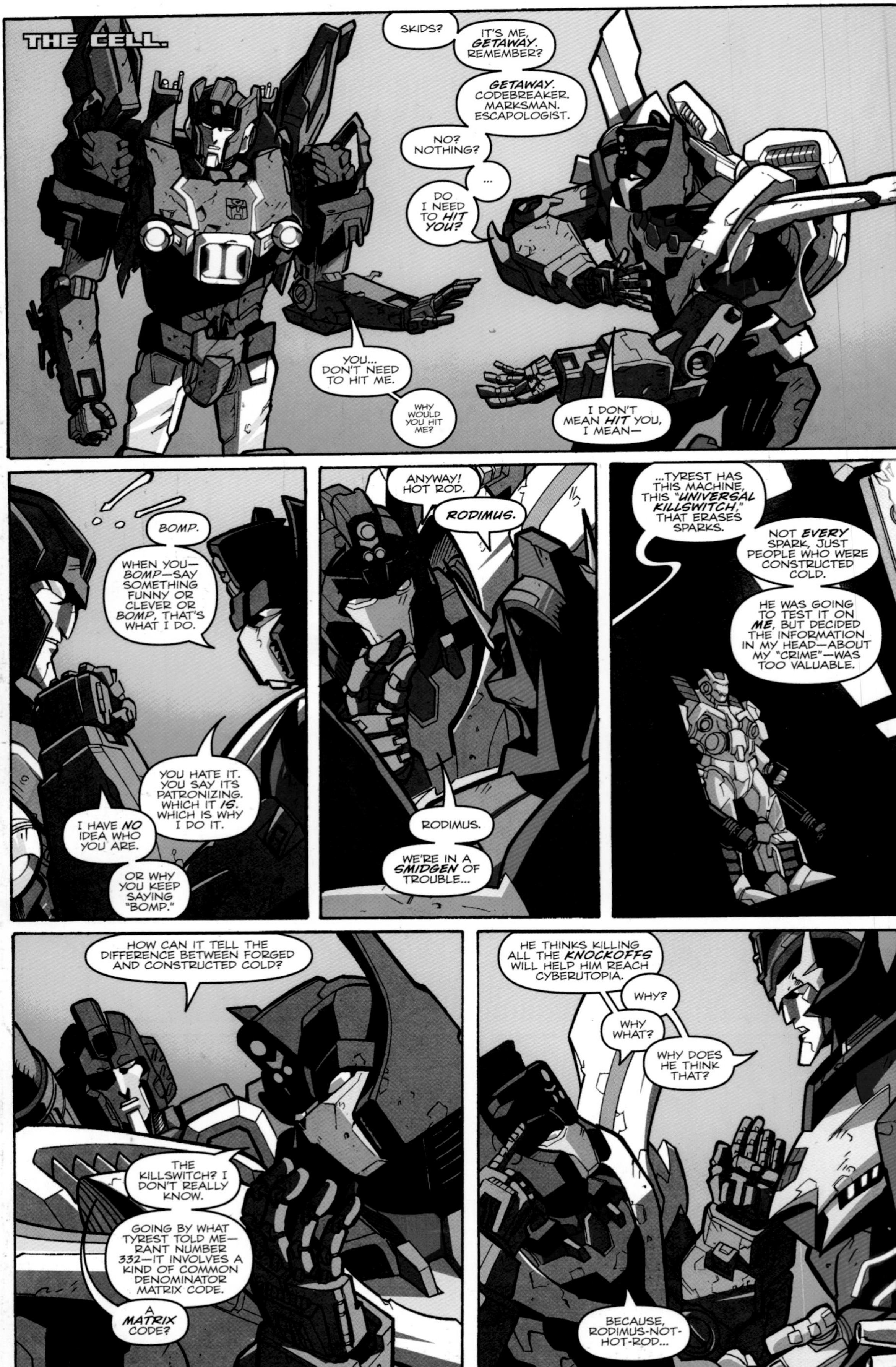
THE CELL.
SKIDS?
IT'S ME, GETAWAY. REMEMBER?
GETAWAY. CODEBREAKER. MARKSMAN. ESCAPOLOGIST.
NO? NOTHING?
...
DO I NEED TO HIT YOU?
YOU... DON'T NEED TO HIT ME.
WHY WOULD YOU HIT ME?
I DON'T MEAN HIT YOU, I MEAN—
BOMP.
WHEN YOU—BOMP—SAY SOMETHING FUNNY OR CLEVER OR BOMP, THAT'S WHAT I DO.
YOU HATE IT. YOU SAY ITS PATRONIZING. WHICH IT IS. WHICH IS WHY I DO IT.
I HAVE NO IDEA WHO YOU ARE.
OR WHY YOU KEEP SAYING "BOMP."
ANYWAY! HOT ROD.
RODIMUS.
RODIMUS.
WE'RE IN A SMIDGEN OF TROUBLE...
...TYREST HAS THIS MACHINE, THIS "UNIVERSAL KILLSWITCH," THAT ERASES SPARKS.
NOT EVERY SPARK, JUST PEOPLE WHO WERE CONSTRUCTED COLD.
HE WAS GOING TO TEST IT ON ME, BUT DECIDED THE INFORMATION IN MY HEAD—ABOUT MY "CRIME"—WAS TOO VALUABLE.
HOW CAN IT TELL THE DIFFERENCE BETWEEN FORGED AND CONSTRUCTED COLD?
THE KILLSWITCH? I DON'T REALLY KNOW.
GOING BY WHAT TYREST TOLD ME—RANT NUMBER 332—IT INVOLVES A KIND OF COMMON DENOMINATOR MATRIX CODE.
A MATRIX CODE?
HE THINKS KILLING ALL THE KNOCKOFFS WILL HELP HIM REACH CYBERUTOPIA.
WHY?
WHY WHAT?
WHY DOES HE THINK THAT?
BECAUSE, RODIMUS-NOT-HOT-ROD...

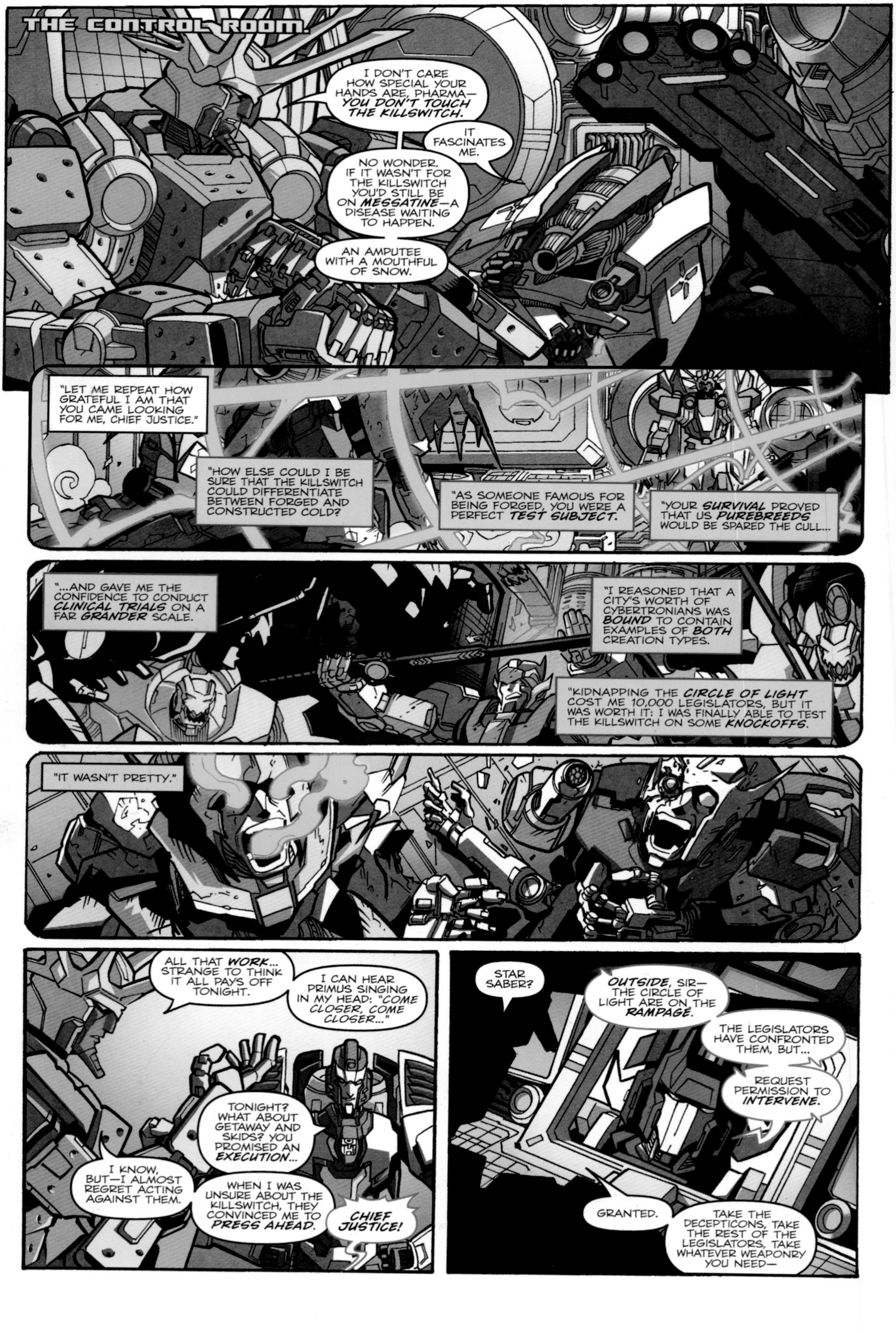
THE CONTROL ROOM.
I DON'T CARE HOW SPECIAL YOUR HANDS ARE, PHARMA— YOU DON'T TOUCH THE KILLSWITCH.
IT FASCINATES ME.
NO WONDER. IF IT WASN'T FOR THE KILLSWITCH YOU'D STILL BE ON MESSATINE—A DISEASE WAITING TO HAPPEN.
AN AMPUTEE WITH A MOUTHFUL OF SNOW.
"LET ME REPEAT HOW GRATEFUL I AM THAT YOU CAME LOOKING FOR ME, CHIEF JUSTICE."
"HOW ELSE COULD I BE SURE THAT THE KILLSWITCH COULD DIFFERENTIATE BETWEEN FORGED AND CONSTRUCTED COLD?
"AS SOMEONE FAMOUS FOR BEING FORGED, YOU WERE A PERFECT TEST SUBJECT.
"YOUR SURVIVAL PROVED THAT US PUREBREEDS WOULD BE SPARED THE CULL...
"...AND GAVE ME THE CONFIDENCE TO CONDUCT CLINICAL TRIALS ON A FAR GRANDER SCALE.
"I REASONED THAT A CITY'S WORTH OF CYBERTRONIANS WAS BOUND TO CONTAIN EXAMPLES OF BOTH CREATION TYPES.
"KIDNAPPING THE CIRCLE OF LIGHT COST ME 10,000 LEGISLATORS, BUT IT WAS WORTH IT: I WAS FINALLY ABLE TO TEST THE KILLSWITCH ON SOME KNOCKOFFS.
"IT WASN'T PRETTY."
ALL THAT WORK... STRANGE TO THINK IT ALL PAYS OFF TONIGHT.
I CAN HEAR PRIMUS SINGING IN MY HEAD: "COME CLOSER, COME CLOSER..."
TONIGHT? WHAT ABOUT GETAWAY AND SKIDS? YOU PROMISED AN EXECUTION...
I KNOW, BUT—I ALMOST REGRET ACTING AGAINST THEM.
WHEN I WAS UNSURE ABOUT THE KILLSWITCH, THEY CONVINCED ME TO PRESS AHEAD.
CHIEF JUSTICE!
STAR SABER?
OUTSIDE, SIR— THE CIRCLE OF LIGHT ARE ON THE RAMPAGE.
THE LEGISLATORS HAVE CONFRONTED THEM, BUT...
REQUEST PERMISSION TO INTERVENE.
GRANTED.
TAKE THE DECEPTICONS, TAKE THE REST OF THE LEGISLATORS, TAKE WHATEVER WEAPONRY YOU NEED—

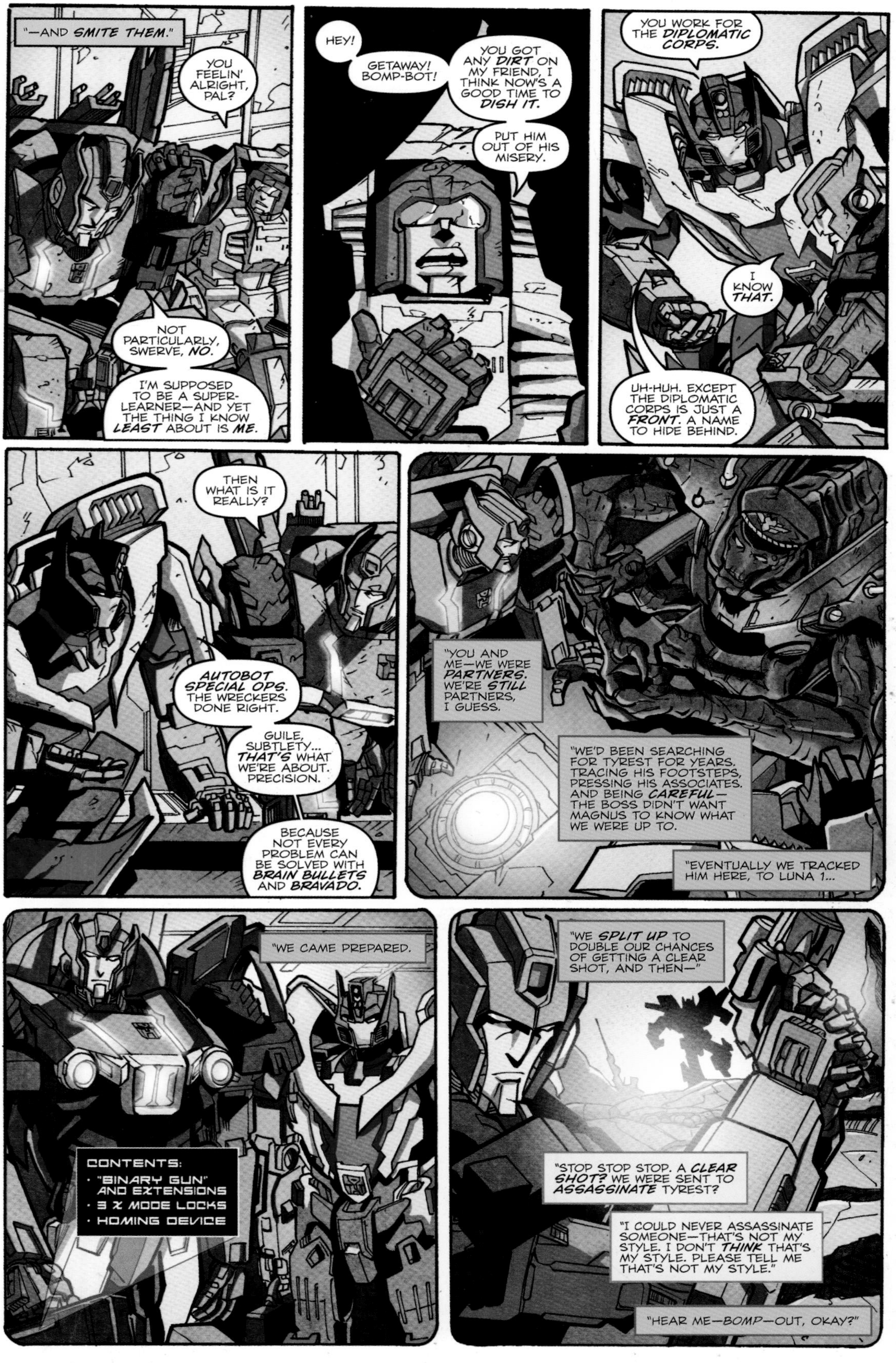
"—AND SMITE THEM."
YOU FEELIN' ALRIGHT, PAL?
NOT PARTICULARLY, SWERVE, NO.
I'M SUPPOSED TO BE A SUPER-LEARNER—AND YET THE THING I KNOW LEAST ABOUT IS ME.
HEY!
GETAWAY! BOMP-BOT!
YOU GOT ANY DIRT ON MY FRIEND, I THINK NOW'S A GOOD TIME TO DISH IT.
PUT HIM OUT OF HIS MISERY.
YOU WORK FOR THE DIPLOMATIC CORPS.
I KNOW THAT.
UH-HUH. EXCEPT THE DIPLOMATIC CORPS IS JUST A FRONT. A NAME TO HIDE BEHIND.
THEN WHAT IS IT REALLY?
AUTOBOT SPECIAL OPS. THE WRECKERS DONE RIGHT.
GUILE, SUBTLETY... THAT'S WHAT WE'RE ABOUT. PRECISION.
BECAUSE NOT EVERY PROBLEM CAN BE SOLVED WITH BRAIN BULLETS AND BRAVADO.
"YOU AND ME—WE WERE PARTNERS. WE'RE STILL PARTNERS, I GUESS.
"WE'D BEEN SEARCHING FOR TYREST FOR YEARS. TRACING HIS FOOTSTEPS, PRESSING HIS ASSOCIATES. AND BEING CAREFUL—THE BOSS DIDN'T WANT MAGNUS TO KNOW WHAT WE WERE UP TO.
"EVENTUALLY WE TRACKED HIM HERE, TO LUNA 1...
"WE CAME PREPARED.
CONTENTS:
• "BINARY GUN" AND EXTENSIONS
• 3 X MODE LOCKS
• HOMING DEVICE
"WE SPLIT UP TO DOUBLE OUR CHANCES OF GETTING A CLEAR SHOT, AND THEN—"
"STOP STOP STOP. A CLEAR SHOT? WE WERE SENT TO ASSASSINATE TYREST?
"I COULD NEVER ASSASSINATE SOMEONE—THAT'S NOT MY STYLE. I DON'T THINK THAT'S MY STYLE. PLEASE TELL ME THAT'S NOT MY STYLE."
"HEAR ME—BOMP—OUT, OKAY?"

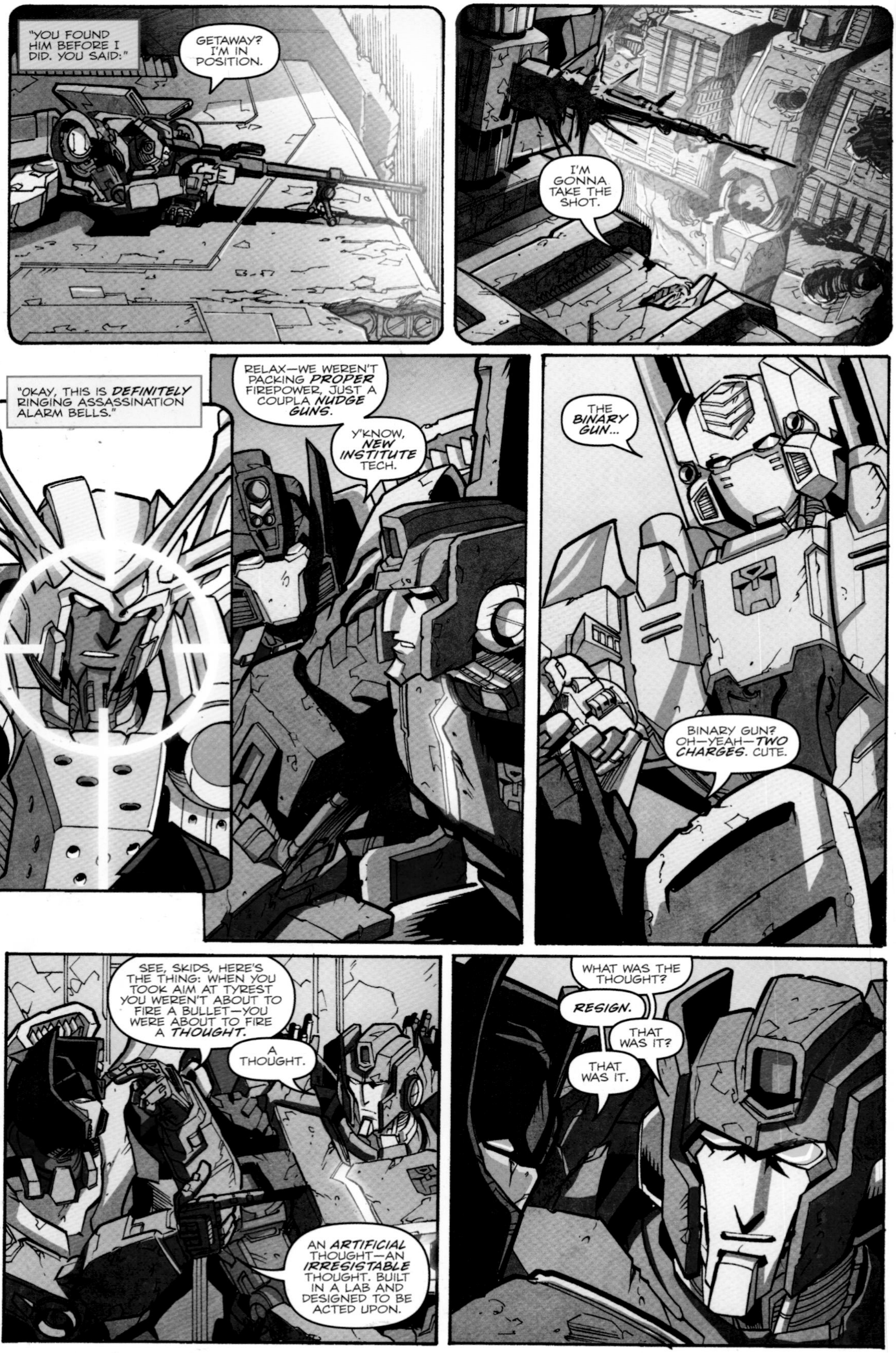

"YOU FOUND HIM BEFORE I DID. YOU SAID:"
GETAWAY? I'M IN POSITION.
I'M GONNA TAKE THE SHOT.
"OKAY, THIS IS DEFINITELY RINGING ASSASSINATION ALARM BELLS."
RELAX—WE WEREN'T PACKING PROPER FIREPOWER, JUST A COUPLA NUDGE GUNS.
Y'KNOW, NEW INSTITUTE TECH.
THE BINARY GUN...
BINARY GUN? OH—YEAH—TWO CHARGES. CUTE.
SEE, SKIDS, HERE'S THE THING: WHEN YOU TOOK AIM AT TYREST YOU WEREN'T ABOUT TO FIRE A BULLET—YOU WERE ABOUT TO FIRE A THOUGHT.
A THOUGHT.
AN ARTIFICIAL THOUGHT—AN IRRESISTABLE THOUGHT. BUILT IN A LAB AND DESIGNED TO BE ACTED UPON.
WHAT WAS THE THOUGHT?
RESIGN.
THAT WAS IT?
THAT WAS IT.

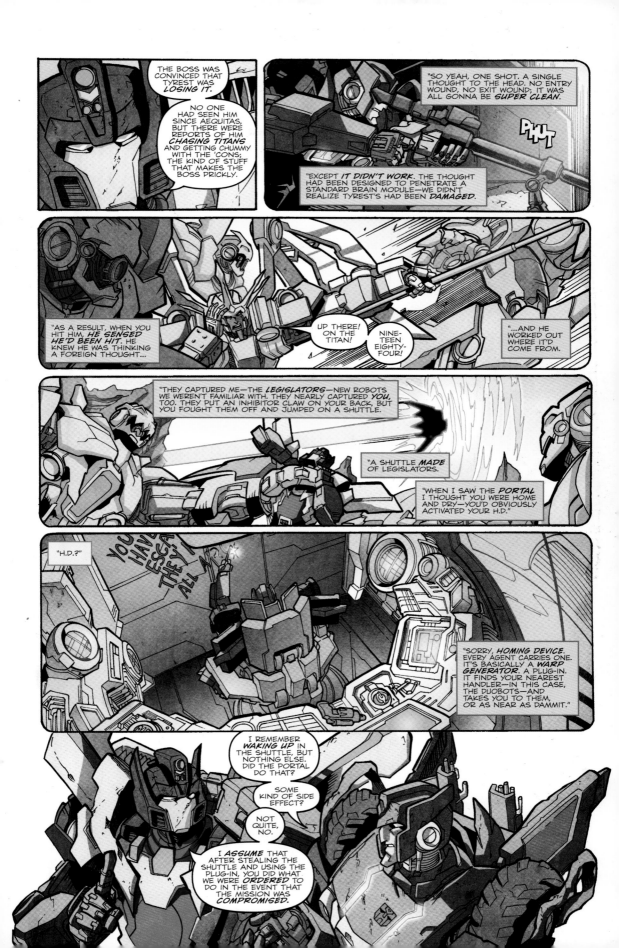

THE BOSS WAS CONVINCED THAT TYREST WAS *LOSING IT*.

NO ONE HAD SEEN HIM SINCE AEQUITAS, BUT THERE WERE REPORTS OF HIM *CHASING TITANS* AND GETTING CHUMMY WITH THE 'CONS; THE KIND OF STUFF THAT MAKES THE BOSS PRICKLY.

"SO YEAH, ONE SHOT. A SINGLE THOUGHT TO THE HEAD. NO ENTRY WOUND, NO EXIT WOUND; IT WAS ALL GONNA BE *SUPER CLEAN*.

PHHT

"EXCEPT *IT DIDN'T WORK*. THE THOUGHT HAD BEEN DESIGNED TO PENETRATE A STANDARD BRAIN MODULE—WE DIDN'T REALIZE TYREST'S HAD BEEN *DAMAGED*.

"AS A RESULT, WHEN YOU HIT HIM, *HE SENSED HE'D BEEN HIT*. HE KNEW HE WAS THINKING A FOREIGN THOUGHT...

UP THERE! ON THE TITAN!

NINE-TEEN EIGHTY-FOUR!

"...AND HE WORKED OUT WHERE IT'D COME FROM.

"THEY CAPTURED ME—THE *LEGISLATORS*—NEW ROBOTS WE WEREN'T FAMILIAR WITH. THEY NEARLY CAPTURED *YOU*, TOO. THEY PUT AN INHIBITOR CLAW ON YOUR BACK, BUT YOU FOUGHT THEM OFF AND JUMPED ON A SHUTTLE.

"A SHUTTLE *MADE* OF LEGISLATORS.

"WHEN I SAW THE *PORTAL* I THOUGHT YOU WERE HOME AND DRY—YOU'D OBVIOUSLY ACTIVATED YOUR H.D."

"H.D.?"

YOU HAVE ESCA THEY ALL

"SORRY, *HOMING DEVICE*. EVERY AGENT CARRIES ONE. IT'S BASICALLY A *WARP GENERATOR*. A PLUG-IN. IT FINDS YOUR NEAREST HANDLER—IN THIS CASE, THE DUOBOTS—AND TAKES YOU TO THEM, OR AS NEAR AS DAMMIT."

I REMEMBER *WAKING UP* IN THE SHUTTLE, BUT NOTHING ELSE. DID THE PORTAL DO THAT?

SOME KIND OF SIDE EFFECT?

NOT QUITE, NO.

I *ASSUME* THAT AFTER STEALING THE SHUTTLE AND USING THE PLUG-IN, YOU DID WHAT WE WERE *ORDERED* TO DO IN THE EVENT THAT THE MISSION WAS *COMPROMISED*.

"YOU TOOK YOUR GUN...

"...AND YOU TURNED IT ON YOURSELF.

"TWO CHARGES, REMEMBER? AND THE SECOND WAS A BLANK.

"A BLANK DESIGNED TO DESTROY EVERY INCRIMINATING MEMORY—EVERY MEMORY OF ME, OF THE BOSS... AND OF THE MISSION ITSELF, OF COURSE.

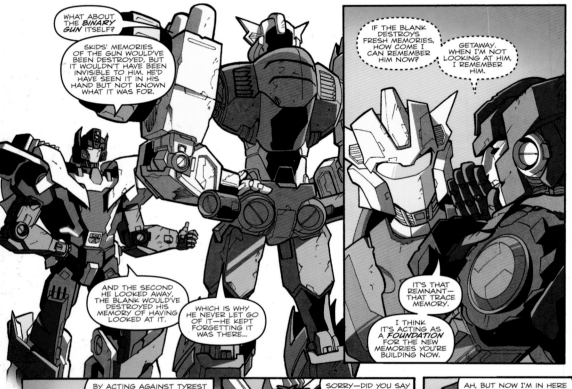

WHAT ABOUT THE BINARY GUN ITSELF?

SKIDS' MEMORIES OF THE GUN WOULD'VE BEEN DESTROYED, BUT IT WOULDN'T HAVE BEEN INVISIBLE TO HIM. HE'D HAVE SEEN IT IN HIS HAND BUT NOT KNOWN WHAT IT WAS FOR.

IF THE BLANK DESTROYS FRESH MEMORIES, HOW COME I CAN REMEMBER HIM NOW?

GETAWAY. WHEN I'M NOT LOOKING AT HIM, I REMEMBER HIM.

AND THE SECOND HE LOOKED AWAY, THE BLANK WOULD'VE DESTROYED HIS MEMORY OF HAVING LOOKED AT IT.

WHICH IS WHY HE NEVER LET GO OF IT—HE KEPT FORGETTING IT WAS THERE...

IT'S THAT REMNANT—THAT TRACE MEMORY.

I THINK IT'S ACTING AS A FOUNDATION FOR THE NEW MEMORIES YOU'RE BUILDING NOW.

BY ACTING AGAINST TYREST I THINK WE CONVINCED HIM OF THE RIGHTNESS OF HIS CAUSE. THE BOSS WOULD'VE CALLED IT AN UNINTENDED CONSEQUENCE.

THIS "BOSS"— IT'S PROWL, RIGHT?

C'MON, WE'RE ALL THINKING IT.

GIVE YOURSELF A BONUS POINT, HOT SHOT.

SORRY—DID YOU SAY ESCAPOLOGIST?

I MIGHT'VE DONE.

TAILGATE, GETAWAY'S BEEN A PRISONER FOR MONTHS. IF HE COULD'VE ESCAPED, HE WOULD'VE ESCAPED.

AH, BUT NOW I'M IN HERE WITH ALL OF YOU, I HAVE SOMETHING I DIDN'T HAVE BEFORE.

A FRESH SET OF KEYS.

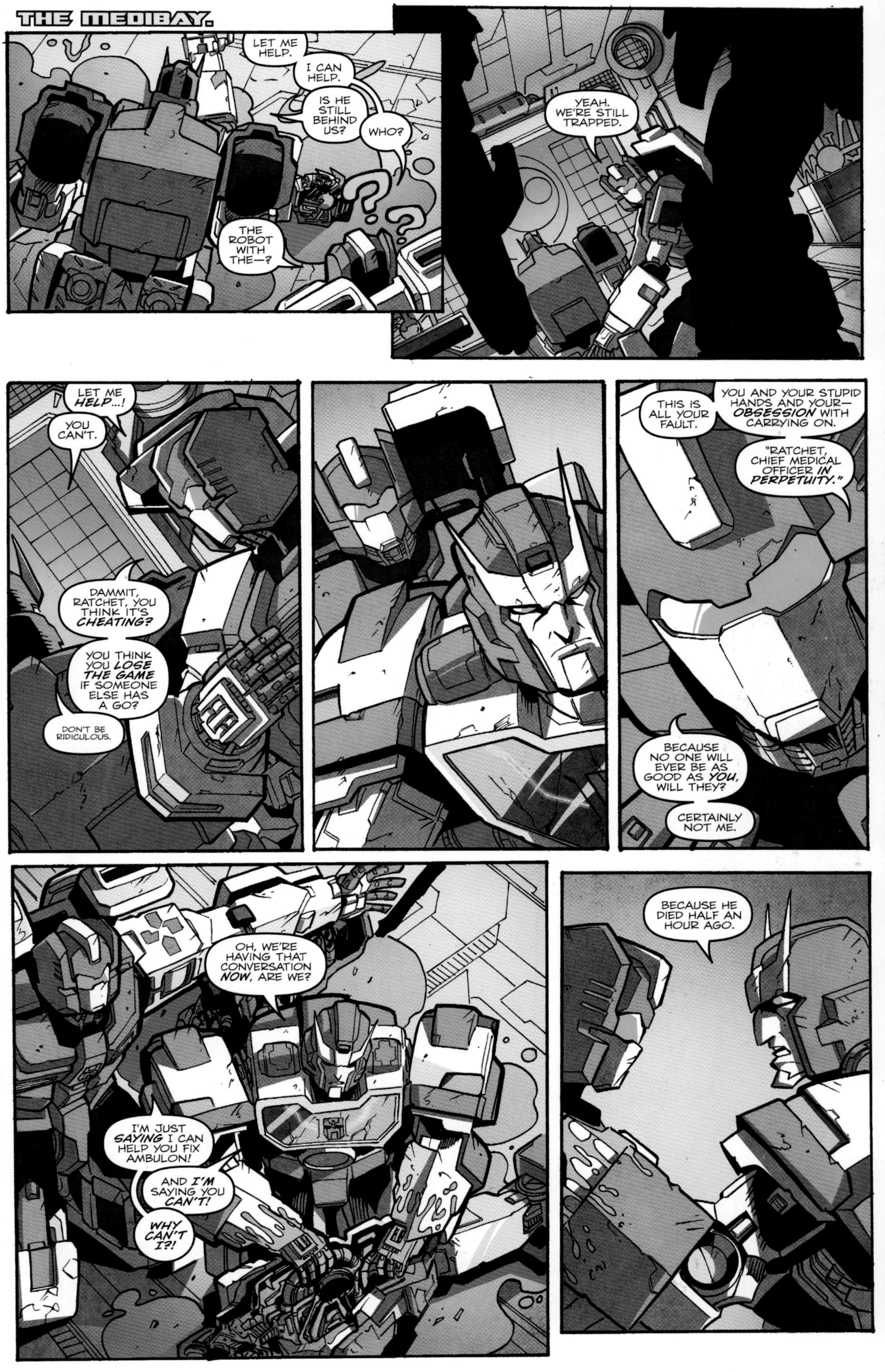
THE MEDIBAY.
LET ME HELP.
I CAN HELP.
IS HE STILL BEHIND US?
WHO?
THE ROBOT WITH THE—?
YEAH. WE'RE STILL TRAPPED.
LET ME HELP...!
YOU CAN'T.
DAMMIT, RATCHET, YOU THINK IT'S CHEATING?
YOU THINK YOU LOSE THE GAME IF SOMEONE ELSE HAS A GO?
DON'T BE RIDICULOUS.
THIS IS ALL YOUR FAULT.
YOU AND YOUR STUPID HANDS AND YOUR— OBSESSION WITH CARRYING ON.
"RATCHET, CHIEF MEDICAL OFFICER IN PERPETUITY."
BECAUSE NO ONE WILL EVER BE AS GOOD AS YOU, WILL THEY?
CERTAINLY NOT ME.
OH, WE'RE HAVING THAT CONVERSATION NOW, ARE WE?
I'M JUST SAYING I CAN HELP YOU FIX AMBULON!
AND I'M SAYING YOU CAN'T!
WHY CAN'T I?!
BECAUSE HE DIED HALF AN HOUR AGO.

"...AND TOLD US TO SLIDE THEM OVER THE BASE OF EVERY ELECTROBAR AT *EXACTLY* THE SAME TIME."

VZZZZ-KOOM

"AND THEN WE JUST WALKED OUT OF THERE! WELL, *MOST* OF US."

YOU OKAY, TAILGATE? HERE, LET ME...

SERVOS IN THE LEGS SEIZING UP, THAT'S ALL. EVER GET THAT?

BIT OF SERVO TROUBLE? NO?

I'M SORRY. THIS MIGHT BE TEMPORARY, THIS MIGHT NOT. YOUR ILLNESS IS ENTERING ITS FINAL—

THERE'S A *CURE*, RATCHET! A CURE FOR MY CYBERCROSIS!

ULTRA MAGNUS WAS DYING, THEN HE *WASN'T*; HE SAID TYREST'S DOCTORS COULD WORK MIRACLES AND—AND—I DON'T HAVE TO DIE!

WHAT DID GETAWAY MEAN, "LURED US HERE"?

ALL I KNOW IS I DON'T BELIEVE IT.

I DON'T BELIEVE HE WAS HIDING INSIDE THAT THING THE WHOLE TIME.

SO COME ON, WHERE'S THE NEAREST MEDIBAY?

IT'S OVER THERE, BUT— I DON'T KNOW, TAILGATE.

THE MEDIBAY'S USELESS WITHOUT THE RIGHT MEDIC.

—TIME FOR THE *SHOWDOWN*.

IF THERE *IS* A CURE FOR CYBERCROSIS, IT'S INSIDE PHARMA'S HEAD.

ALRIGHT, EVERYONE—

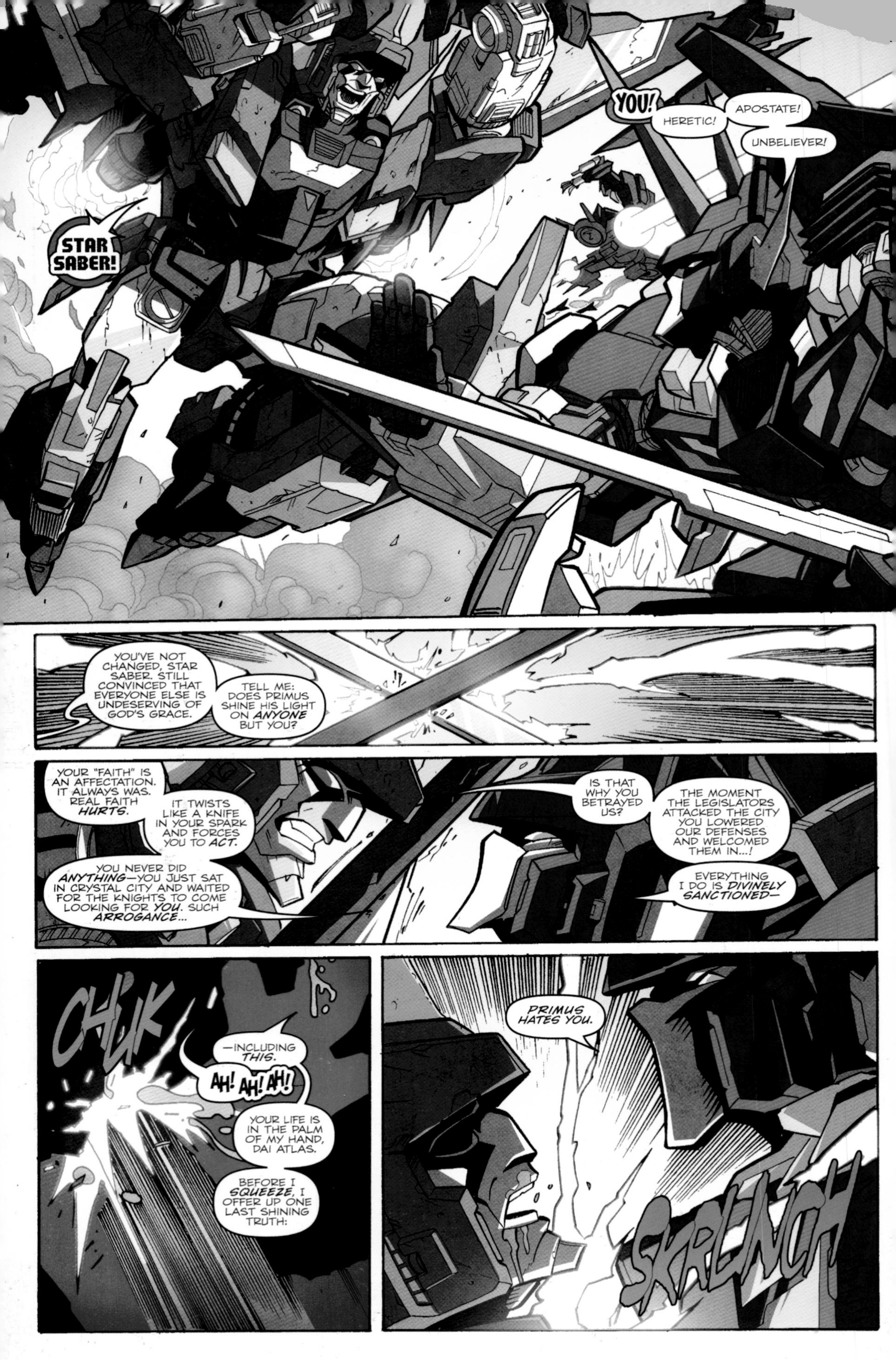

STAR SABER!
YOU!
HERETIC!
APOSTATE!
UNBELIEVER!
YOU'VE NOT CHANGED, STAR SABER. STILL CONVINCED THAT EVERYONE ELSE IS UNDESERVING OF GOD'S GRACE.
TELL ME: DOES PRIMUS SHINE HIS LIGHT ON ANYONE BUT YOU?
YOUR "FAITH" IS AN AFFECTATION. IT ALWAYS WAS. REAL FAITH HURTS.
IT TWISTS LIKE A KNIFE IN YOUR SPARK AND FORCES YOU TO ACT.
YOU NEVER DID ANYTHING—YOU JUST SAT IN CRYSTAL CITY AND WAITED FOR THE KNIGHTS TO COME LOOKING FOR YOU. SUCH ARROGANCE...
IS THAT WHY YOU BETRAYED US?
THE MOMENT THE LEGISLATORS ATTACKED THE CITY YOU LOWERED OUR DEFENSES AND WELCOMED THEM IN...!
EVERYTHING I DO IS DIVINELY SANCTIONED—
CHUK
—INCLUDING THIS.
AH! AH! AH!
YOUR LIFE IS IN THE PALM OF MY HAND, DAI ATLAS.
BEFORE I SQUEEZE, I OFFER UP ONE LAST SHINING TRUTH:
PRIMUS HATES YOU.
SKRUNCH

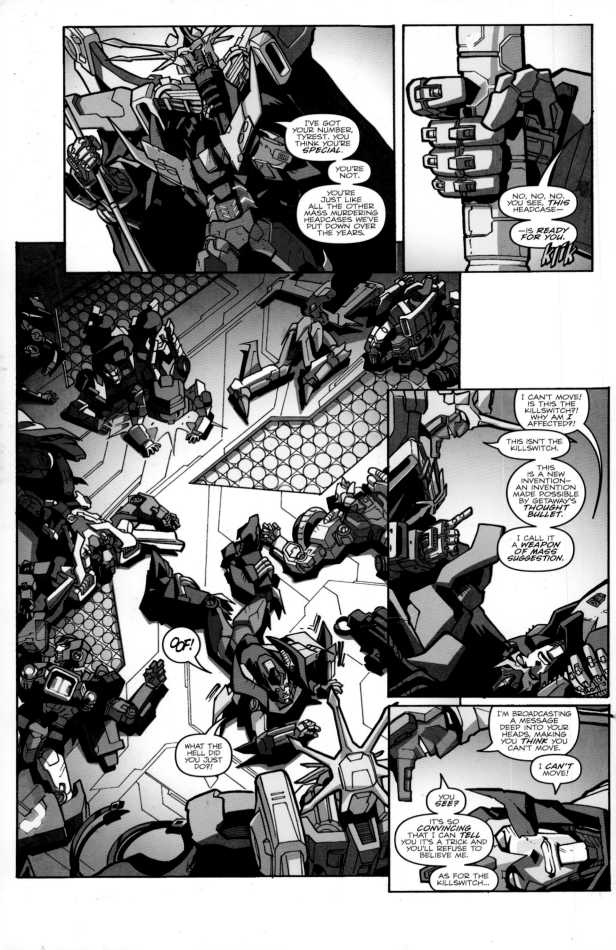

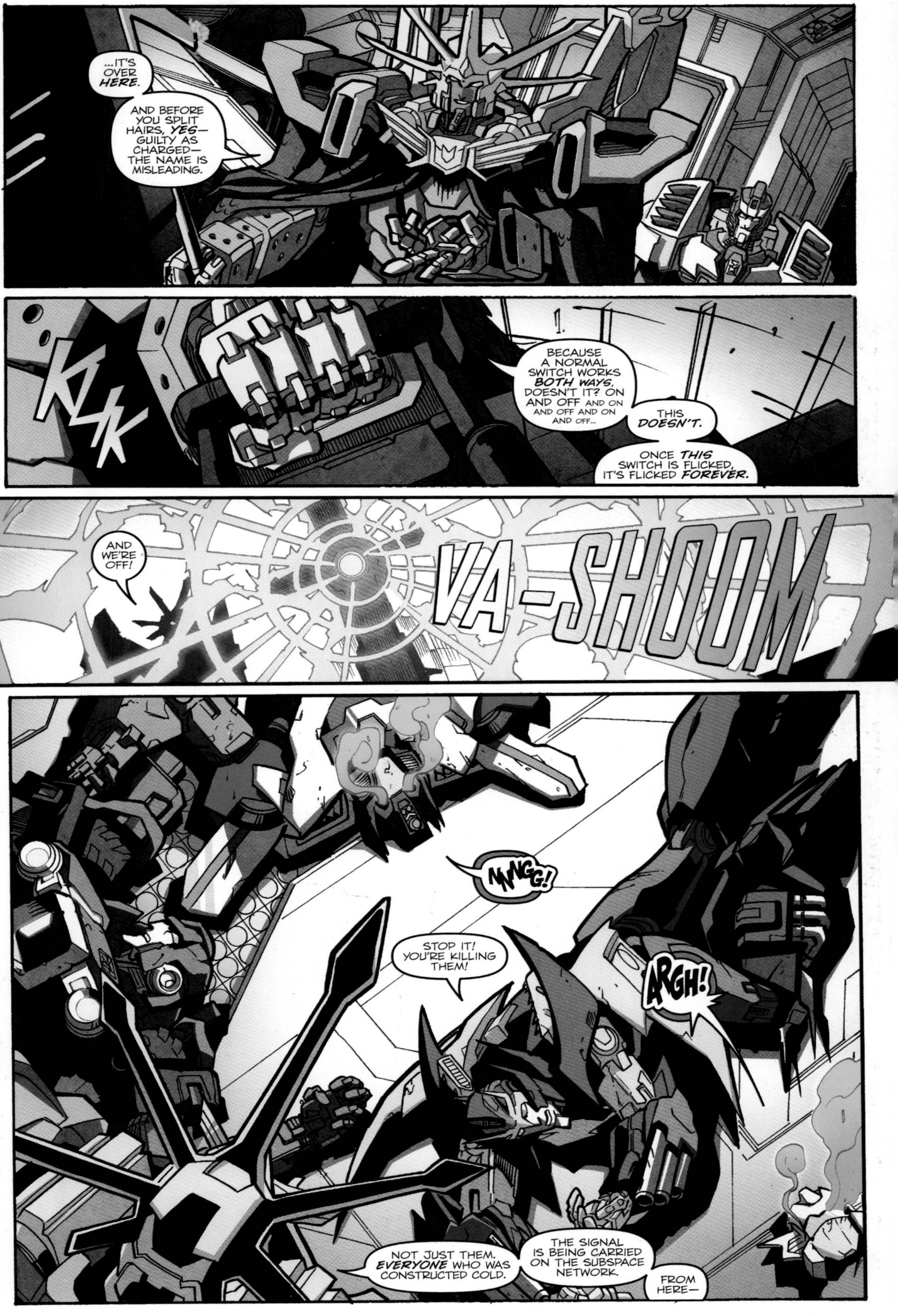
...IT'S OVER *HERE*.
AND BEFORE YOU SPLIT HAIRS, *YES*— GUILTY AS CHARGED— THE NAME IS MISLEADING.
KLIK
BECAUSE A NORMAL SWITCH WORKS *BOTH WAYS*, DOESN'T IT? ON AND OFF AND ON AND OFF AND ON AND OFF...
THIS *DOESN'T*.
ONCE *THIS* SWITCH IS FLICKED, IT'S FLICKED *FOREVER*.
AND WE'RE OFF!
VA-SHOOM
NNNGG!
STOP IT! YOU'RE KILLING THEM!
ARGH!
NOT JUST THEM. *EVERYONE* WHO WAS CONSTRUCTED COLD.
THE SIGNAL IS BEING CARRIED ON THE SUBSPACE NETWORK.
FROM HERE—

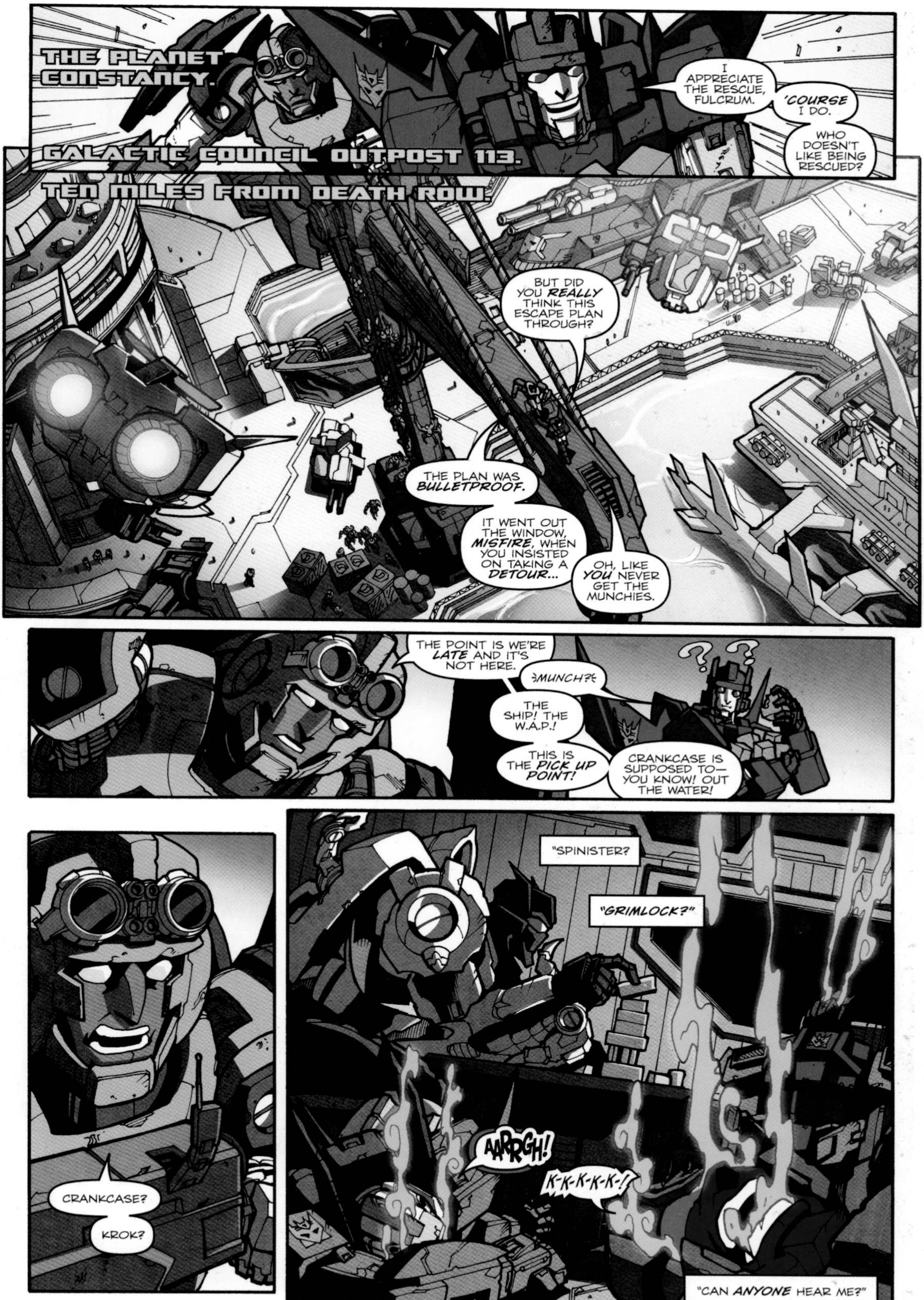
THE PLANET CONSTANCY.
I APPRECIATE THE RESCUE, FULCRUM.
'COURSE I DO.
WHO DOESN'T LIKE BEING RESCUED?
GALACTIC COUNCIL OUTPOST 113.
TEN MILES FROM DEATH ROW.
BUT DID YOU REALLY THINK THIS ESCAPE PLAN THROUGH?
THE PLAN WAS BULLETPROOF.
IT WENT OUT THE WINDOW, MISFIRE, WHEN YOU INSISTED ON TAKING A DETOUR...
OH, LIKE YOU NEVER GET THE MUNCHIES.
THE POINT IS WE'RE LATE AND IT'S NOT HERE.
MUNCH?
THE SHIP! THE W.A.P.!
THIS IS THE PICK UP POINT!
CRANKCASE IS SUPPOSED TO— YOU KNOW! OUT THE WATER!
CRANKCASE?
KROK?
"SPINISTER?
"GRIMLOCK?"
AARRGH!
K-K-K-K-K-!
"CAN ANYONE HEAR ME?"

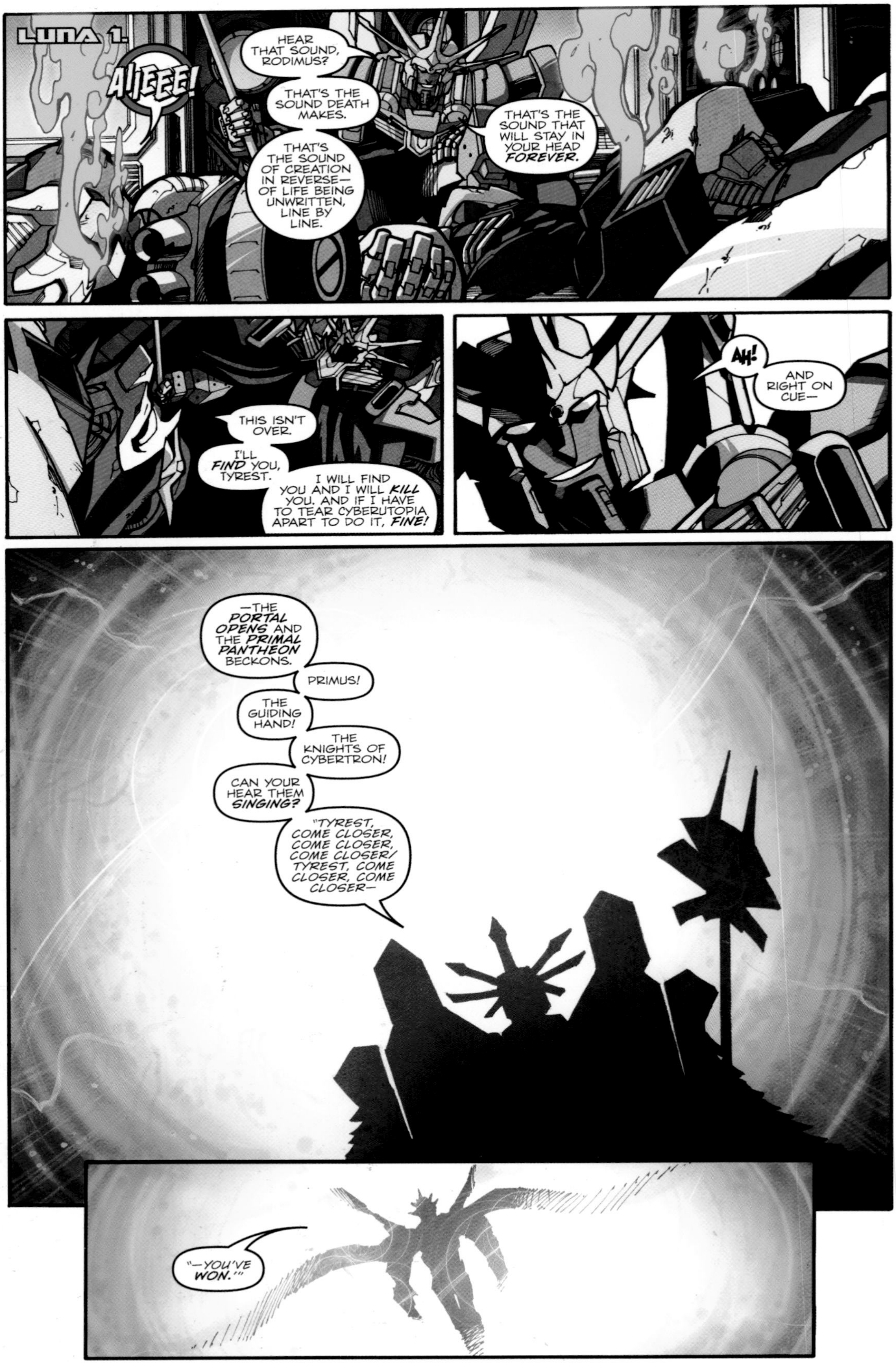
LUNA 1.
AIIEEE!
HEAR THAT SOUND, RODIMUS?
THAT'S THE SOUND DEATH MAKES.
THAT'S THE SOUND OF CREATION IN REVERSE— OF LIFE BEING UNWRITTEN, LINE BY LINE.
THAT'S THE SOUND THAT WILL STAY IN YOUR HEAD FOREVER.
THIS ISN'T OVER.
I'LL FIND YOU, TYREST.
I WILL FIND YOU AND I WILL KILL YOU. AND IF I HAVE TO TEAR CYBERUTOPIA APART TO DO IT, FINE!
AH!
AND RIGHT ON CUE—
—THE PORTAL OPENS AND THE PRIMAL PANTHEON BECKONS.
PRIMUS!
THE GUIDING HAND!
THE KNIGHTS OF CYBERTRON!
CAN YOUR HEAR THEM SINGING?
"TYREST, COME CLOSER, COME CLOSER, COME CLOSER/ TYREST, COME CLOSER, COME CLOSER—
"—YOU'VE WON.'"

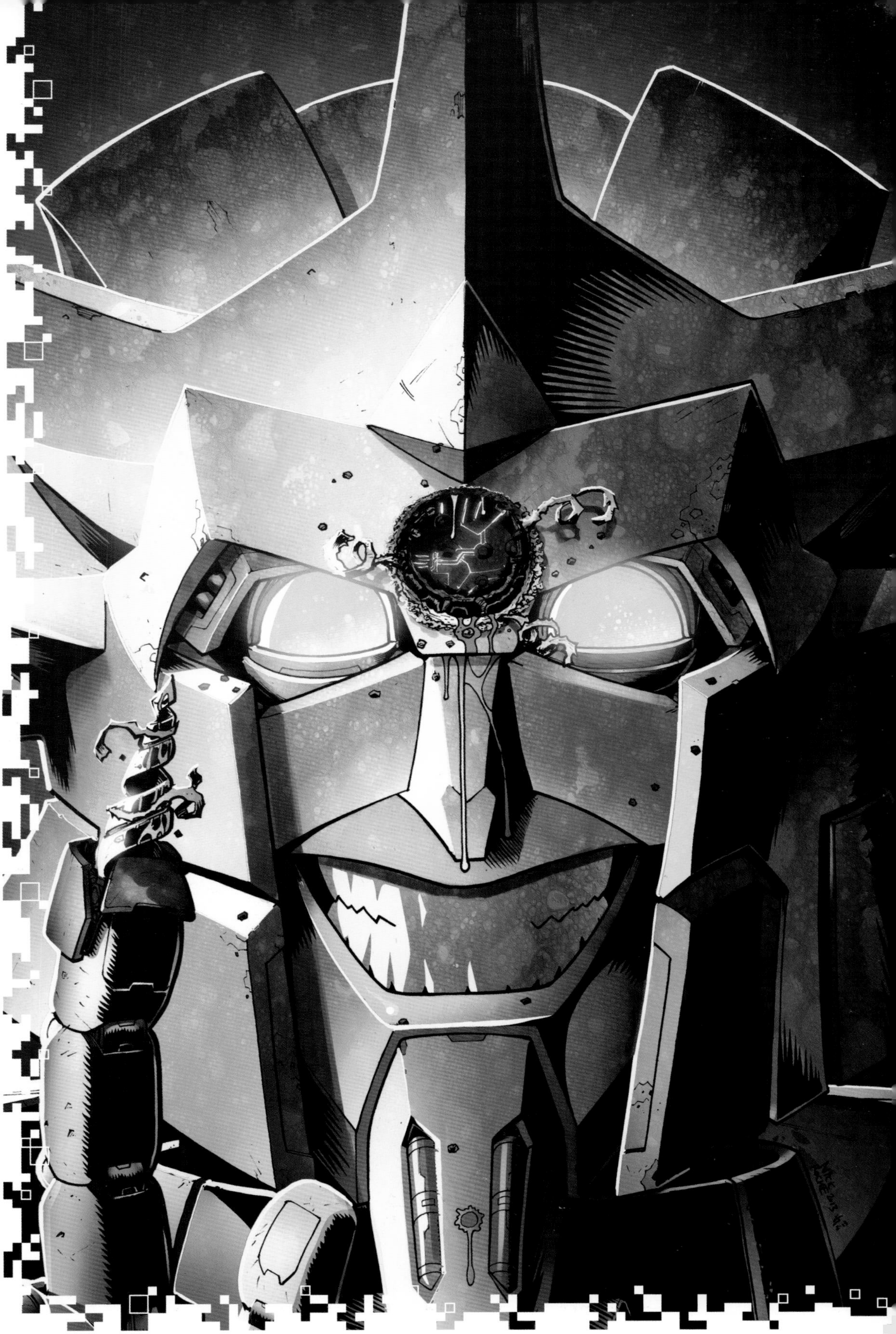

MORE THAN MEETS THE EYE #20 COVER B

by **NICK ROCHE** Colors by **JOANA LAFUENTE**

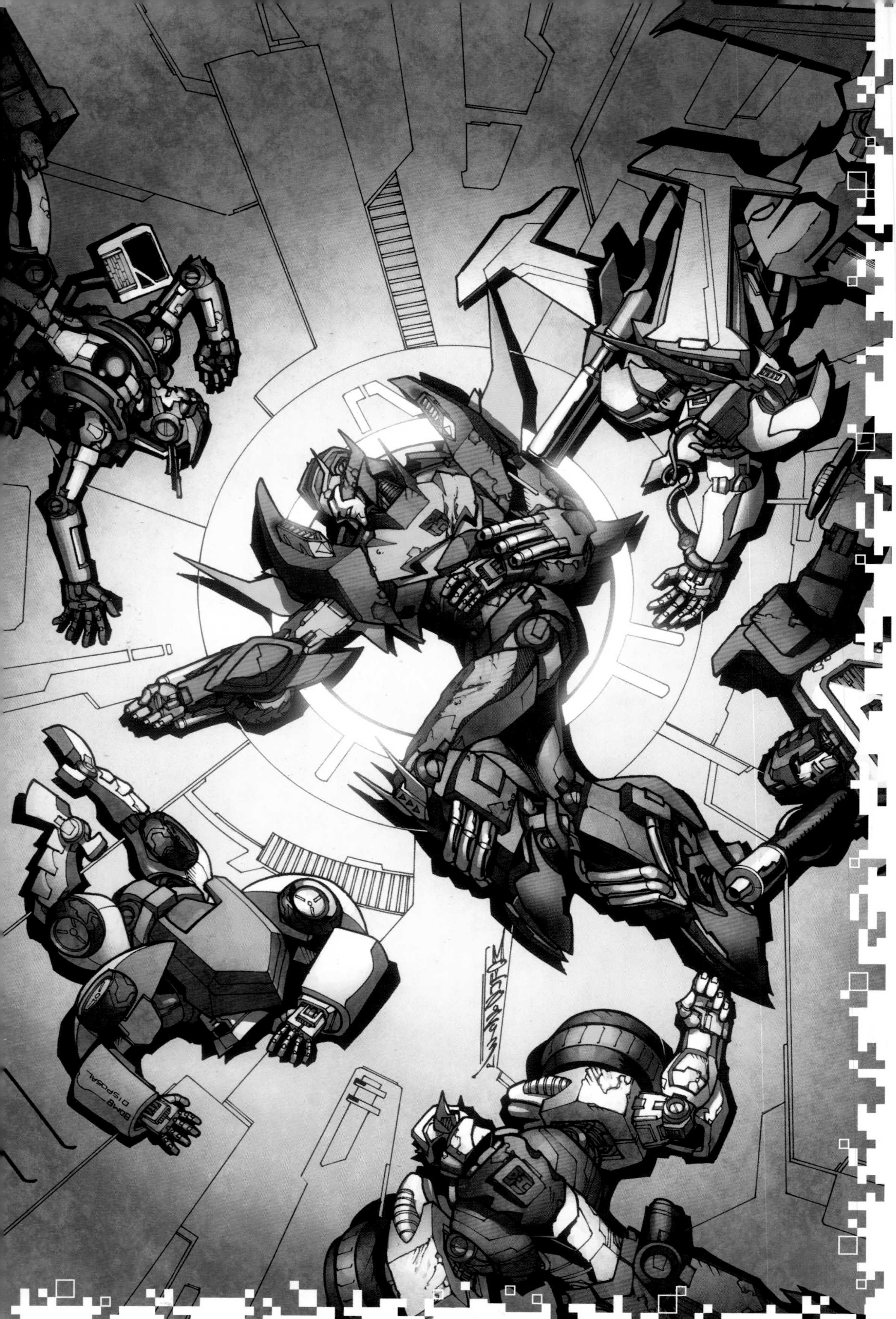
BOMB DISPOSAL

MORE THAN MEETS THE EYE #21 COVER A

by **ALEX MILNE** Colors by **JOSH PEREZ**

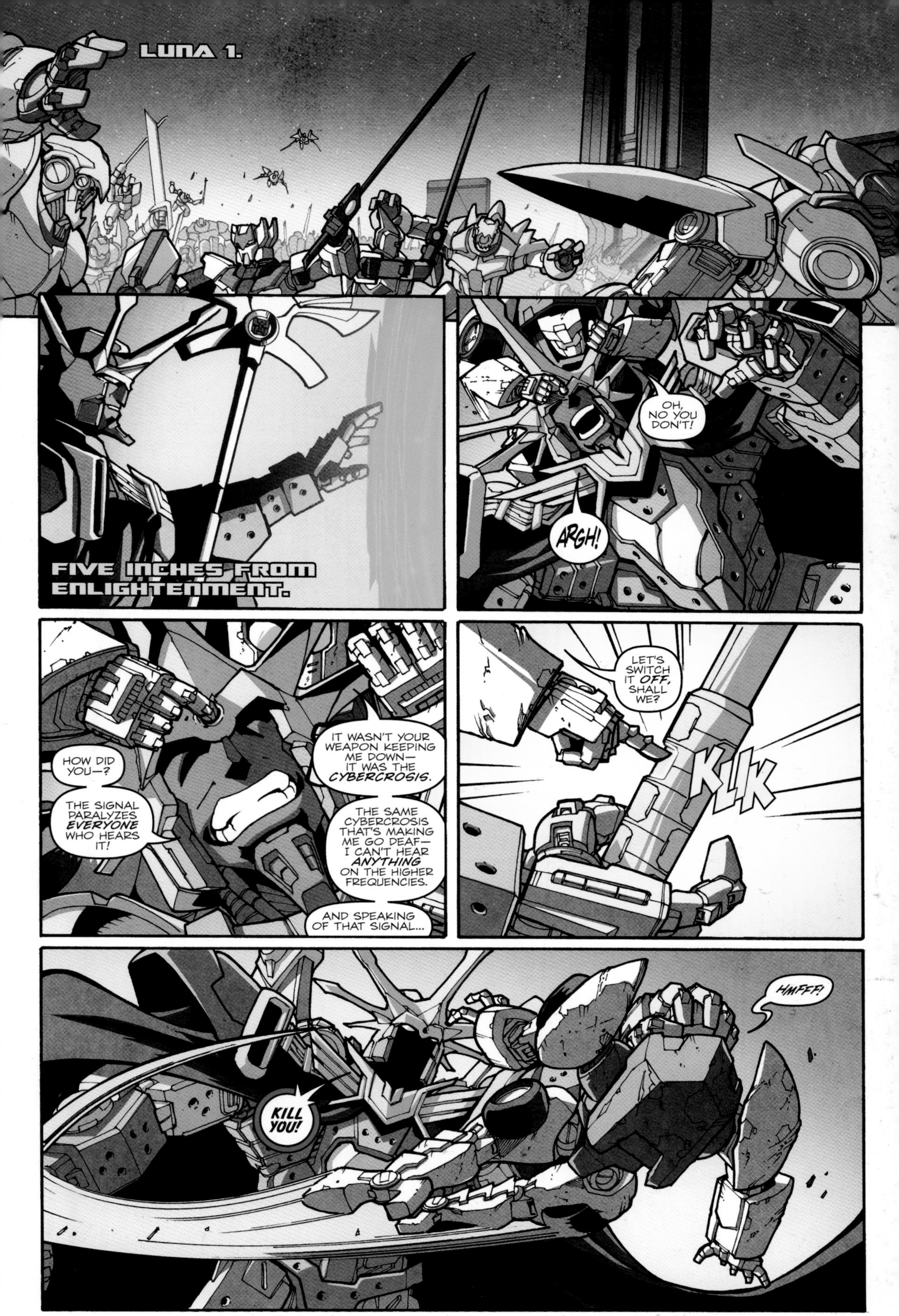
LUNA 1.
FIVE INCHES FROM ENLIGHTENMENT.
OH, NO YOU DON'T!
ARGH!
HOW DID YOU—?
THE SIGNAL PARALYZES EVERYONE WHO HEARS IT!
IT WASN'T YOUR WEAPON KEEPING ME DOWN— IT WAS THE CYBERCROSIS.
THE SAME CYBERCROSIS THAT'S MAKING ME GO DEAF— I CAN'T HEAR ANYTHING ON THE HIGHER FREQUENCIES.
AND SPEAKING OF THAT SIGNAL...
LET'S SWITCH IT OFF, SHALL WE?
KLIK
HMFFF!
KILL YOU!

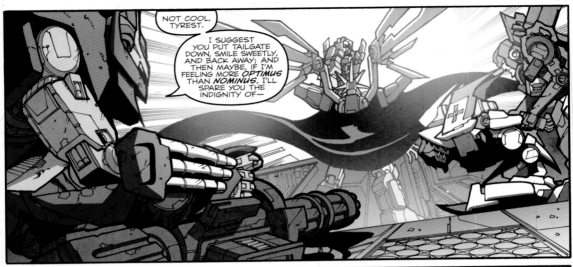

NOT COOL, TYREST.

I SUGGEST YOU PUT TAILGATE DOWN, SMILE SWEETLY, AND BACK AWAY; AND THEN MAYBE, IF I'M FEELING MORE *OPTIMUS* THAN *NOMINUS*, I'LL SPARE YOU THE INDIGNITY OF—

RODIMUS! *FOCUS!*

UNLESS WE TURN OFF THE KILLSWITCH, CHROMEDOME AND THE OTHERS WILL BE DEAD IN *MINUTES!*

I TOLD YOU— THE KILLSWITCH *CAN'T* BE TURNED OFF!

TEAR IT DOWN, BLOW IT UP, DOESN'T MATTER— THE DAMAGE IS ALREADY DONE!

NOW—I WANT EVERYONE WITHIN KISSING DISTANCE OF THE FLOOR. NO ONE LOOK UP 'TIL I'M THROUGH THE PORTAL.

DO IT! OR I'LL LOBOTOMIZE THE SHIP'S MASCOT.

TAILGATE, I—

SHOOT HIM, RODIMUS! *SHOOT HIM!*

01 : 12 : 15 : 59

I'M *DYING!* PROPER, FULL ON *DYING!*

CYBERCROSIS! THE BIG C! I'VE ONLY GOT A DAY AND A HALF LEFT!

NOW *SHOOT HIM!*

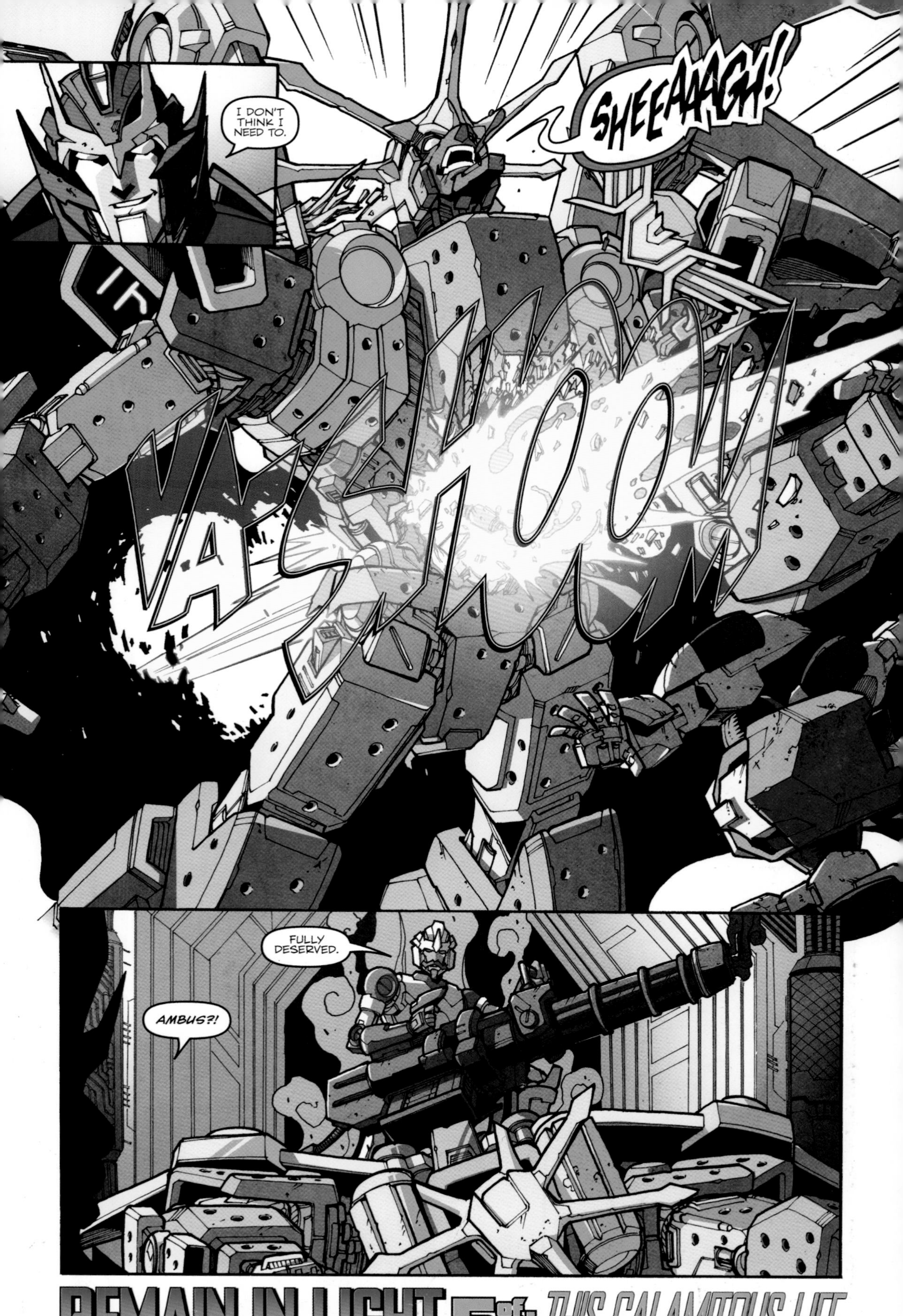
I DON'T THINK I NEED TO.
SHEEAAAGH!
VASHOOM
FULLY DESERVED.
AMBUS?!

REMAIN IN LIGHT 5 of 5: THIS CALAMITOUS LIFE

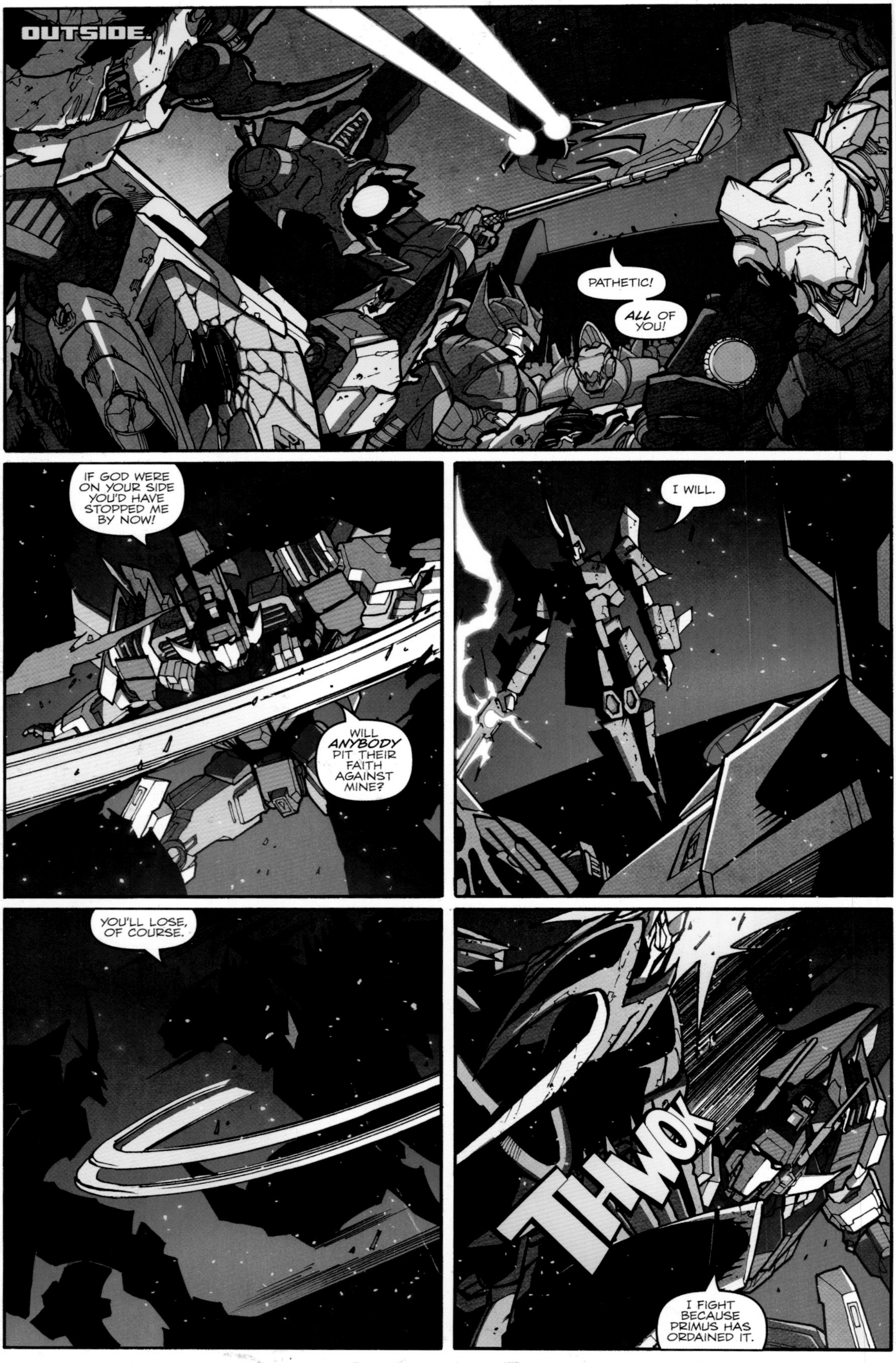
OUTSIDE.
PATHETIC!
ALL OF YOU!
IF GOD WERE ON YOUR SIDE YOU'D HAVE STOPPED ME BY NOW!
WILL ANYBODY PIT THEIR FAITH AGAINST MINE?
I WILL.
YOU'LL LOSE, OF COURSE.
THWOK
I FIGHT BECAUSE PRIMUS HAS ORDAINED IT.

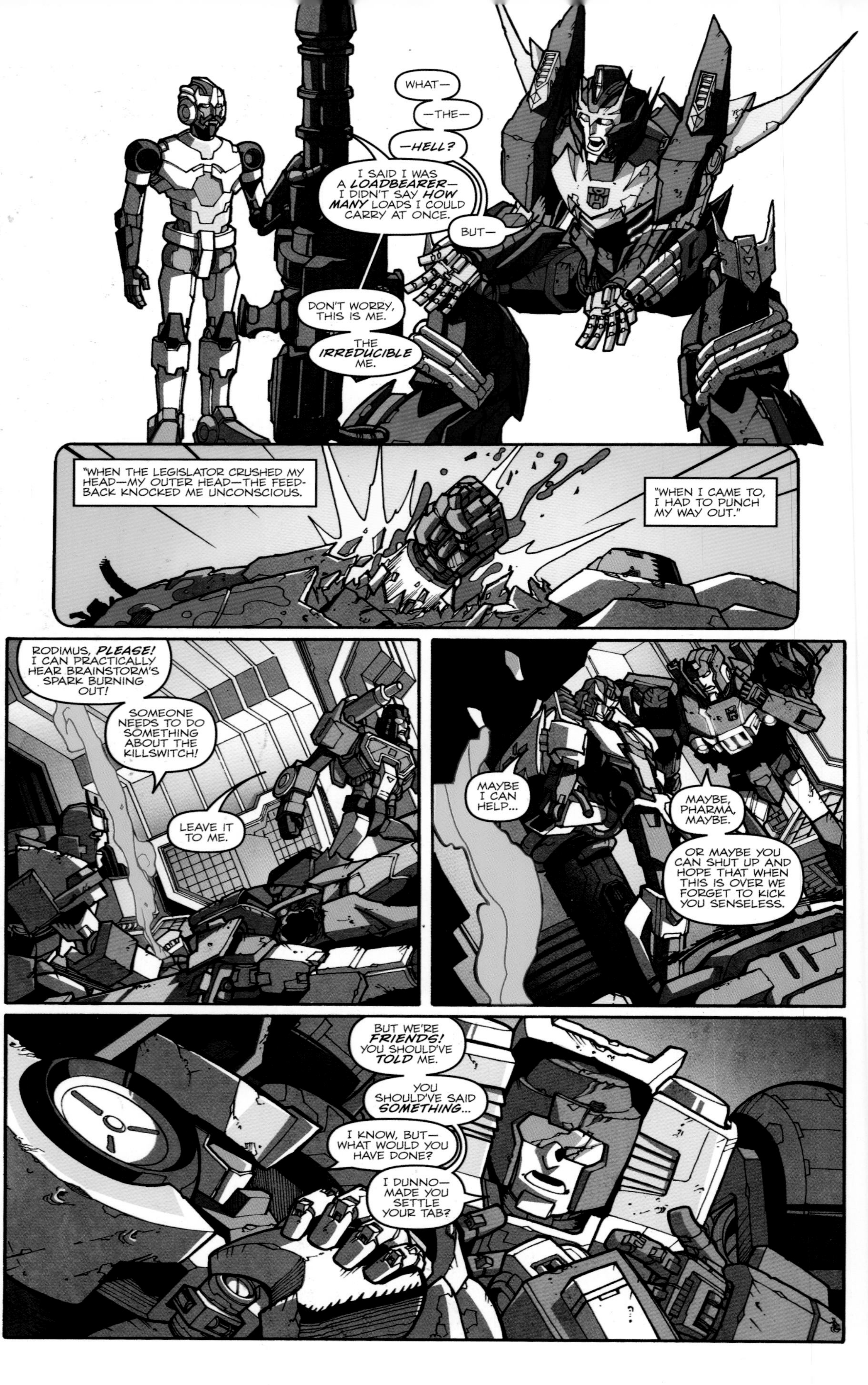

WHAT—
—THE—
—HELL?
I SAID I WAS A LOADBEARER— I DIDN'T SAY HOW MANY LOADS I COULD CARRY AT ONCE.
BUT—
DON'T WORRY, THIS IS ME.
THE IRREDUCIBLE ME.
"WHEN THE LEGISLATOR CRUSHED MY HEAD—MY OUTER HEAD—THE FEED-BACK KNOCKED ME UNCONSCIOUS.
"WHEN I CAME TO, I HAD TO PUNCH MY WAY OUT."
RODIMUS, PLEASE! I CAN PRACTICALLY HEAR BRAINSTORM'S SPARK BURNING OUT!
SOMEONE NEEDS TO DO SOMETHING ABOUT THE KILLSWITCH!
LEAVE IT TO ME.
MAYBE I CAN HELP...
MAYBE, PHARMA, MAYBE.
OR MAYBE YOU CAN SHUT UP AND HOPE THAT WHEN THIS IS OVER WE FORGET TO KICK YOU SENSELESS.
BUT WE'RE FRIENDS! YOU SHOULD'VE TOLD ME.
YOU SHOULD'VE SAID SOMETHING...
I KNOW, BUT— WHAT WOULD YOU HAVE DONE?
I DUNNO— MADE YOU SETTLE YOUR TAB?

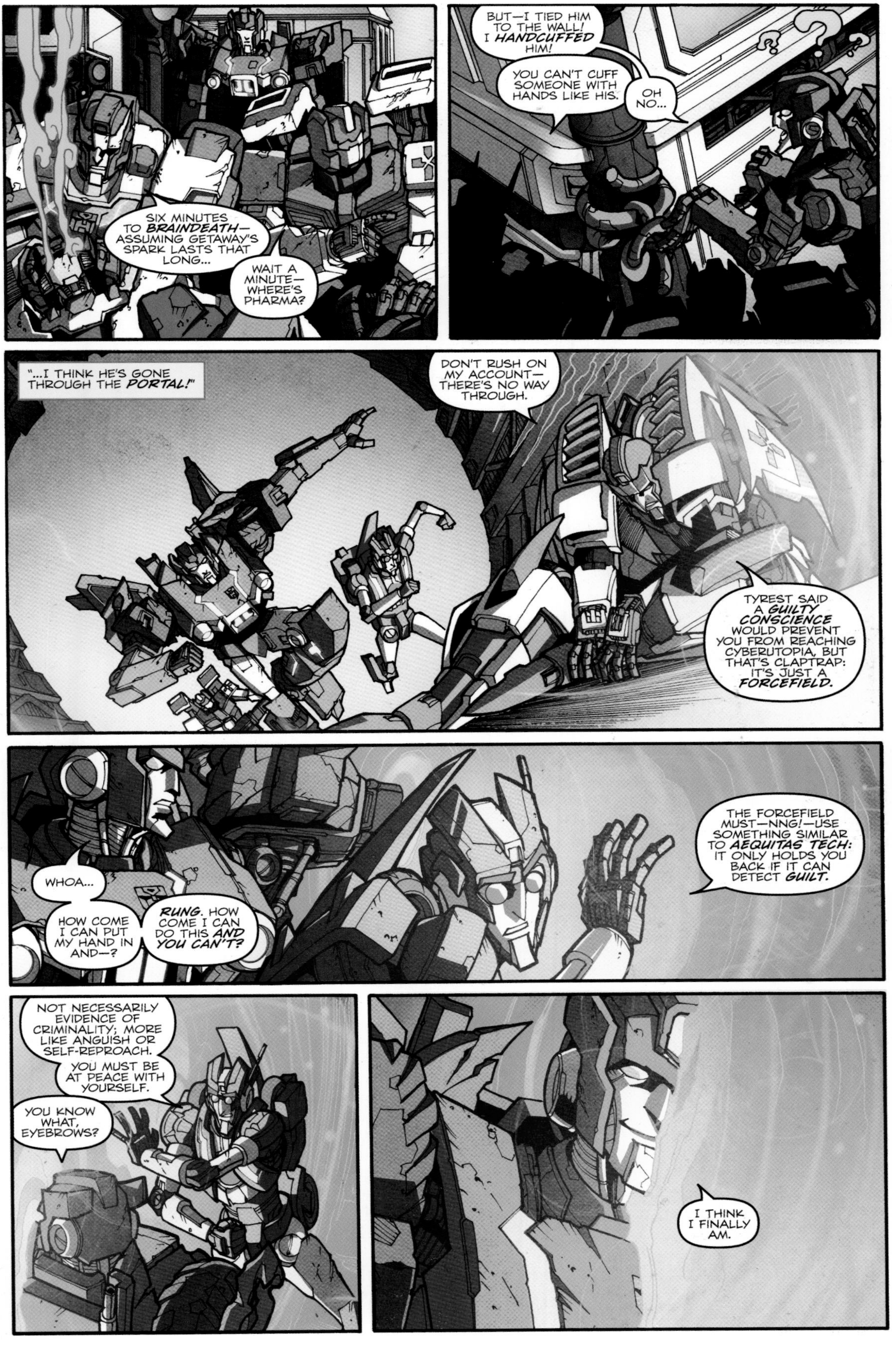

SIX MINUTES TO BRAINDEATH— ASSUMING GETAWAY'S SPARK LASTS THAT LONG...
WAIT A MINUTE— WHERE'S PHARMA?
BUT—I TIED HIM TO THE WALL! I HANDCUFFED HIM!
YOU CAN'T CUFF SOMEONE WITH HANDS LIKE HIS.
OH NO...
"...I THINK HE'S GONE THROUGH THE PORTAL!"
DON'T RUSH ON MY ACCOUNT— THERE'S NO WAY THROUGH.
TYREST SAID A GUILTY CONSCIENCE WOULD PREVENT YOU FROM REACHING CYBERUTOPIA, BUT THAT'S CLAPTRAP: IT'S JUST A FORCEFIELD.
WHOA...
HOW COME I CAN PUT MY HAND IN AND—?
RUNG. HOW COME I CAN DO THIS AND YOU CAN'T?
THE FORCEFIELD MUST—NNG!—USE SOMETHING SIMILAR TO AEQUITAS TECH: IT ONLY HOLDS YOU BACK IF IT CAN DETECT GUILT.
NOT NECESSARILY EVIDENCE OF CRIMINALITY; MORE LIKE ANGUISH OR SELF-REPROACH.
YOU MUST BE AT PEACE WITH YOURSELF.
YOU KNOW WHAT, EYEBROWS?
I THINK I FINALLY AM.

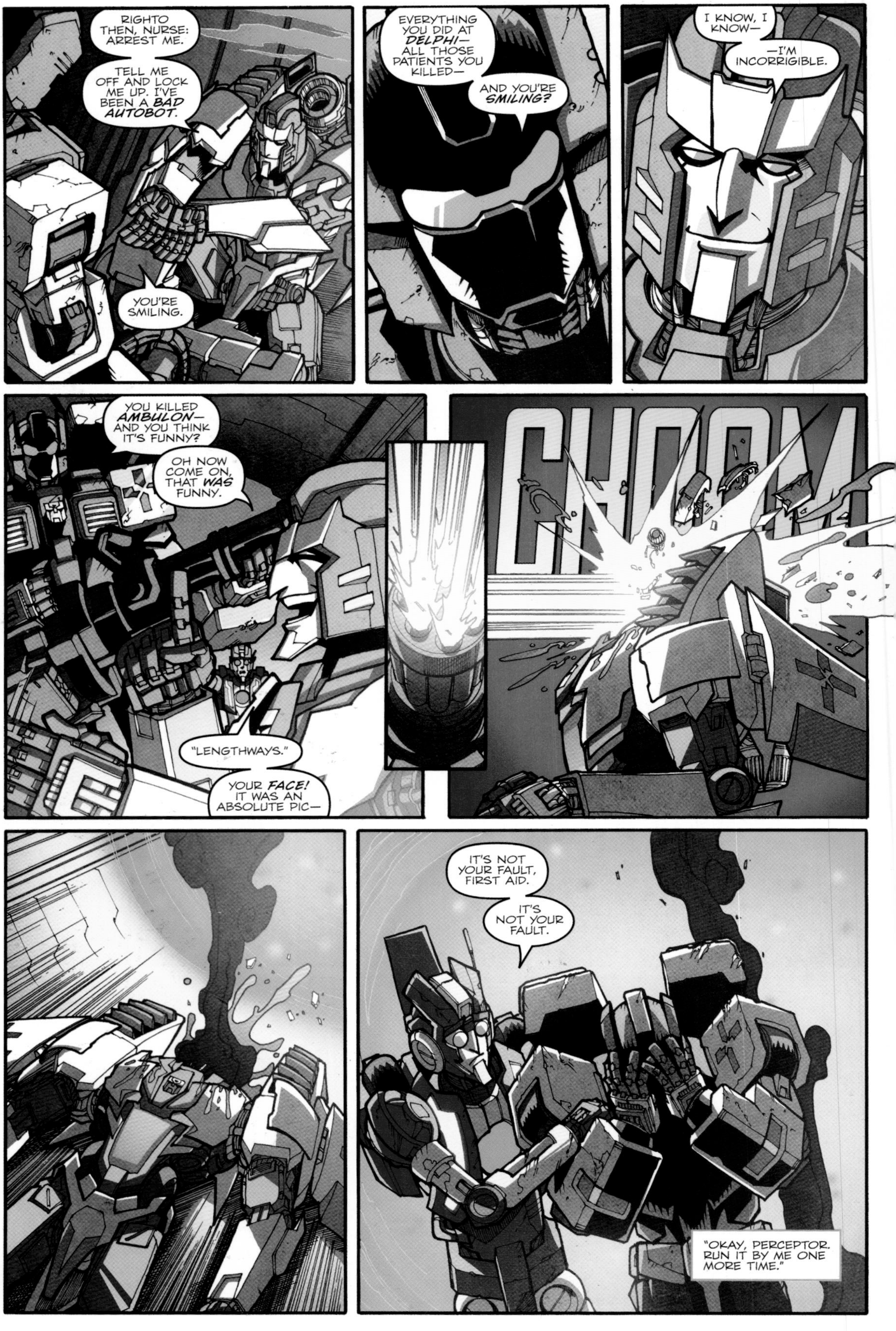

RIGHTO THEN, NURSE: ARREST ME.
TELL ME OFF AND LOCK ME UP. I'VE BEEN A BAD AUTOBOT.
YOU'RE SMILING.
EVERYTHING YOU DID AT DELPHI— ALL THOSE PATIENTS YOU KILLED—
AND YOU'RE SMILING?
I KNOW, I KNOW—
—I'M INCORRIGIBLE.
YOU KILLED AMBULON— AND YOU THINK IT'S FUNNY?
OH NOW COME ON, THAT WAS FUNNY.
"LENGTHWAYS."
YOUR FACE! IT WAS AN ABSOLUTE PIC—
CHOOM
IT'S NOT YOUR FAULT, FIRST AID.
IT'S NOT YOUR FAULT.
"OKAY, PERCEPTOR. RUN IT BY ME ONE MORE TIME."

EVERYONE WHO WAS **CONSTRUCTED COLD** HAS A SPECIAL SPARKCODE.

UNTIL TODAY, I THOUGHT THE CODE WAS A BYPRODUCT OF THE SPARK-SPLICING PROCESS, BUT IT'S NOT—IT'S COPIED DIRECTLY FROM THE MATRIX.

THE KILLSWITCH SCRAMBLES THE SPARKCODE. IF WE CAN **REINSTATE** THE CODE BY TAKING A NEW COPY FROM WHAT'S LEFT OF THE MATRIX, WE SHOULD BE ABLE TO REVERSE THE EFFECTS OF THE KILLSWITCH.

IS IT GOING TO KILL ME?

HONESTLY? I DON'T KNOW. IT'LL CERTAINLY TEAR THE MATRIX APART.

THERE GOES OUR MAP.

JUST GIVE ME A MOMENT TO FINALIZE THE SETTINGS.

MINIMUS— MAGNUS— C'MERE A MINUTE.

NEARBY.

I'M TELLING YOU, TYREST'S ALIVE—HE'S TRYING TO SAY SOMETHING.

HE'S SAYING...

WHAT'S HE SAYING?

SOMETHING ABOUT **WINNING.**

ONE

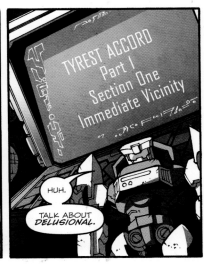

TYREST ACCORD
Part I
Section One
Immediate Vicinity

HUH.

TALK ABOUT **DELUSIONAL.**

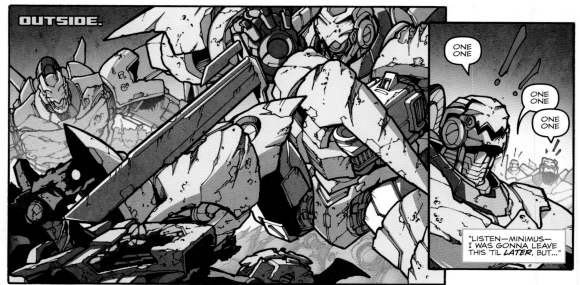

OUTSIDE.

ONE ONE

ONE ONE

ONE ONE

"LISTEN—MINIMUS—I WAS GONNA LEAVE THIS 'TIL *LATER*, BUT..."

...GETAWAY SAID YOU *LURED US HERE*.

HE THINKS THAT RATHER THAN TELEPORT HERE, YOU USED YOUR RECALL TRIGGER TO GIVE TYREST REMOTE ACCESS TO YOUR BODY, KNOWING WE'D FOLLOW YOU.

BUT IT'S AN INTERESTING WORD TO USE, ISN'T IT?

"LURED."

...

RODIMUS—CAPTAIN—I'VE BEEN UNHAPPY FOR A WHILE NOW.

WITH YOU, I MEAN. WITH YOUR *LEADERSHIP*.

SO YOU *DID* LURE US HERE!

WAIT—

MY *LEADERSHIP*?

I'VE HAD MISGIVINGS FROM THE OUTSET—WHEN WE WERE LEAVING CYBERTRON, AND YOU REFUSED TO SPEAK TO BUMBLEBEE.

THEN THERE WAS THE *SPARKEATER*, AND YOU RISKING RUNG'S LIFE, AND THEN—

AND THEN WHEN FORTRESS MAXIMUS TOOK HOSTAGES AND YOU MADE SWERVE SHOOT, EVEN THOUGH MAX HAD BEEN *PACIFIED*.

YOU ARRESTED CYCLONUS ON THE *FLIMSIEST* OF PRETEXTS, YOU *ANTAGONIZED* THE GALACTIC COUNCIL, AND AS FOR YOUR *STAGGERINGLY IMMATURE* REACTION WHEN *THUNDER*—

OKAY!

MESSAGE RECEIVED AND UNDERSTOOD.

ACTUALLY, NO, MESSAGE *NOT* UNDERSTOOD: YOU DIDN'T LIKE MY *STYLE* SO YOU THOUGHT YOU'D GET ME ARRESTED *AND PUT TO DEATH?*

YOU WERE CLOSE TO FALLING FOUL OF THE *FIT PERSONS ACT!*

I THOUGHT TYREST WOULD *REPRIMAND* YOU AND IT WOULD—I DON'T KNOW—*SHOCK* OR, OR, OR *SHAME* YOU INTO ACTING MORE RESPONSIBLY.

I DIDN'T KNOW—I *OBVIOUSLY* DIDN'T KNOW TYREST HAD BECOME UNHINGED.

MAGNUS— (I'M GONNA CALL YOU MAGNUS.)

MAGNUS, IF THIS IS IT— IF I'M GOING TO DIE—I NEED TO COME CLEAN. EVERYTHING YOU'VE JUST SAID—

I'VE DONE WORSE. I'VE DONE *MUCH WORSE.*

I BROUGHT OVERLORD ON BOARD.

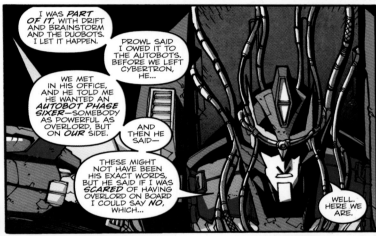

I WAS *PART OF IT,* WITH DRIFT AND BRAINSTORM AND THE DUOBOTS. I LET IT HAPPEN.

PROWL SAID I OWED IT TO THE AUTOBOTS. BEFORE WE LEFT CYBERTRON, HE...

WE MET IN HIS OFFICE, AND HE TOLD ME HE WANTED AN *AUTOBOT PHASE SIXER*—SOMEBODY AS POWERFUL AS OVERLORD, BUT ON *OUR* SIDE.

AND THEN HE SAID—

THESE MIGHT NOT HAVE BEEN HIS EXACT WORDS, BUT HE SAID IF I WAS *SCARED* OF HAVING OVERLORD ON BOARD I COULD SAY *NO,* WHICH...

WELL. HERE WE ARE.

WE'RE NEARLY READY TO GO.

TEN SECONDS.

I DON'T WANT TO DIE.

OF COURSE NOT. OF COURSE YOU DON'T.

NO, I MEAN—

SELF-SACRIFICE, MAGNUS—IT'S *CHEAP.* IT'S A CHEAP WAY OUT.

I NEED TO *LIVE* SO I CAN *MAKE AMENDS* AND—

AAAARRRGH!

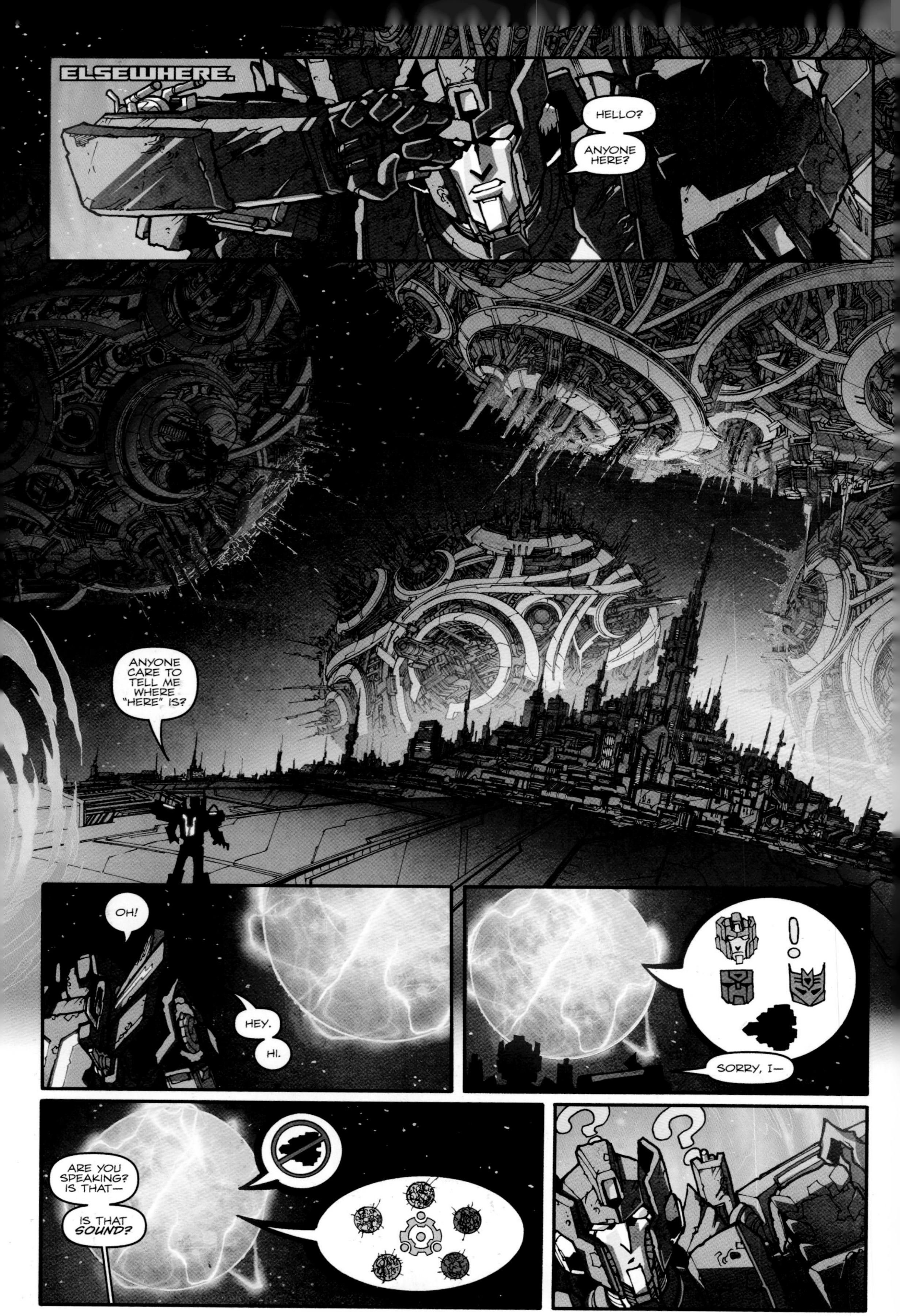
ELSEWHERE.
HELLO?
ANYONE HERE?
ANYONE CARE TO TELL ME WHERE "HERE" IS?
OH!
HEY.
HI.
!
SORRY, I—
ARE YOU SPEAKING? IS THAT—
IS THAT *SOUND?*

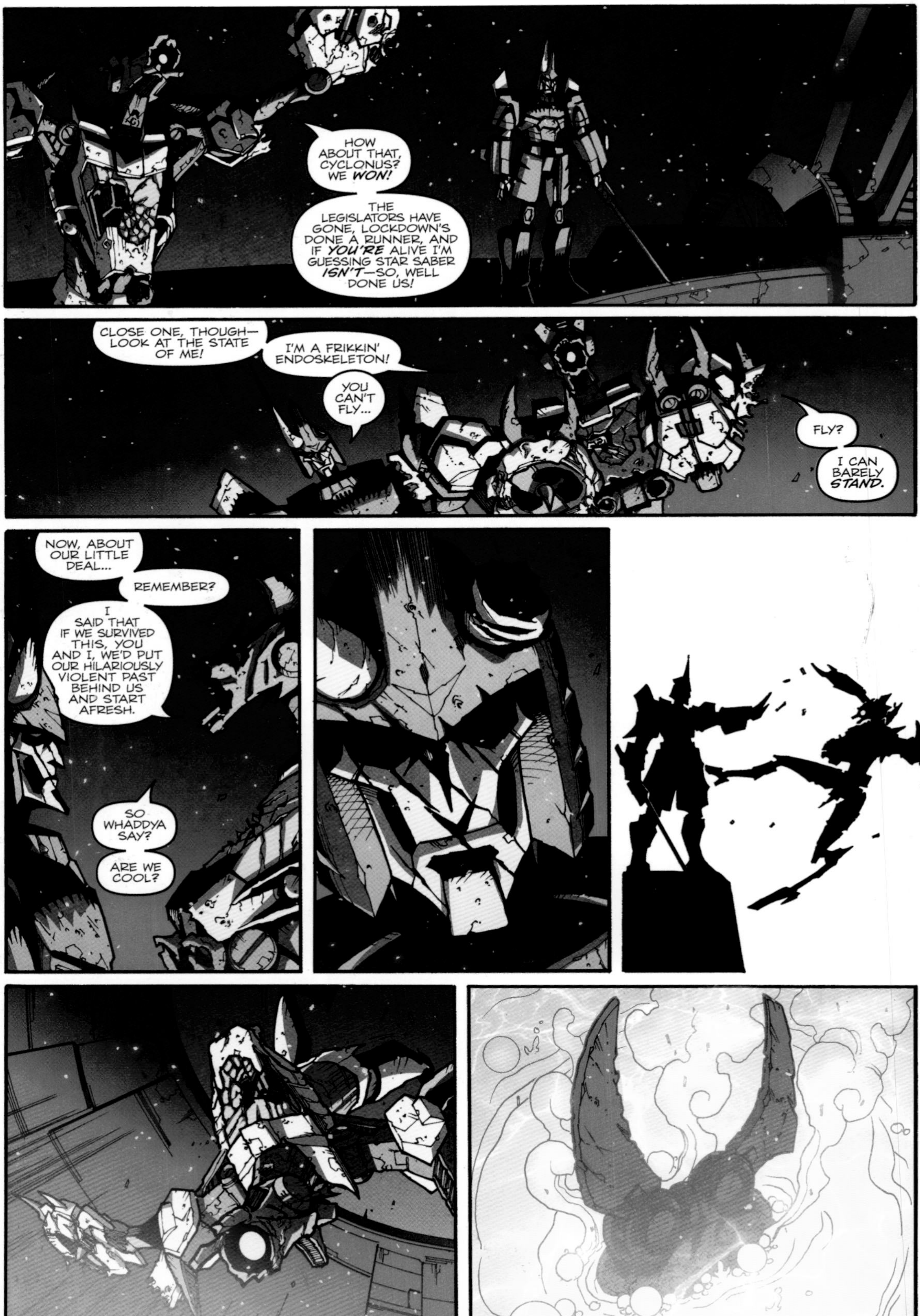
HOW ABOUT THAT, CYCLONUS? WE WON!
THE LEGISLATORS HAVE GONE, LOCKDOWN'S DONE A RUNNER, AND IF YOU'RE ALIVE I'M GUESSING STAR SABER ISN'T—SO, WELL DONE US!
CLOSE ONE, THOUGH—LOOK AT THE STATE OF ME!
I'M A FRIKKIN' ENDOSKELETON!
YOU CAN'T FLY...
FLY?
I CAN BARELY STAND.
NOW, ABOUT OUR LITTLE DEAL...
REMEMBER?
I SAID THAT IF WE SURVIVED THIS, YOU AND I, WE'D PUT OUR HILARIOUSLY VIOLENT PAST BEHIND US AND START AFRESH.
SO WHADDYA SAY?
ARE WE COOL?

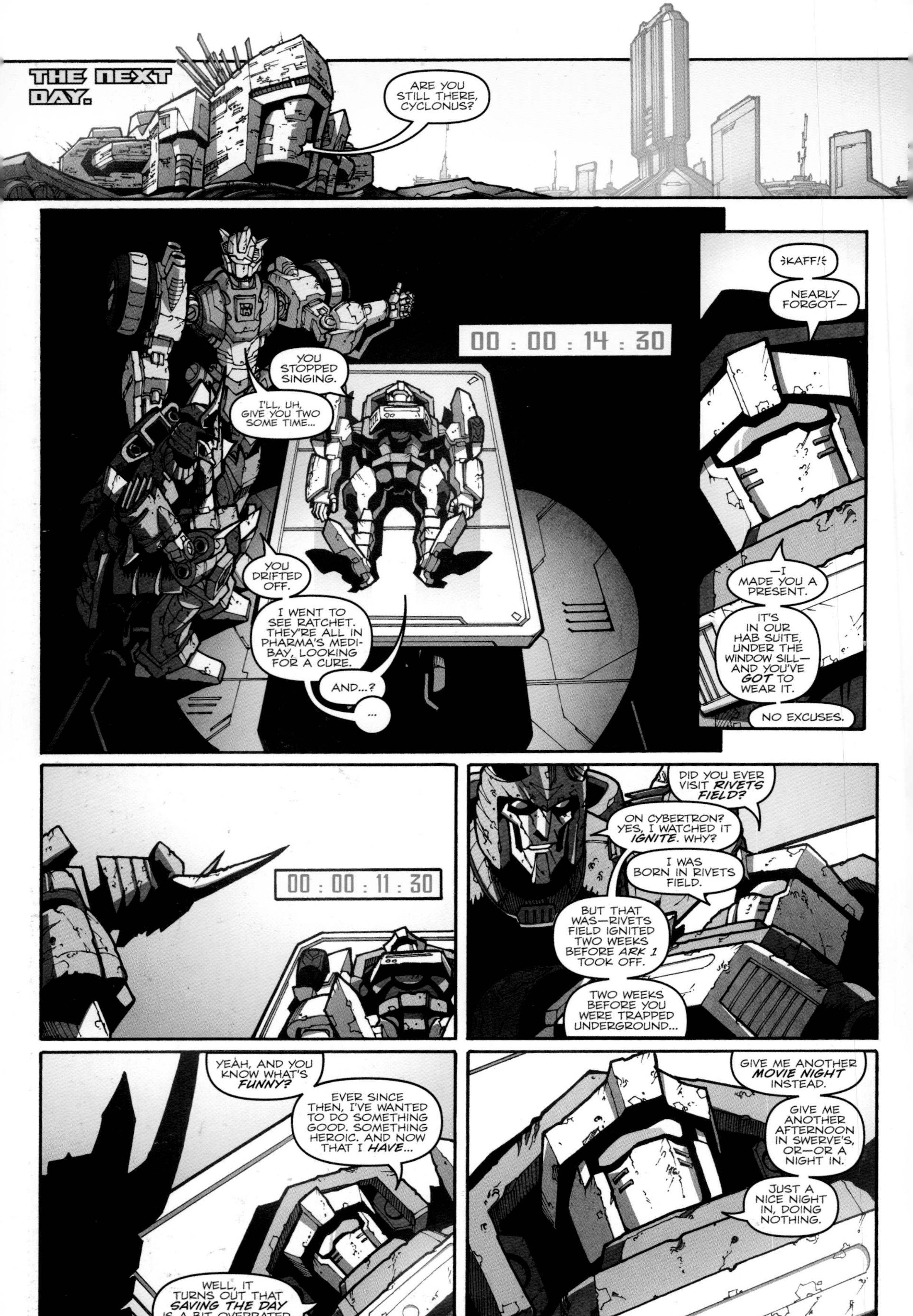
THE NEXT DAY.
ARE YOU STILL THERE, CYCLONUS?
00 : 00 : 14 : 30
YOU STOPPED SINGING.
I'LL, UH, GIVE YOU TWO SOME TIME...
YOU DRIFTED OFF.
I WENT TO SEE RATCHET. THEY'RE ALL IN PHARMA'S MEDI-BAY, LOOKING FOR A CURE.
AND...?
...
KAFF!
NEARLY FORGOT—
—I MADE YOU A PRESENT.
IT'S IN OUR HAB SUITE, UNDER THE WINDOW SILL—AND YOU'VE GOT TO WEAR IT.
NO EXCUSES.
00 : 00 : 11 : 30
DID YOU EVER VISIT RIVETS FIELD?
ON CYBERTRON? YES, I WATCHED IT IGNITE. WHY?
I WAS BORN IN RIVETS FIELD.
BUT THAT WAS—RIVETS FIELD IGNITED TWO WEEKS BEFORE ARK 1 TOOK OFF.
TWO WEEKS BEFORE YOU WERE TRAPPED UNDERGROUND...
YEAH, AND YOU KNOW WHAT'S FUNNY?
EVER SINCE THEN, I'VE WANTED TO DO SOMETHING GOOD. SOMETHING HEROIC. AND NOW THAT I HAVE...
WELL, IT TURNS OUT THAT SAVING THE DAY IS A BIT OVERRATED.
GIVE ME ANOTHER MOVIE NIGHT INSTEAD.
GIVE ME ANOTHER AFTERNOON IN SWERVE'S, OR—OR A NIGHT IN.
JUST A NICE NIGHT IN, DOING NOTHING.

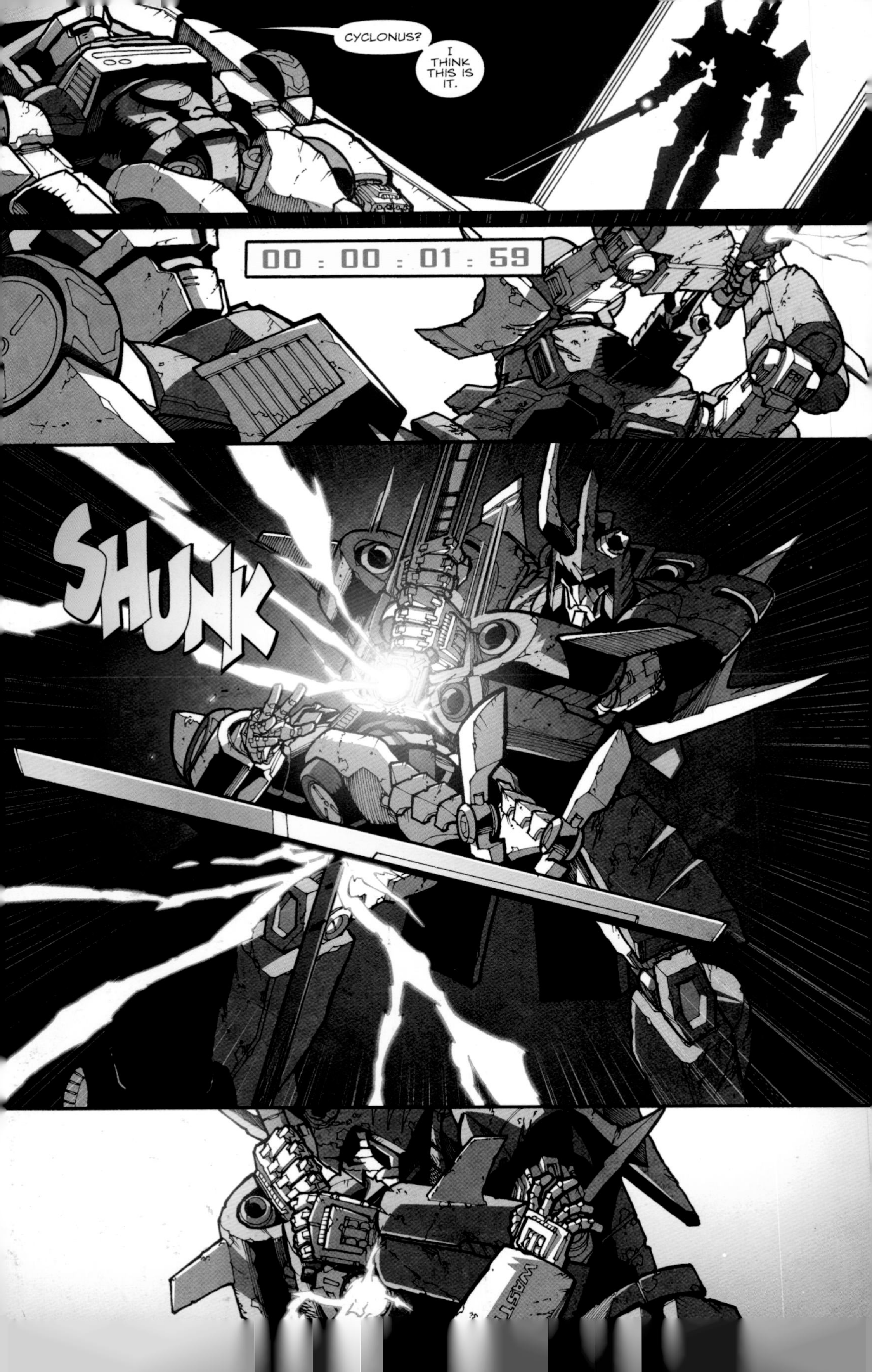
CYCLONUS?
I THINK THIS IS IT.
00 : 00 : 01 : 59
SHUNK

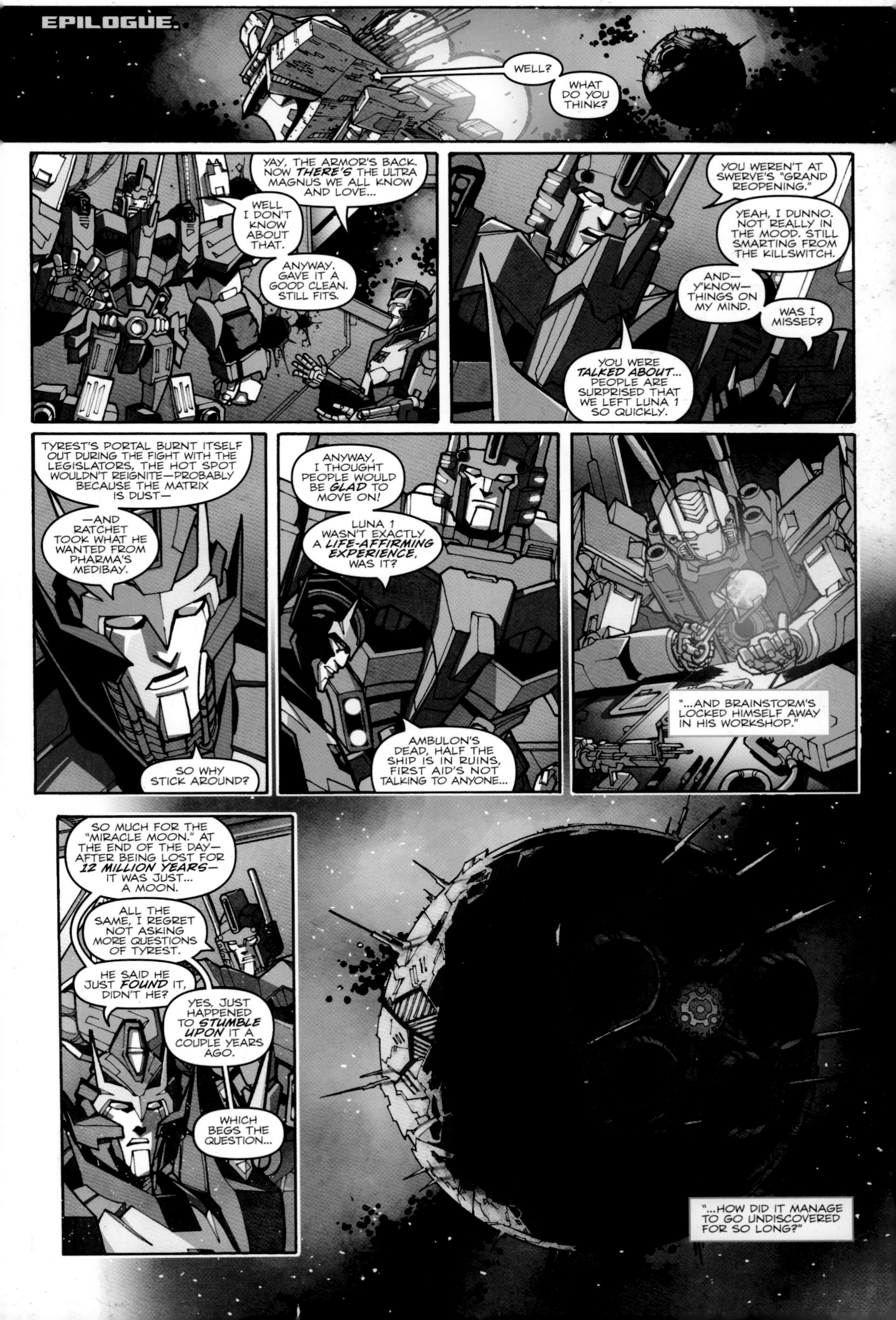
EPILOGUE.
WELL?
WHAT DO YOU THINK?
YAY, THE ARMOR'S BACK. NOW THERE'S THE ULTRA MAGNUS WE ALL KNOW AND LOVE...
WELL I DON'T KNOW ABOUT THAT.
ANYWAY. GAVE IT A GOOD CLEAN. STILL FITS.
YOU WEREN'T AT SWERVE'S "GRAND REOPENING."
YEAH, I DUNNO. NOT REALLY IN THE MOOD. STILL SMARTING FROM THE KILLSWITCH.
AND— Y'KNOW— THINGS ON MY MIND.
WAS I MISSED?
YOU WERE TALKED ABOUT... PEOPLE ARE SURPRISED THAT WE LEFT LUNA 1 SO QUICKLY.
TYREST'S PORTAL BURNT ITSELF OUT DURING THE FIGHT WITH THE LEGISLATORS, THE HOT SPOT WOULDN'T REIGNITE—PROBABLY BECAUSE THE MATRIX IS DUST—
—AND RATCHET TOOK WHAT HE WANTED FROM PHARMA'S MEDIBAY.
SO WHY STICK AROUND?
ANYWAY, I THOUGHT PEOPLE WOULD BE GLAD TO MOVE ON!
LUNA 1 WASN'T EXACTLY A LIFE-AFFIRMING EXPERIENCE, WAS IT?
AMBULON'S DEAD, HALF THE SHIP IS IN RUINS, FIRST AID'S NOT TALKING TO ANYONE...
"...AND BRAINSTORM'S LOCKED HIMSELF AWAY IN HIS WORKSHOP."
SO MUCH FOR THE "MIRACLE MOON." AT THE END OF THE DAY— AFTER BEING LOST FOR 12 MILLION YEARS— IT WAS JUST... A MOON.
ALL THE SAME, I REGRET NOT ASKING MORE QUESTIONS OF TYREST.
HE SAID HE JUST FOUND IT, DIDN'T HE?
YES, JUST HAPPENED TO STUMBLE UPON IT A COUPLE YEARS AGO.
WHICH BEGS THE QUESTION...
"...HOW DID IT MANAGE TO GO UNDISCOVERED FOR SO LONG?"

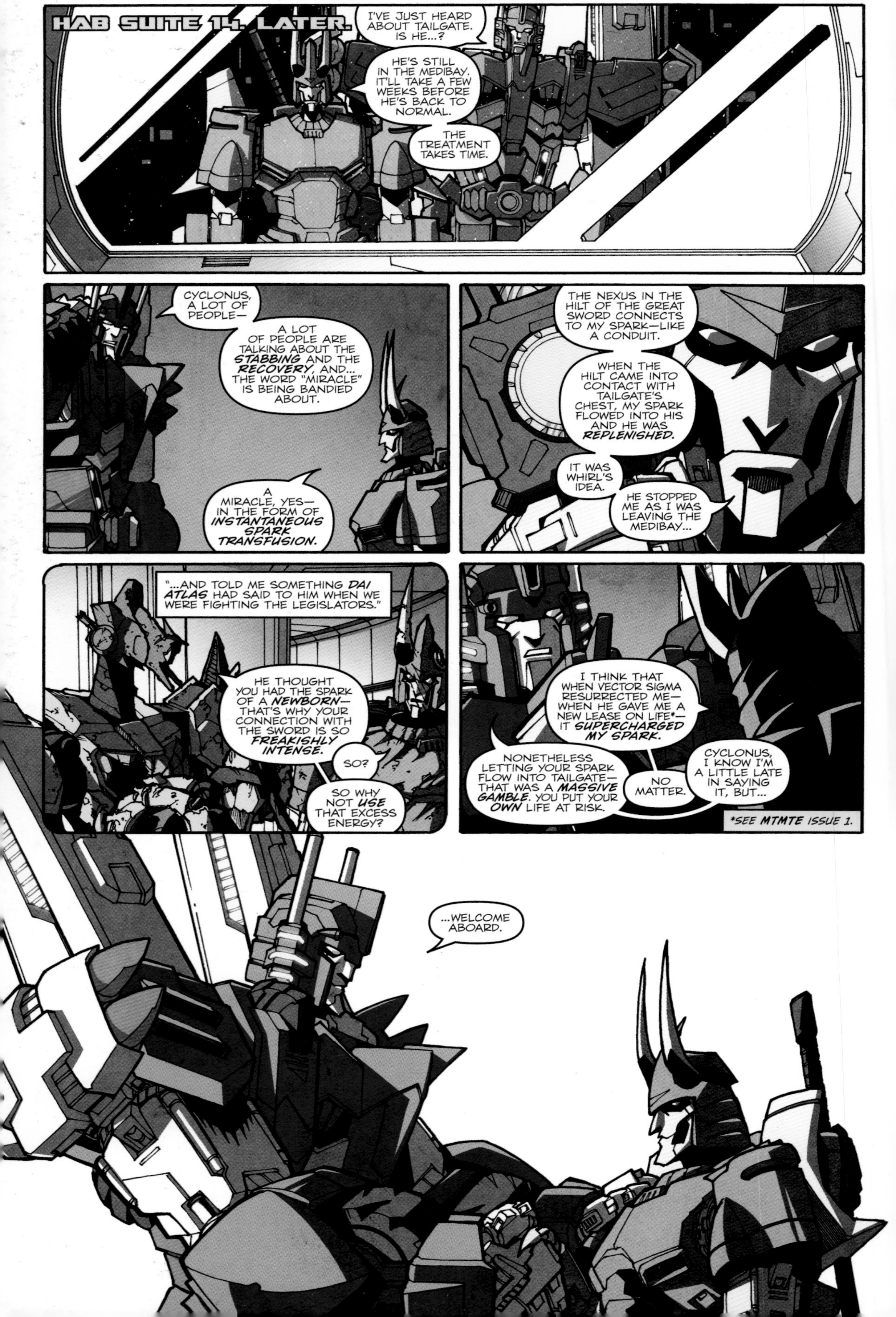
HAB SUITE 14. LATER.
I'VE JUST HEARD ABOUT TAILGATE. IS HE...?
HE'S STILL IN THE MEDIBAY. IT'LL TAKE A FEW WEEKS BEFORE HE'S BACK TO NORMAL.
THE TREATMENT TAKES TIME.
CYCLONUS, A LOT OF PEOPLE—
A LOT OF PEOPLE ARE TALKING ABOUT THE STABBING AND THE RECOVERY, AND... THE WORD "MIRACLE" IS BEING BANDIED ABOUT.
A MIRACLE, YES— IN THE FORM OF INSTANTANEOUS SPARK TRANSFUSION.
THE NEXUS IN THE HILT OF THE GREAT SWORD CONNECTS TO MY SPARK—LIKE A CONDUIT.
WHEN THE HILT CAME INTO CONTACT WITH TAILGATE'S CHEST, MY SPARK FLOWED INTO HIS AND HE WAS REPLENISHED.
IT WAS WHIRL'S IDEA.
HE STOPPED ME AS I WAS LEAVING THE MEDIBAY...
"...AND TOLD ME SOMETHING DAI ATLAS HAD SAID TO HIM WHEN WE WERE FIGHTING THE LEGISLATORS."
HE THOUGHT YOU HAD THE SPARK OF A NEWBORN— THAT'S WHY YOUR CONNECTION WITH THE SWORD IS SO FREAKISHLY INTENSE.
SO?
SO WHY NOT USE THAT EXCESS ENERGY?
I THINK THAT WHEN VECTOR SIGMA RESURRECTED ME— WHEN HE GAVE ME A NEW LEASE ON LIFE*— IT SUPERCHARGED MY SPARK.
NONETHELESS LETTING YOUR SPARK FLOW INTO TAILGATE— THAT WAS A MASSIVE GAMBLE. YOU PUT YOUR OWN LIFE AT RISK.
NO MATTER.
CYCLONUS, I KNOW I'M A LITTLE LATE IN SAYING IT, BUT...
*SEE MTMTE ISSUE 1.
...WELCOME ABOARD.

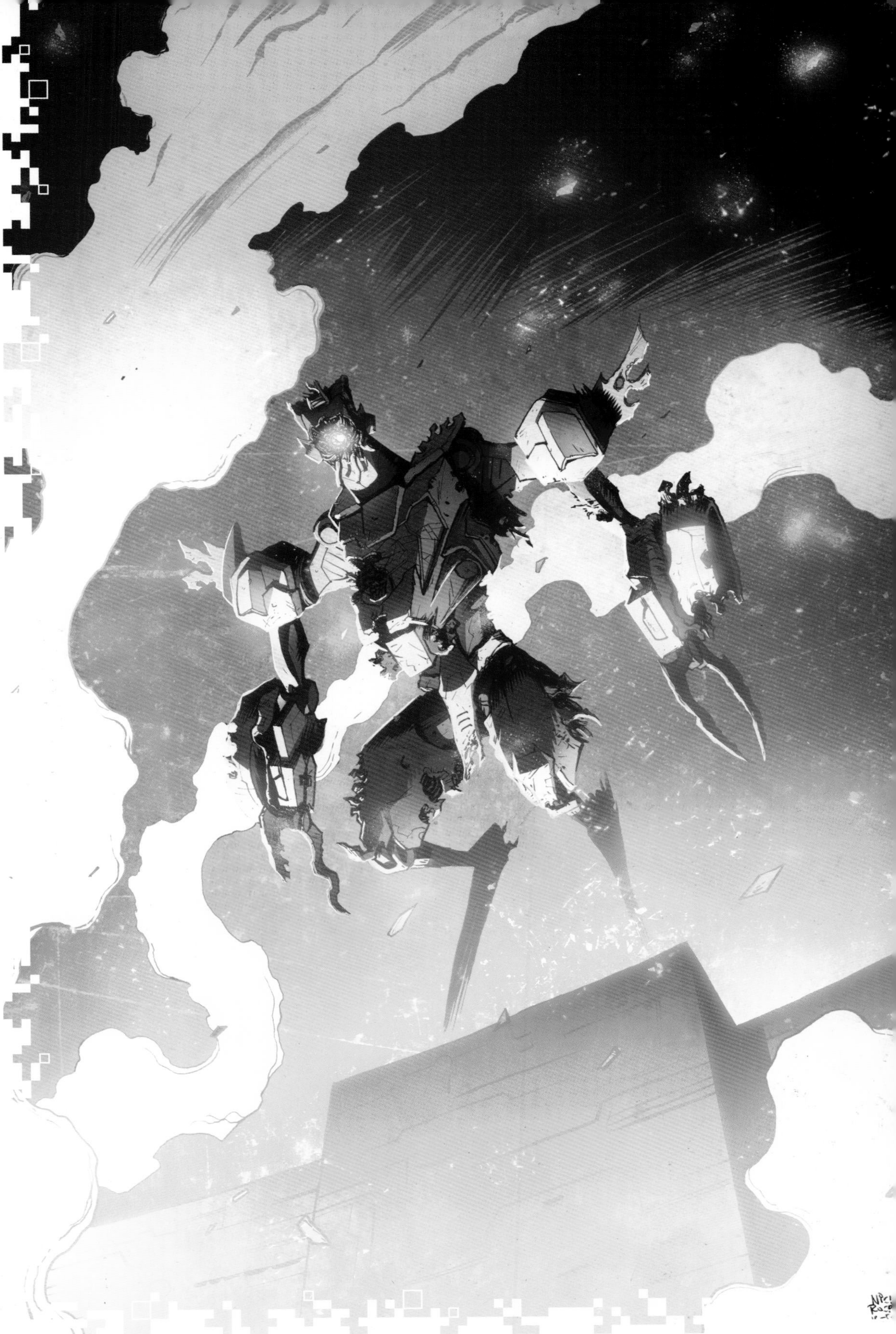

□ MORE THAN MEETS THE EYE #21 COVER B

by **NICK ROCHE** Colors by **JOANA LAFUENTE**

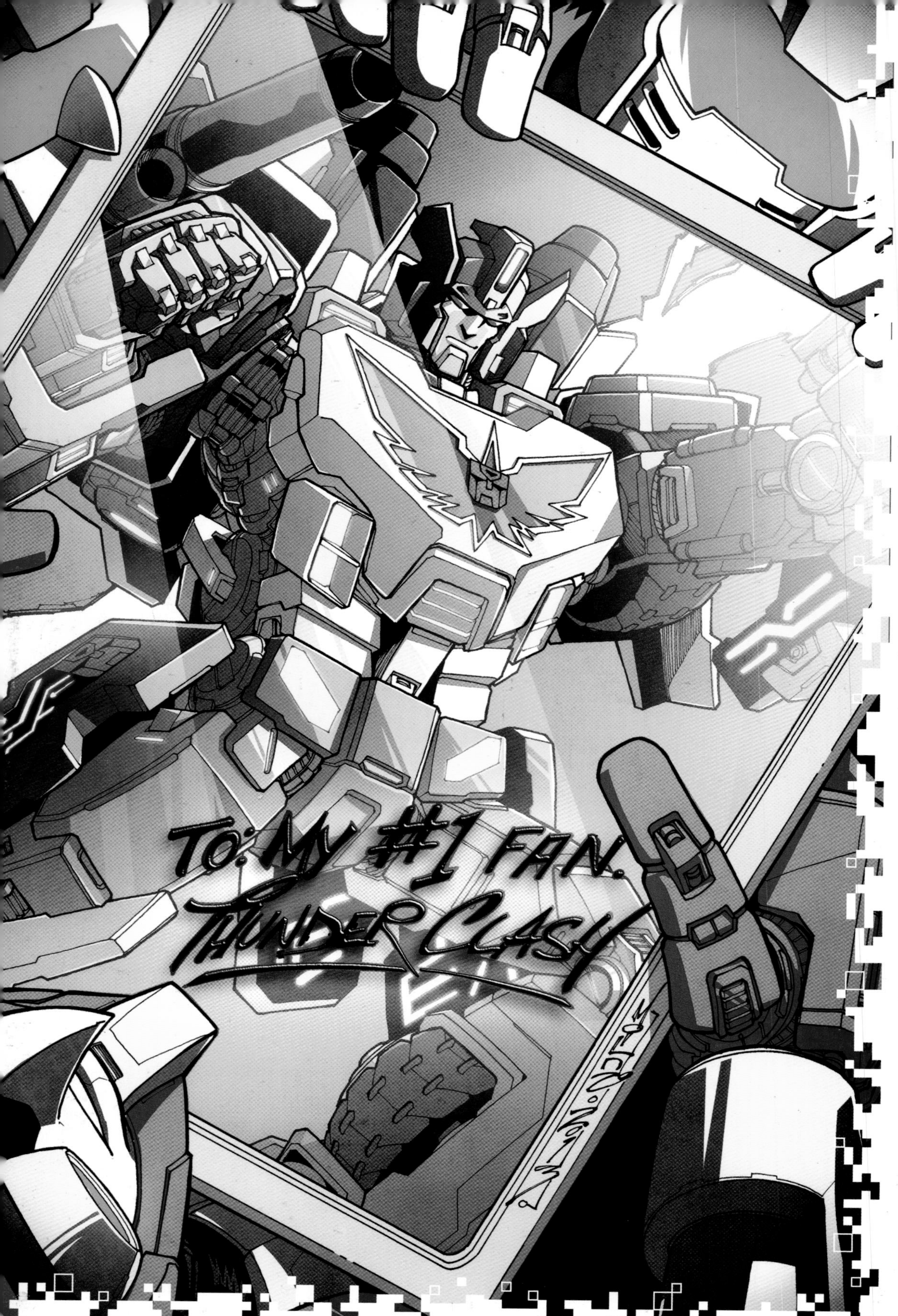
TO: MY #1 FAN.
THUNDER CLASH

MORE THAN MEETS THE EYE #22 COVER A
by **ALEX MILNE** Colors by **JOSH BURCHAM**

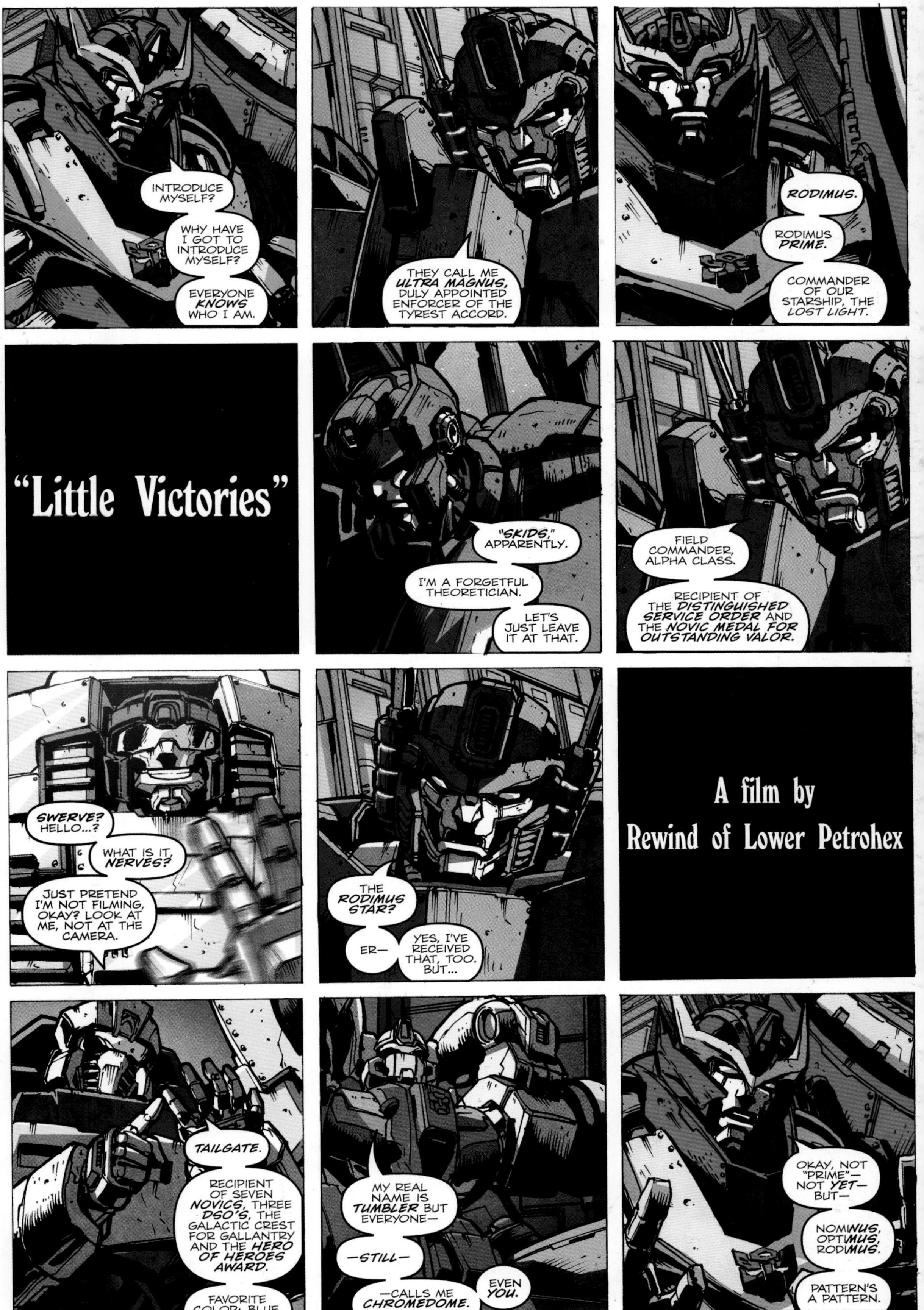
INTRODUCE MYSELF?
WHY HAVE I GOT TO INTRODUCE MYSELF?
EVERYONE KNOWS WHO I AM.
THEY CALL ME ULTRA MAGNUS, DULY APPOINTED ENFORCER OF THE TYREST ACCORD.
RODIMUS.
RODIMUS PRIME.
COMMANDER OF OUR STARSHIP, THE LOST LIGHT.
"Little Victories"
"SKIDS," APPARENTLY.
I'M A FORGETFUL THEORETICIAN.
LET'S JUST LEAVE IT AT THAT.
FIELD COMMANDER, ALPHA CLASS.
RECIPIENT OF THE DISTINGUISHED SERVICE ORDER AND THE NOVIC MEDAL FOR OUTSTANDING VALOR.
SWERVE? HELLO...?
WHAT IS IT, NERVES?
JUST PRETEND I'M NOT FILMING, OKAY? LOOK AT ME, NOT AT THE CAMERA.
THE RODIMUS STAR?
ER—
YES, I'VE RECEIVED THAT, TOO. BUT...
A film by
Rewind of Lower Petrohex
TAILGATE.
RECIPIENT OF SEVEN NOVICS, THREE DSO'S, THE GALACTIC CREST FOR GALLANTRY AND THE HERO OF HEROES AWARD.
FAVORITE COLOR: BLUE.
MY REAL NAME IS TUMBLER BUT EVERYONE—
—STILL—
—CALLS ME CHROMEDOME.
EVEN YOU.
OKAY, NOT "PRIME"—NOT YET—BUT—
NOMINUS, OPTIMUS, RODIMUS.
PATTERN'S A PATTERN.

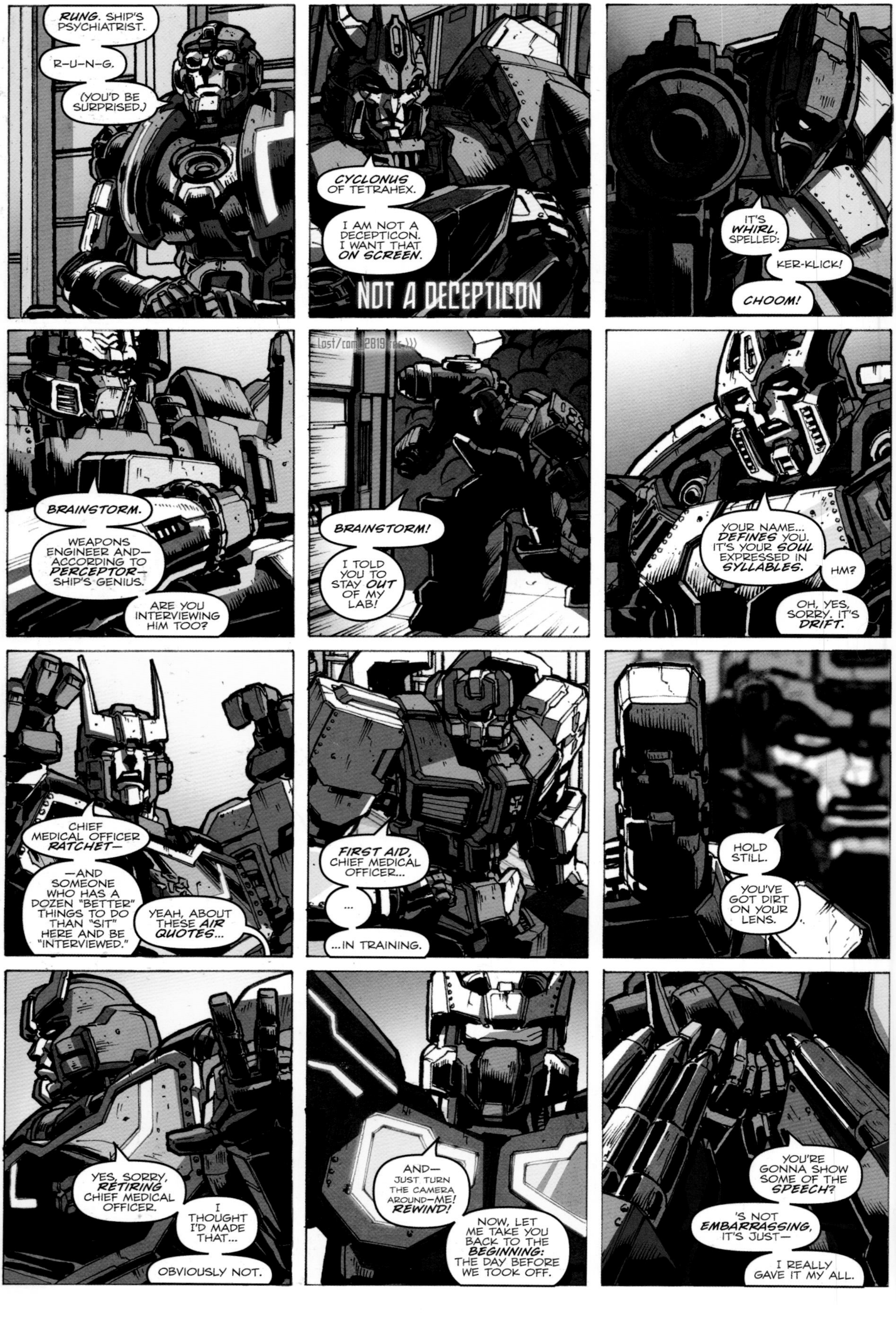
RUNG. SHIP'S PSYCHIATRIST.
R-U-N-G.
(YOU'D BE SURPRISED.)
CYCLONUS OF TETRAHEX.
I AM NOT A DECEPTICON. I WANT THAT ON SCREEN.
NOT A DECEPTICON
IT'S WHIRL, SPELLED:
KER-KLICK!
CHOOM!
BRAINSTORM.
WEAPONS ENGINEER AND— ACCORDING TO PERCEPTOR— SHIP'S GENIUS.
ARE YOU INTERVIEWING HIM TOO?
BRAINSTORM!
I TOLD YOU TO STAY OUT OF MY LAB!
YOUR NAME... DEFINES YOU. IT'S YOUR SOUL EXPRESSED IN SYLLABLES.
HM?
OH, YES, SORRY. IT'S DRIFT.
CHIEF MEDICAL OFFICER RATCHET—
—AND SOMEONE WHO HAS A DOZEN "BETTER" THINGS TO DO THAN "SIT" HERE AND BE "INTERVIEWED."
YEAH, ABOUT THESE AIR QUOTES...
FIRST AID, CHIEF MEDICAL OFFICER...
...
...IN TRAINING.
HOLD STILL.
YOU'VE GOT DIRT ON YOUR LENS.
YES, SORRY, RETIRING CHIEF MEDICAL OFFICER.
I THOUGHT I'D MADE THAT...
OBVIOUSLY NOT.
AND— JUST TURN THE CAMERA AROUND—ME! REWIND!
NOW, LET ME TAKE YOU BACK TO THE BEGINNING: THE DAY BEFORE WE TOOK OFF.
YOU'RE GONNA SHOW SOME OF THE SPEECH?
'S NOT EMBARRASSING, IT'S JUST—
I REALLY GAVE IT MY ALL.

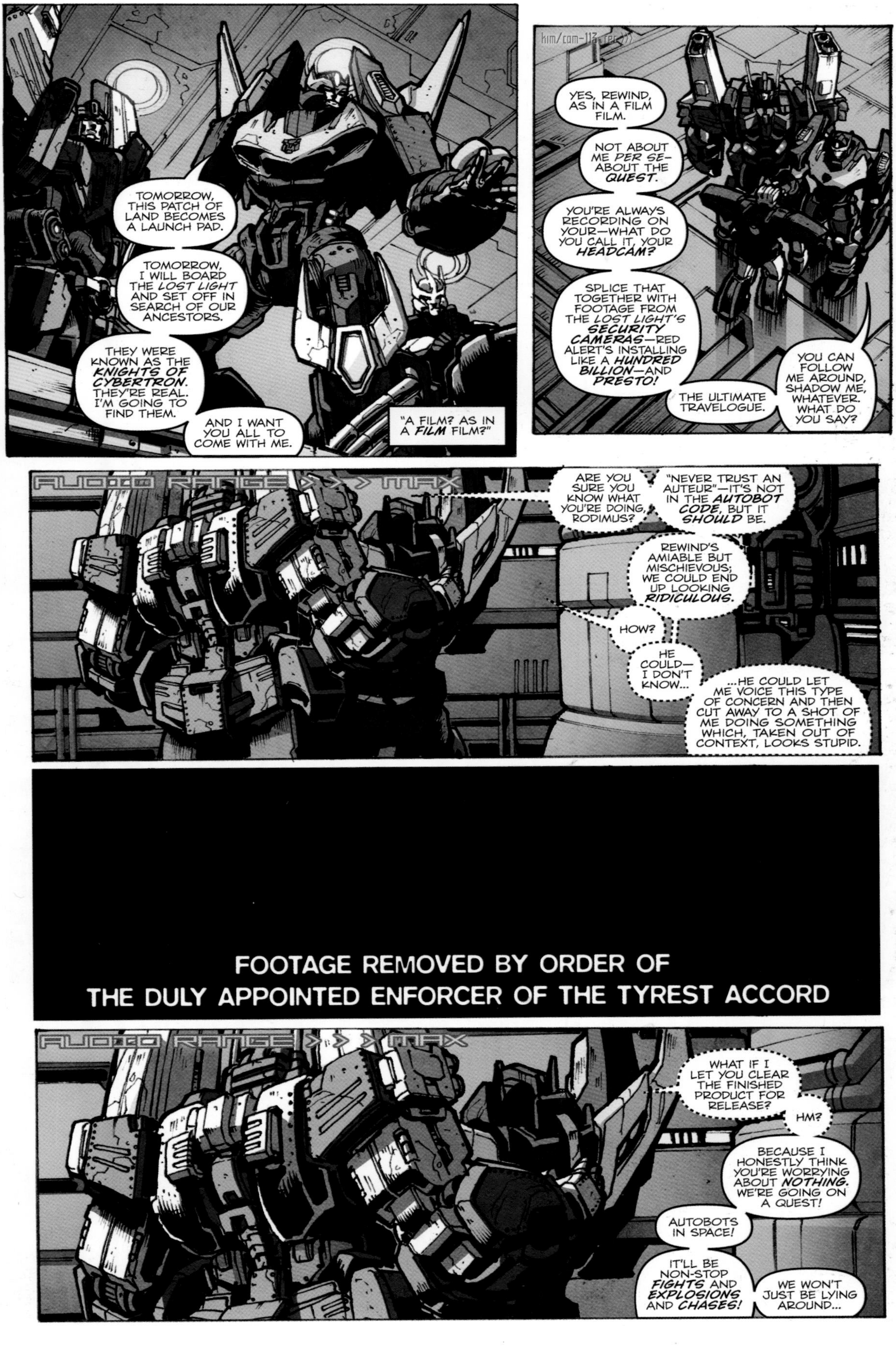
TOMORROW, THIS PATCH OF LAND BECOMES A LAUNCH PAD.
TOMORROW, I WILL BOARD THE LOST LIGHT AND SET OFF IN SEARCH OF OUR ANCESTORS.
THEY WERE KNOWN AS THE KNIGHTS OF CYBERTRON. THEY'RE REAL. I'M GOING TO FIND THEM.
AND I WANT YOU ALL TO COME WITH ME.
"A FILM? AS IN A FILM FILM?"
kim/cam-113.rec
YES, REWIND, AS IN A FILM FILM.
NOT ABOUT ME PER SE—ABOUT THE QUEST.
YOU'RE ALWAYS RECORDING ON YOUR—WHAT DO YOU CALL IT, YOUR HEADCAM?
SPLICE THAT TOGETHER WITH FOOTAGE FROM THE LOST LIGHT'S SECURITY CAMERAS—RED ALERT'S INSTALLING LIKE A HUNDRED BILLION—AND PRESTO!
THE ULTIMATE TRAVELOGUE.
YOU CAN FOLLOW ME AROUND, SHADOW ME, WHATEVER. WHAT DO YOU SAY?
AUDIO RANGE >>> MAX
ARE YOU SURE YOU KNOW WHAT YOU'RE DOING, RODIMUS?
"NEVER TRUST AN AUTEUR"—IT'S NOT IN THE AUTOBOT CODE, BUT IT SHOULD BE.
REWIND'S AMIABLE BUT MISCHIEVOUS; WE COULD END UP LOOKING RIDICULOUS.
HOW?
HE COULD—I DON'T KNOW...
...HE COULD LET ME VOICE THIS TYPE OF CONCERN AND THEN CUT AWAY TO A SHOT OF ME DOING SOMETHING WHICH, TAKEN OUT OF CONTEXT, LOOKS STUPID.
FOOTAGE REMOVED BY ORDER OF THE DULY APPOINTED ENFORCER OF THE TYREST ACCORD
AUDIO RANGE >>> MAX
WHAT IF I LET YOU CLEAR THE FINISHED PRODUCT FOR RELEASE?
HM?
BECAUSE I HONESTLY THINK YOU'RE WORRYING ABOUT NOTHING. WE'RE GOING ON A QUEST!
AUTOBOTS IN SPACE!
IT'LL BE NON-STOP FIGHTS AND EXPLOSIONS AND CHASES!
WE WON'T JUST BE LYING AROUND...

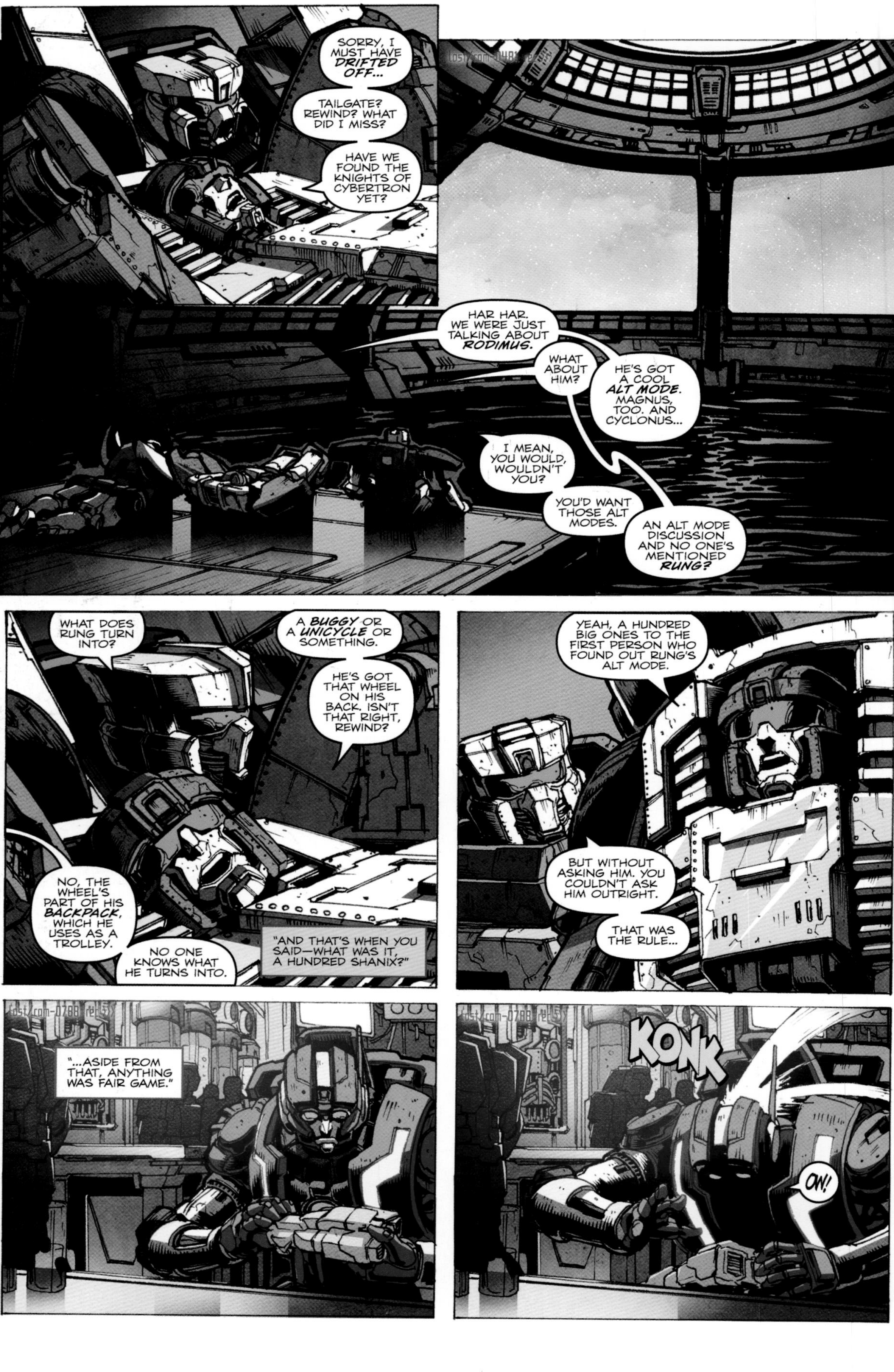
SORRY, I MUST HAVE DRIFTED OFF...
TAILGATE? REWIND? WHAT DID I MISS?
HAVE WE FOUND THE KNIGHTS OF CYBERTRON YET?
HAR HAR. WE WERE JUST TALKING ABOUT RODIMUS.
WHAT ABOUT HIM?
HE'S GOT A COOL ALT MODE. MAGNUS, TOO. AND CYCLONUS...
I MEAN, YOU WOULD, WOULDN'T YOU?
YOU'D WANT THOSE ALT MODES.
AN ALT MODE DISCUSSION AND NO ONE'S MENTIONED RUNG?
WHAT DOES RUNG TURN INTO?
A BUGGY OR A UNICYCLE OR SOMETHING.
HE'S GOT THAT WHEEL ON HIS BACK. ISN'T THAT RIGHT, REWIND?
NO, THE WHEEL'S PART OF HIS BACKPACK, WHICH HE USES AS A TROLLEY.
NO ONE KNOWS WHAT HE TURNS INTO.
"AND THAT'S WHEN YOU SAID—WHAT WAS IT, A HUNDRED SHANIX?"
YEAH, A HUNDRED BIG ONES TO THE FIRST PERSON WHO FOUND OUT RUNG'S ALT MODE.
BUT WITHOUT ASKING HIM. YOU COULDN'T ASK HIM OUTRIGHT.
THAT WAS THE RULE...
"...ASIDE FROM THAT, ANYTHING WAS FAIR GAME."
KONK
OW!

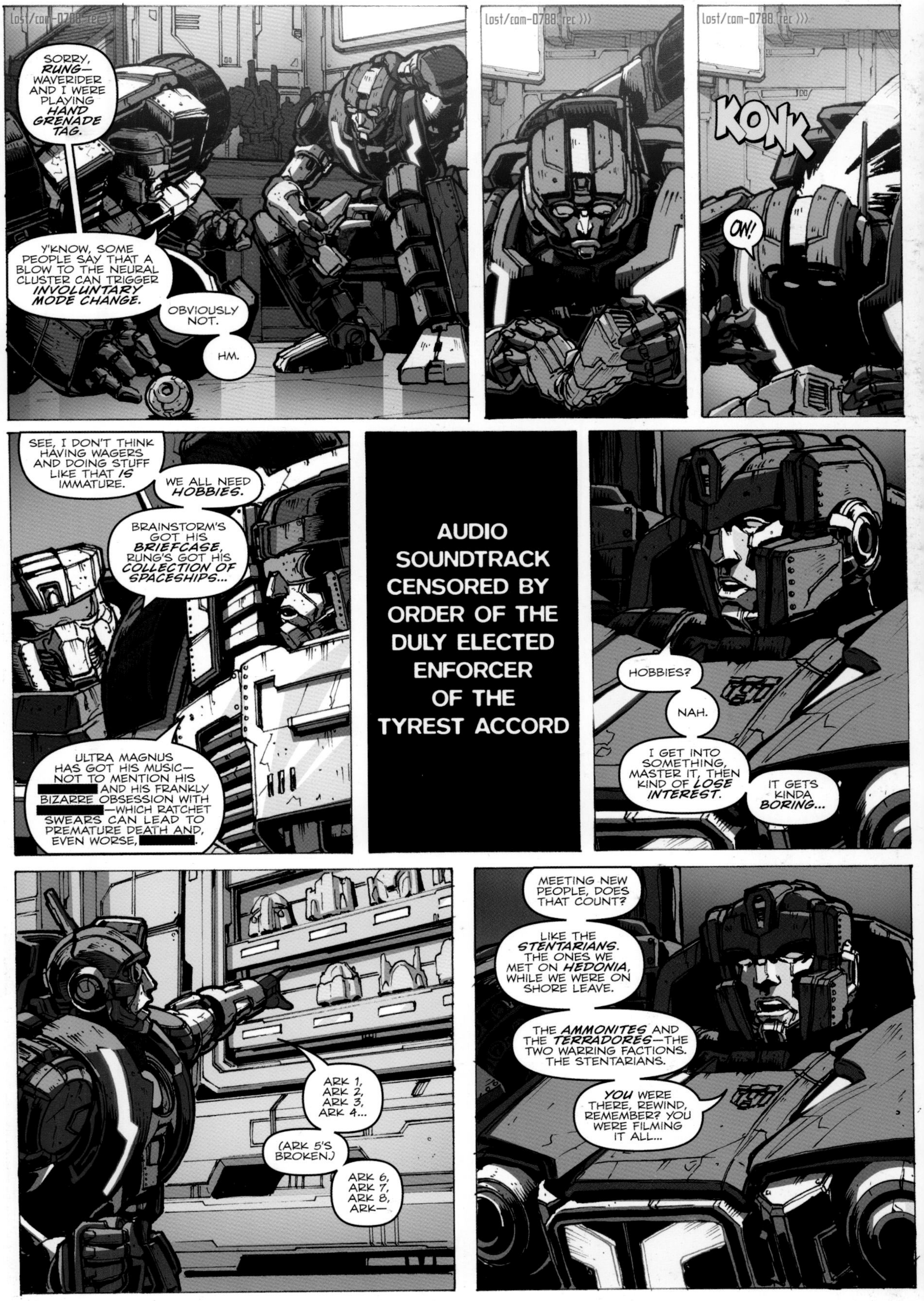
lost/cam-0788 rec)))
SORRY, RUNG— WAVERIDER AND I WERE PLAYING HAND GRENADE TAG.
Y'KNOW, SOME PEOPLE SAY THAT A BLOW TO THE NEURAL CLUSTER CAN TRIGGER INVOLUNTARY MODE CHANGE.
OBVIOUSLY NOT.
HM.
lost/cam-0788 rec)))
lost/cam-0788 rec)))
KONK
OW!
SEE, I DON'T THINK HAVING WAGERS AND DOING STUFF LIKE THAT IS IMMATURE.
WE ALL NEED HOBBIES.
BRAINSTORM'S GOT HIS BRIEFCASE, RUNG'S GOT HIS COLLECTION OF SPACESHIPS...
ULTRA MAGNUS HAS GOT HIS MUSIC— NOT TO MENTION HIS [redacted] AND HIS FRANKLY BIZARRE OBSESSION WITH [redacted]—WHICH RATCHET SWEARS CAN LEAD TO PREMATURE DEATH AND, EVEN WORSE, [redacted].
AUDIO SOUNDTRACK CENSORED BY ORDER OF THE DULY ELECTED ENFORCER OF THE TYREST ACCORD
HOBBIES?
NAH.
I GET INTO SOMETHING, MASTER IT, THEN KIND OF LOSE INTEREST.
IT GETS KINDA BORING...
ARK 1, ARK 2, ARK 3, ARK 4...
(ARK 5'S BROKEN.)
ARK 6, ARK 7, ARK 8, ARK—
MEETING NEW PEOPLE, DOES THAT COUNT?
LIKE THE STENTARIANS. THE ONES WE MET ON HEDONIA, WHILE WE WERE ON SHORE LEAVE.
THE AMMONITES AND THE TERRADORES—THE TWO WARRING FACTIONS. THE STENTARIANS.
YOU WERE THERE, REWIND, REMEMBER? YOU WERE FILMING IT ALL...

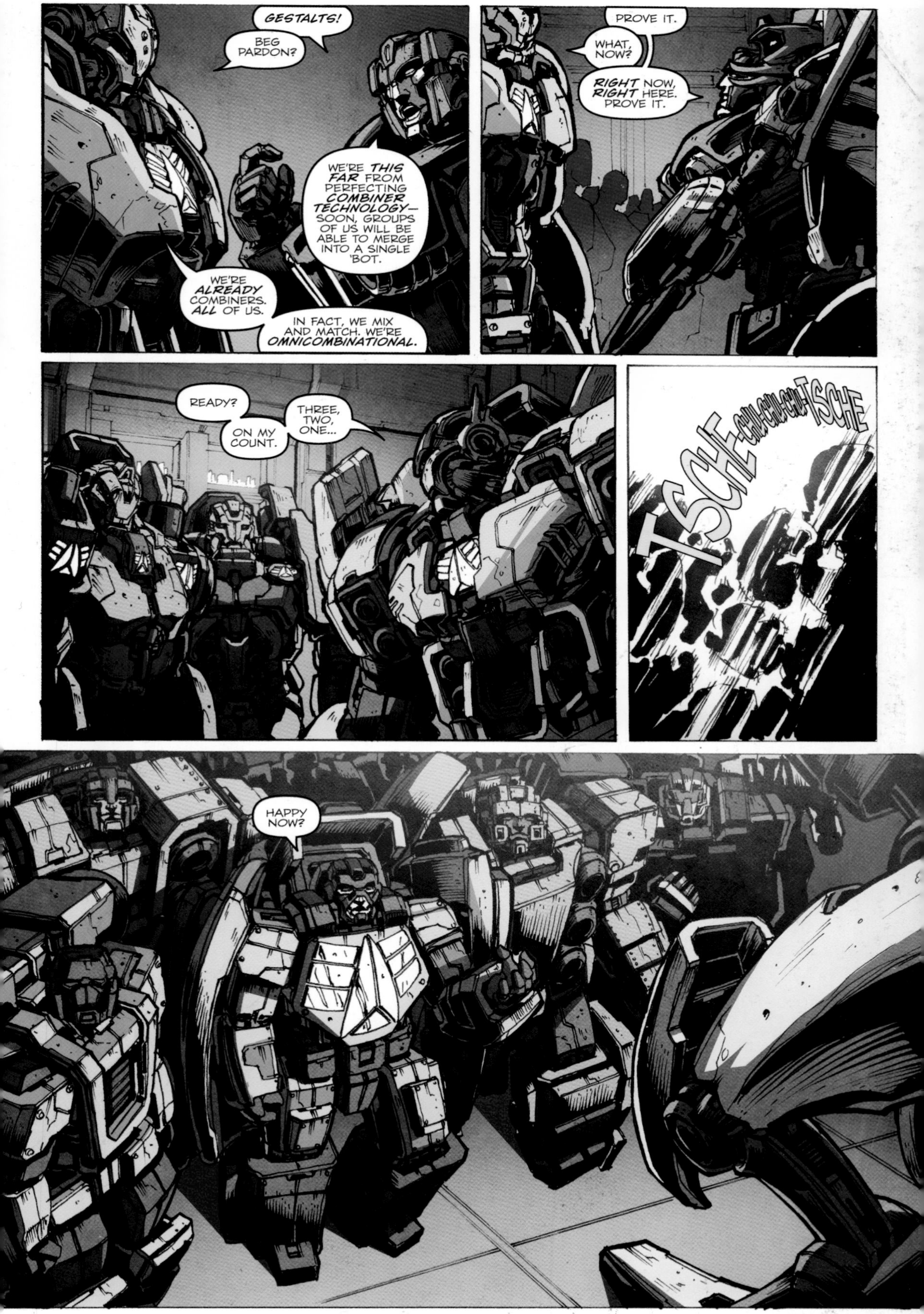
GESTALTS!
BEG PARDON?
WE'RE THIS FAR FROM PERFECTING COMBINER TECHNOLOGY— SOON, GROUPS OF US WILL BE ABLE TO MERGE INTO A SINGLE 'BOT.
WE'RE ALREADY COMBINERS. ALL OF US.
IN FACT, WE MIX AND MATCH. WE'RE OMNICOMBINATIONAL.
PROVE IT.
WHAT, NOW?
RIGHT NOW, RIGHT HERE. PROVE IT.
READY?
ON MY COUNT.
THREE, TWO, ONE...
TSCHE-CHU-CHU-CHU-TSCHE
HAPPY NOW?

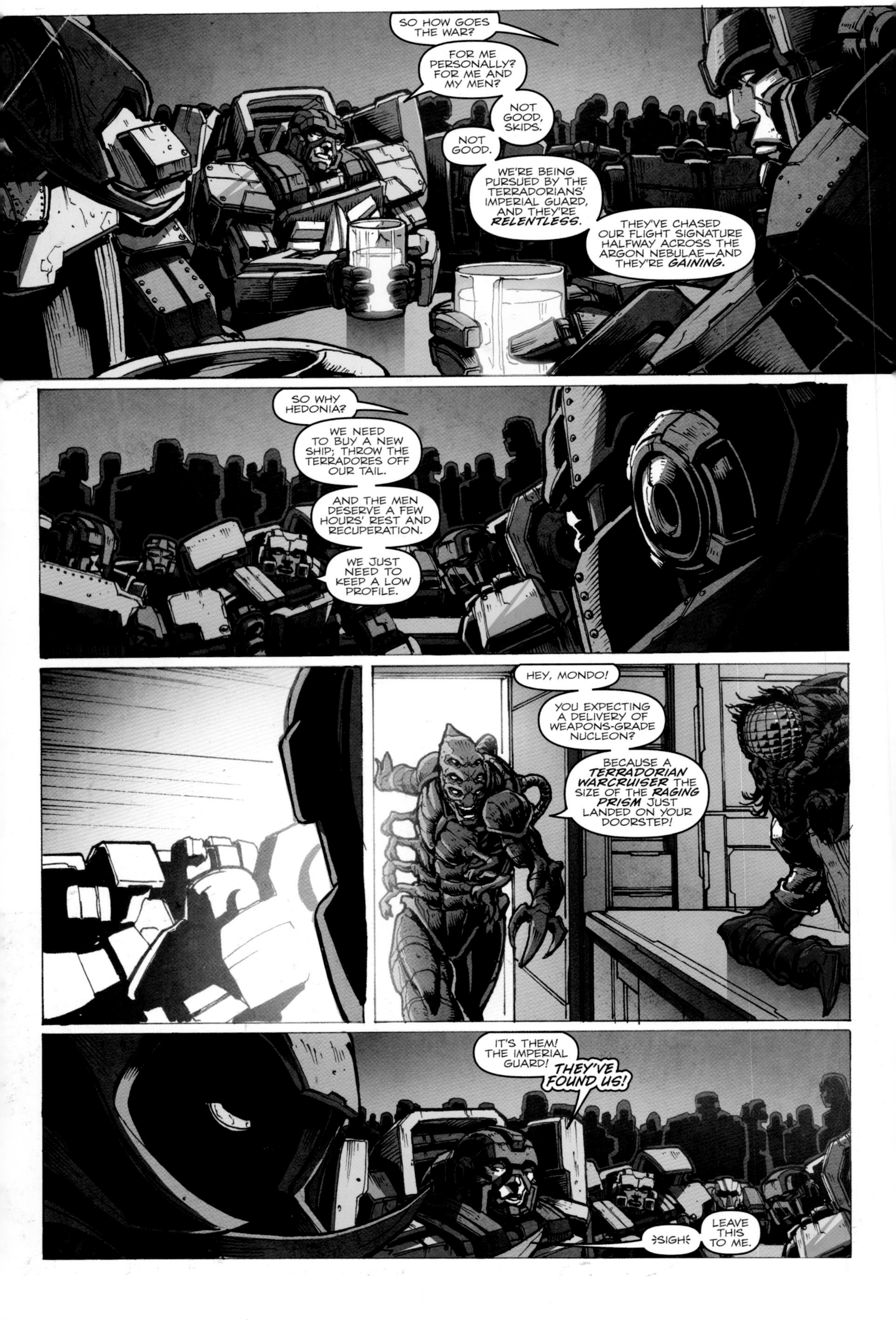
SO HOW GOES THE WAR?
FOR ME PERSONALLY? FOR ME AND MY MEN?
NOT GOOD, SKIDS.
NOT GOOD.
WE'RE BEING PURSUED BY THE TERRADORIANS' IMPERIAL GUARD, AND THEY'RE RELENTLESS.
THEY'VE CHASED OUR FLIGHT SIGNATURE HALFWAY ACROSS THE ARGON NEBULAE—AND THEY'RE GAINING.
SO WHY HEDONIA?
WE NEED TO BUY A NEW SHIP; THROW THE TERRADORES OFF OUR TAIL.
AND THE MEN DESERVE A FEW HOURS' REST AND RECUPERATION.
WE JUST NEED TO KEEP A LOW PROFILE.
HEY, MONDO!
YOU EXPECTING A DELIVERY OF WEAPONS-GRADE NUCLEON?
BECAUSE A TERRADORIAN WARCRUISER THE SIZE OF THE RAGING PRISM JUST LANDED ON YOUR DOORSTEP!
IT'S THEM! THE IMPERIAL GUARD! THEY'VE FOUND US!
SIGH
LEAVE THIS TO ME.

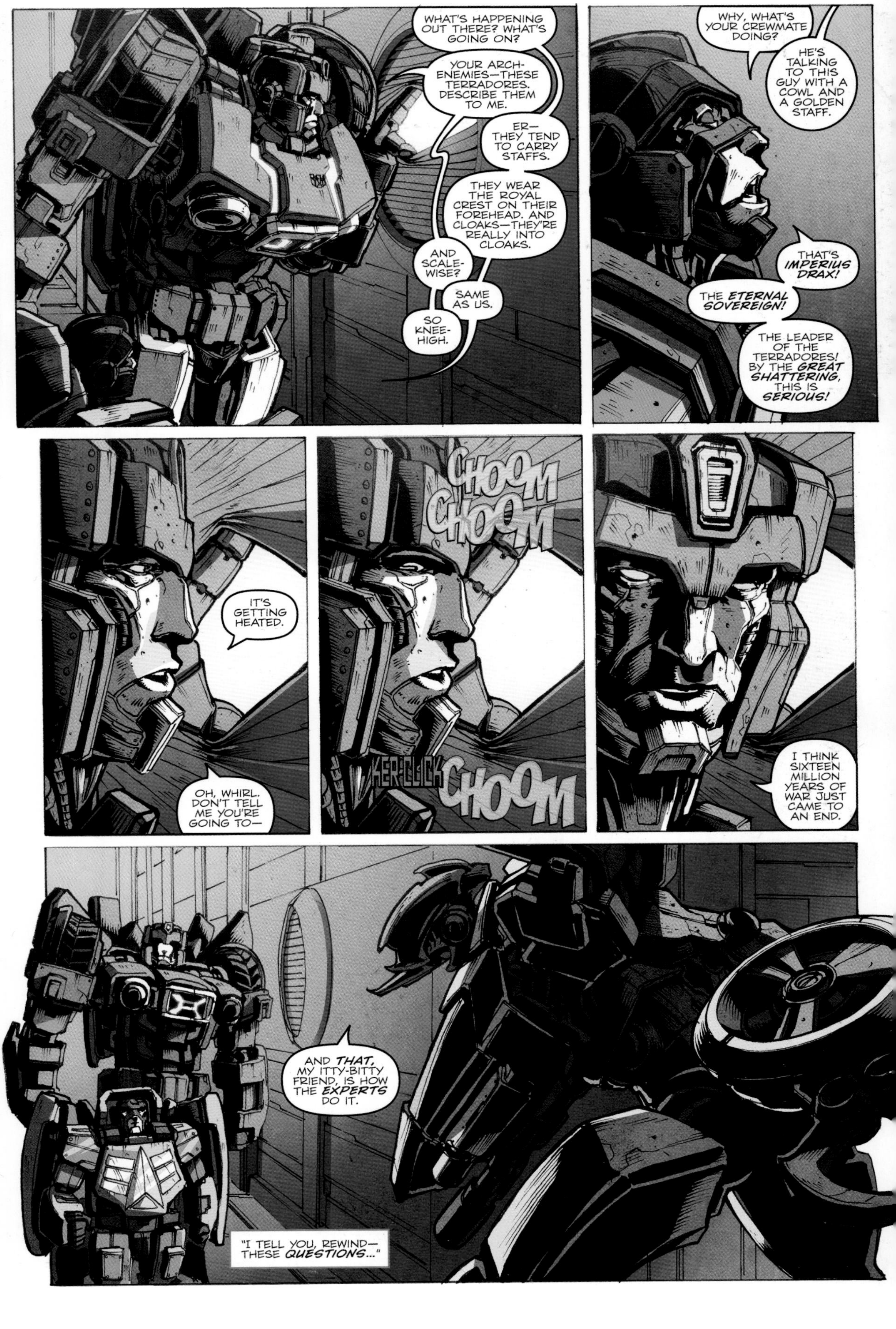
WHAT'S HAPPENING OUT THERE? WHAT'S GOING ON?
YOUR ARCH-ENEMIES—THESE TERRADORES. DESCRIBE THEM TO ME.
ER—THEY TEND TO CARRY STAFFS.
THEY WEAR THE ROYAL CREST ON THEIR FOREHEAD. AND CLOAKS—THEY'RE REALLY INTO CLOAKS.
AND SCALE-WISE?
SAME AS US.
SO KNEE-HIGH.
WHY, WHAT'S YOUR CREWMATE DOING?
HE'S TALKING TO THIS GUY WITH A COWL AND A GOLDEN STAFF.
THAT'S IMPERIUS DRAX!
THE ETERNAL SOVEREIGN!
THE LEADER OF THE TERRADORES! BY THE GREAT SHATTERING, THIS IS SERIOUS!
IT'S GETTING HEATED.
OH, WHIRL. DON'T TELL ME YOU'RE GOING TO—
CHOOM
CHOOM
KER-CLICK
CHOOM
I THINK SIXTEEN MILLION YEARS OF WAR JUST CAME TO AN END.
AND THAT, MY ITTY-BITTY FRIEND, IS HOW THE EXPERTS DO IT.
"I TELL YOU, REWIND—THESE QUESTIONS..."

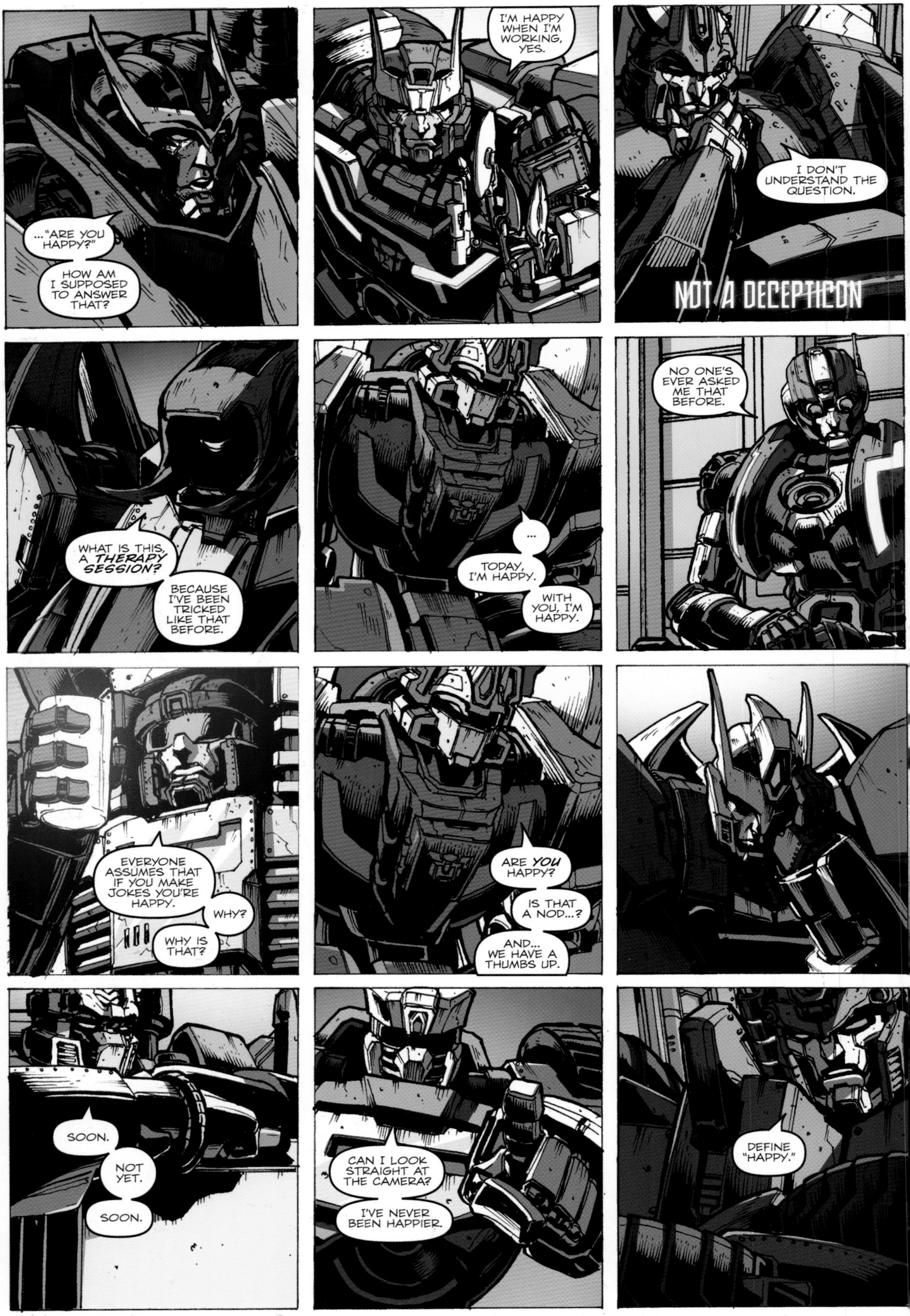
..."ARE YOU HAPPY?"
HOW AM I SUPPOSED TO ANSWER THAT?
I'M HAPPY WHEN I'M WORKING, YES.
I DON'T UNDERSTAND THE QUESTION.
NOT A DECEPTICON
WHAT IS THIS, A THERAPY SESSION?
BECAUSE I'VE BEEN TRICKED LIKE THAT BEFORE.
...
TODAY, I'M HAPPY.
WITH YOU, I'M HAPPY.
NO ONE'S EVER ASKED ME THAT BEFORE.
EVERYONE ASSUMES THAT IF YOU MAKE JOKES YOU'RE HAPPY.
WHY?
WHY IS THAT?
ARE YOU HAPPY?
IS THAT A NOD...?
AND... WE HAVE A THUMBS UP.
SOON.
NOT YET.
SOON.
CAN I LOOK STRAIGHT AT THE CAMERA?
I'VE NEVER BEEN HAPPIER.
DEFINE "HAPPY."

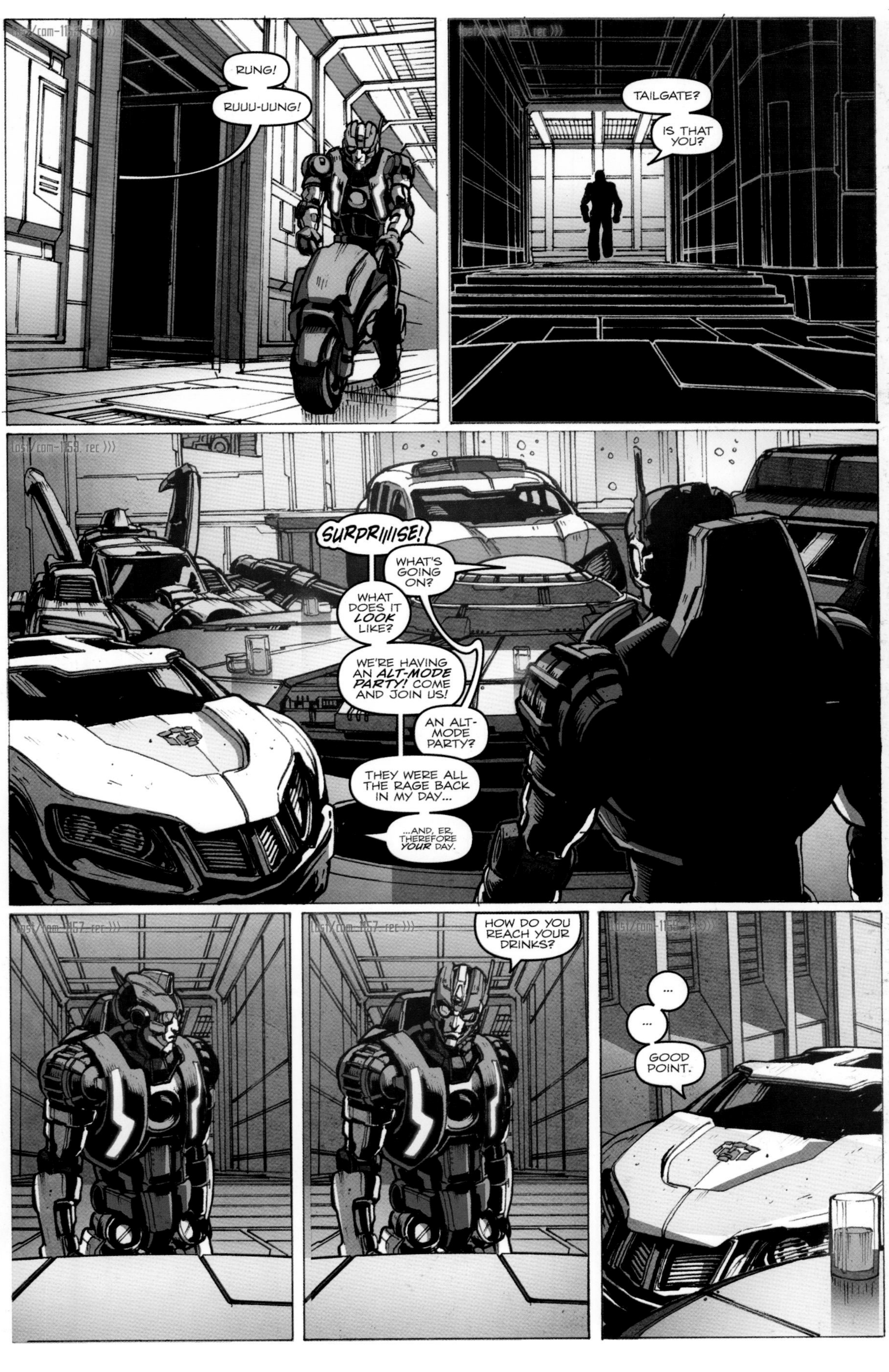
RUNG!
RUUU-UUNG!
TAILGATE?
IS THAT YOU?
SURPRIIIISE!
WHAT'S GOING ON?
WHAT DOES IT *LOOK* LIKE?
WE'RE HAVING AN ***ALT-MODE PARTY!*** COME AND JOIN US!
AN ALT-MODE PARTY?
THEY WERE ALL THE RAGE BACK IN MY DAY...
...AND, ER, THEREFORE ***YOUR*** DAY.
HOW DO YOU REACH YOUR DRINKS?
...
...
GOOD POINT.

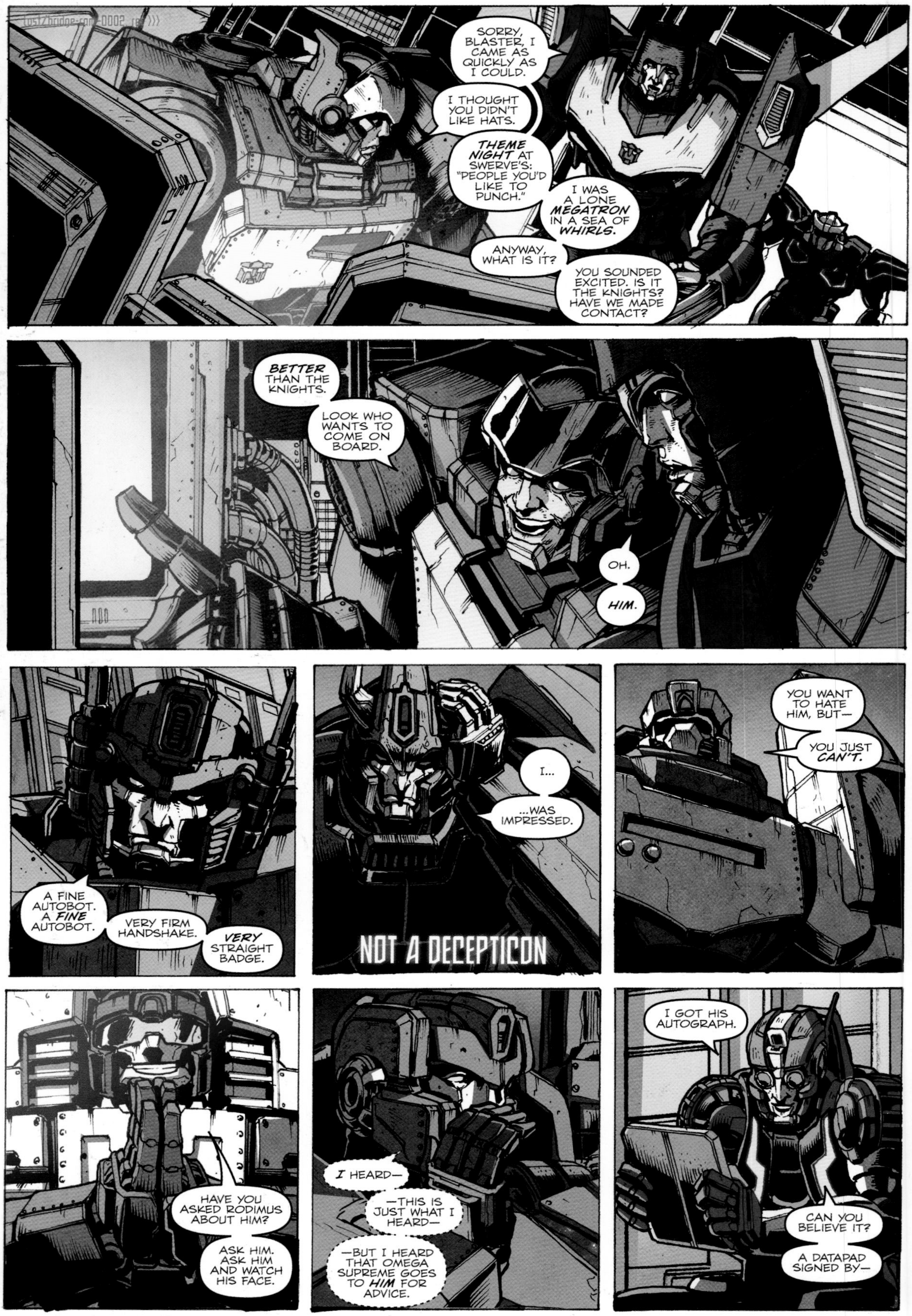
SORRY, BLASTER, I CAME AS QUICKLY AS I COULD.
I THOUGHT YOU DIDN'T LIKE HATS.
THEME NIGHT AT SWERVE'S: "PEOPLE YOU'D LIKE TO PUNCH."
I WAS A LONE MEGATRON IN A SEA OF WHIRLS.
ANYWAY, WHAT IS IT?
YOU SOUNDED EXCITED. IS IT THE KNIGHTS? HAVE WE MADE CONTACT?
BETTER THAN THE KNIGHTS.
LOOK WHO WANTS TO COME ON BOARD.
OH.
HIM.
A FINE AUTOBOT. A FINE AUTOBOT.
VERY FIRM HANDSHAKE.
VERY STRAIGHT BADGE.
I...
...WAS IMPRESSED.
NOT A DECEPTICON
YOU WANT TO HATE HIM, BUT—
YOU JUST CAN'T.
HAVE YOU ASKED RODIMUS ABOUT HIM?
ASK HIM. ASK HIM AND WATCH HIS FACE.
I HEARD—
—THIS IS JUST WHAT I HEARD—
—BUT I HEARD THAT OMEGA SUPREME GOES TO HIM FOR ADVICE.
I GOT HIS AUTOGRAPH.
CAN YOU BELIEVE IT?
A DATAPAD SIGNED BY—

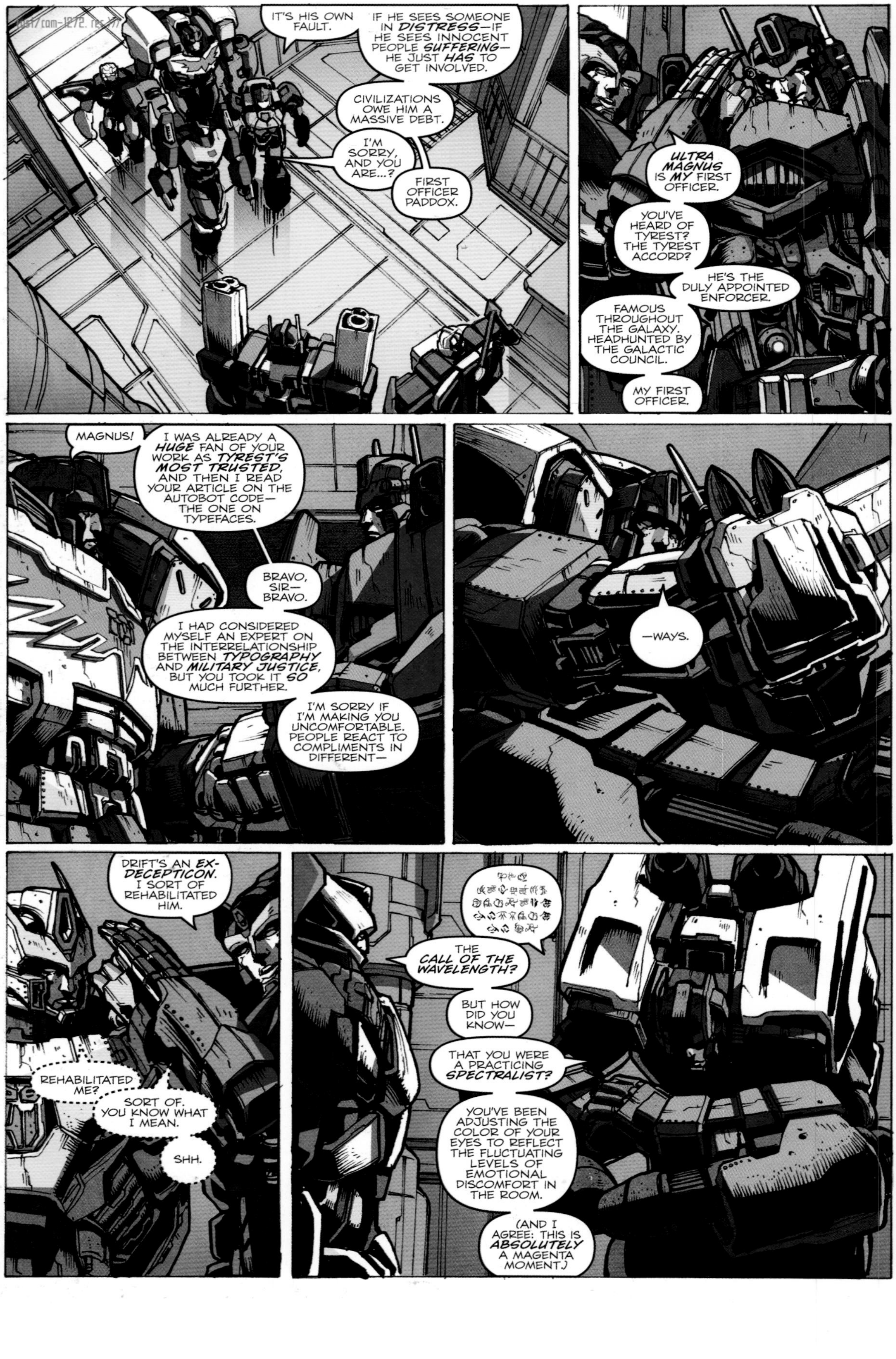
IT'S HIS OWN FAULT.
IF HE SEES SOMEONE IN DISTRESS—IF HE SEES INNOCENT PEOPLE SUFFERING—HE JUST HAS TO GET INVOLVED.
CIVILIZATIONS OWE HIM A MASSIVE DEBT.
I'M SORRY, AND YOU ARE...?
FIRST OFFICER PADDOX.
ULTRA MAGNUS IS MY FIRST OFFICER.
YOU'VE HEARD OF TYREST? THE TYREST ACCORD?
HE'S THE DULY APPOINTED ENFORCER.
FAMOUS THROUGHOUT THE GALAXY. HEADHUNTED BY THE GALACTIC COUNCIL.
MY FIRST OFFICER.
MAGNUS!
I WAS ALREADY A HUGE FAN OF YOUR WORK AS TYREST'S MOST TRUSTED, AND THEN I READ YOUR ARTICLE ON THE AUTOBOT CODE—THE ONE ON TYPEFACES.
BRAVO, SIR—BRAVO.
I HAD CONSIDERED MYSELF AN EXPERT ON THE INTERRELATIONSHIP BETWEEN TYPOGRAPHY AND MILITARY JUSTICE, BUT YOU TOOK IT SO MUCH FURTHER.
I'M SORRY IF I'M MAKING YOU UNCOMFORTABLE. PEOPLE REACT TO COMPLIMENTS IN DIFFERENT—
—WAYS.
DRIFT'S AN EX-DECEPTICON. I SORT OF REHABILITATED HIM.
REHABILITATED ME?
SORT OF. YOU KNOW WHAT I MEAN.
SHH.
THE CALL OF THE WAVELENGTH?
BUT HOW DID YOU KNOW—
THAT YOU WERE A PRACTICING SPECTRALIST?
YOU'VE BEEN ADJUSTING THE COLOR OF YOUR EYES TO REFLECT THE FLUCTUATING LEVELS OF EMOTIONAL DISCOMFORT IN THE ROOM.
(AND I AGREE: THIS IS ABSOLUTELY A MAGENTA MOMENT.)

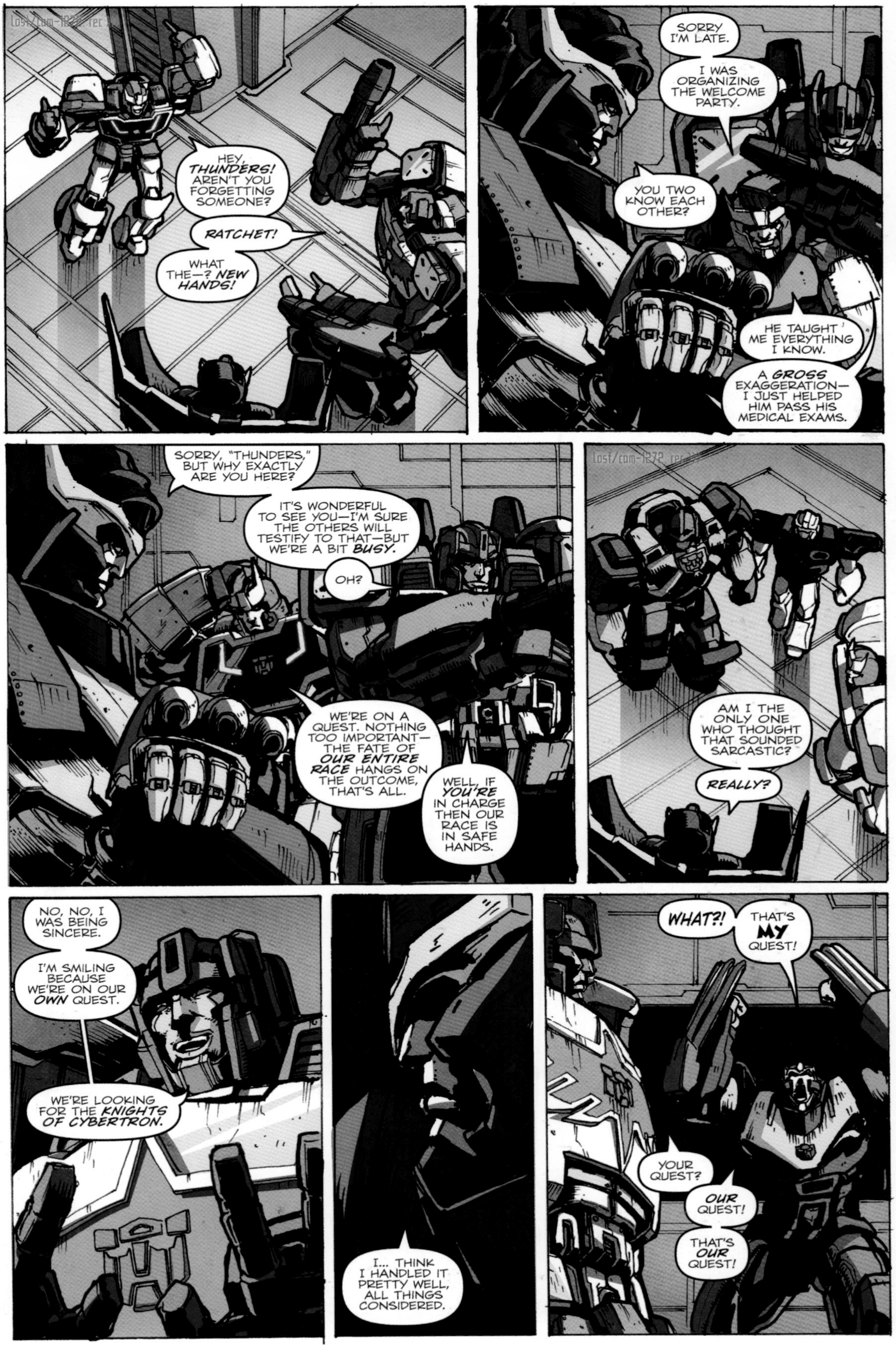
HEY, THUNDERS! AREN'T YOU FORGETTING SOMEONE?
RATCHET!
WHAT THE—? NEW HANDS!
SORRY I'M LATE.
I WAS ORGANIZING THE WELCOME PARTY.
YOU TWO KNOW EACH OTHER?
HE TAUGHT ME EVERYTHING I KNOW.
A GROSS EXAGGERATION— I JUST HELPED HIM PASS HIS MEDICAL EXAMS.
SORRY, "THUNDERS," BUT WHY EXACTLY ARE YOU HERE?
IT'S WONDERFUL TO SEE YOU—I'M SURE THE OTHERS WILL TESTIFY TO THAT—BUT WE'RE A BIT BUSY.
OH?
WE'RE ON A QUEST. NOTHING TOO IMPORTANT—THE FATE OF OUR ENTIRE RACE HANGS ON THE OUTCOME, THAT'S ALL.
WELL, IF YOU'RE IN CHARGE THEN OUR RACE IS IN SAFE HANDS.
AM I THE ONLY ONE WHO THOUGHT THAT SOUNDED SARCASTIC?
REALLY?
NO, NO, I WAS BEING SINCERE.
I'M SMILING BECAUSE WE'RE ON OUR OWN QUEST.
WE'RE LOOKING FOR THE KNIGHTS OF CYBERTRON.
I... THINK I HANDLED IT PRETTY WELL, ALL THINGS CONSIDERED.
WHAT?!
THAT'S MY QUEST!
YOUR QUEST?
OUR QUEST!
THAT'S OUR QUEST!

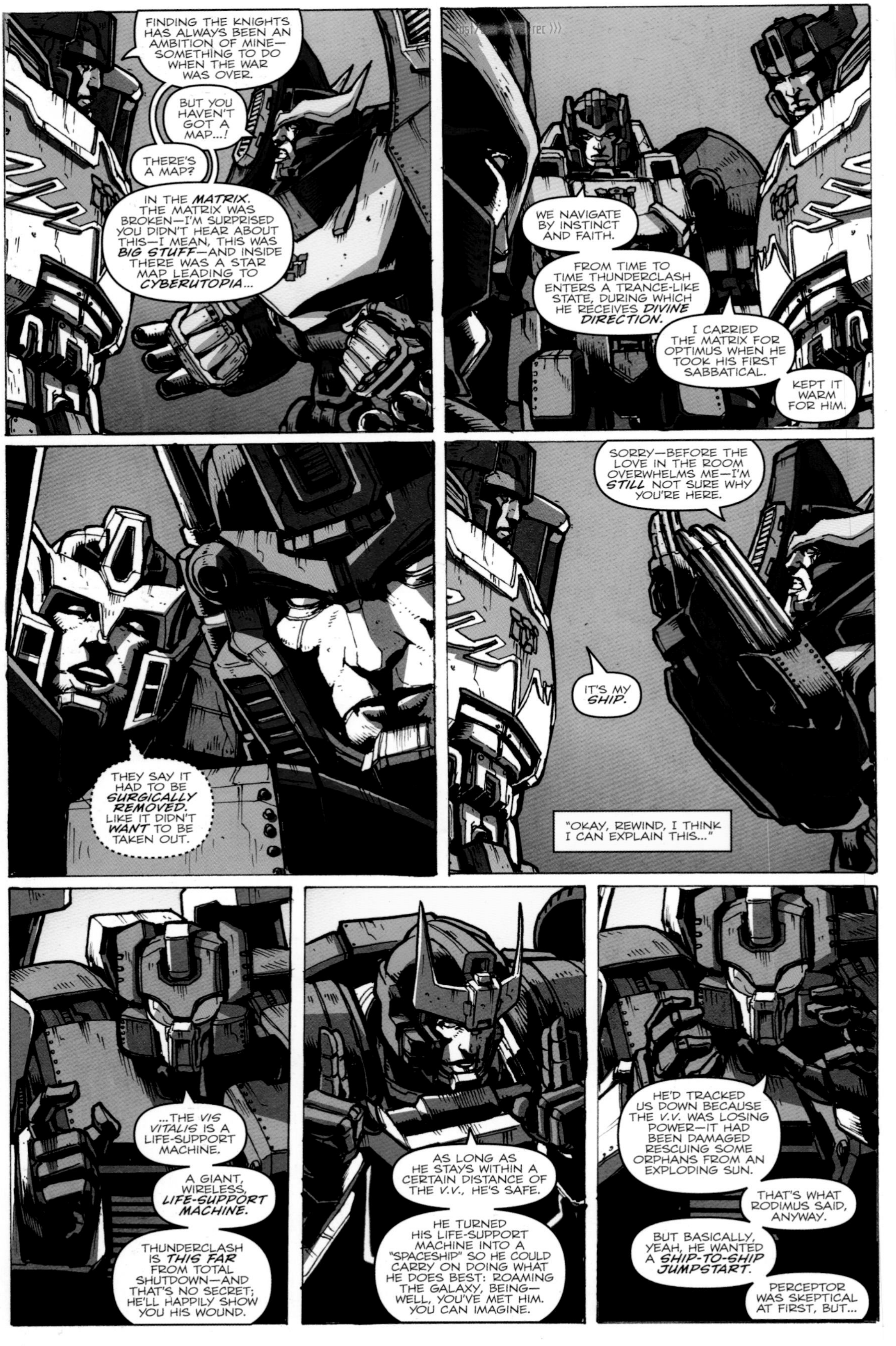
FINDING THE KNIGHTS HAS ALWAYS BEEN AN AMBITION OF MINE—SOMETHING TO DO WHEN THE WAR WAS OVER.
BUT YOU HAVEN'T GOT A MAP...!
THERE'S A MAP?
IN THE MATRIX. THE MATRIX WAS BROKEN—I'M SURPRISED YOU DIDN'T HEAR ABOUT THIS—I MEAN, THIS WAS BIG STUFF—AND INSIDE THERE WAS A STAR MAP LEADING TO CYBERUTOPIA...
WE NAVIGATE BY INSTINCT AND FAITH.
FROM TIME TO TIME THUNDERCLASH ENTERS A TRANCE-LIKE STATE, DURING WHICH HE RECEIVES DIVINE DIRECTION.
I CARRIED THE MATRIX FOR OPTIMUS WHEN HE TOOK HIS FIRST SABBATICAL.
KEPT IT WARM FOR HIM.
THEY SAY IT HAD TO BE SURGICALLY REMOVED. LIKE IT DIDN'T WANT TO BE TAKEN OUT.
SORRY—BEFORE THE LOVE IN THE ROOM OVERWHELMS ME—I'M STILL NOT SURE WHY YOU'RE HERE.
IT'S MY SHIP.
"OKAY, REWIND, I THINK I CAN EXPLAIN THIS..."
...THE VIS VITALIS IS A LIFE-SUPPORT MACHINE.
A GIANT, WIRELESS, LIFE-SUPPORT MACHINE.
THUNDERCLASH IS THIS FAR FROM TOTAL SHUTDOWN—AND THAT'S NO SECRET; HE'LL HAPPILY SHOW YOU HIS WOUND.
AS LONG AS HE STAYS WITHIN A CERTAIN DISTANCE OF THE V.V., HE'S SAFE.
HE TURNED HIS LIFE-SUPPORT MACHINE INTO A "SPACESHIP" SO HE COULD CARRY ON DOING WHAT HE DOES BEST: ROAMING THE GALAXY, BEING—WELL, YOU'VE MET HIM. YOU CAN IMAGINE.
HE'D TRACKED US DOWN BECAUSE THE V.V. WAS LOSING POWER—IT HAD BEEN DAMAGED RESCUING SOME ORPHANS FROM AN EXPLODING SUN.
THAT'S WHAT RODIMUS SAID, ANYWAY.
BUT BASICALLY, YEAH, HE WANTED A SHIP-TO-SHIP JUMPSTART.
PERCEPTOR WAS SKEPTICAL AT FIRST, BUT...

WE'VE BEEN FIGHTING THE *TERRADORES* FOR *SO LONG* WE THOUGHT WE'D REACHED AN ETERNAL STALEMATE.

AND THEN— THREE WEEKS AGO—THEIR LEADER, IMPERIUS DRAX, WAS *ASSASSINATED* ON HEDONIA.

HIS SUCCESSOR IS DETERMINED TO WIN *AT ANY COST*—EVEN IF IT MEANS REACHING OUT TO THE *DARK CYCLOPS.*

EVEN IF IT MEANS OUR *PLANET* IS DESTROYED IN THE PROCESS.

WE'VE BEEN SPYING ON YOU AUTOBOTS FOR *YEARS,* PASSING ALL YOUR SECRETS BACK TO OUR WEAPONS ENGINEERS.

BUT IN THE LAST FEW DAYS, EVERY UNDERCOVER AGENT HAS BEEN *RECALLED* AHEAD OF THE *BIG PUSH*—AND WE'VE BEEN TOLD TO STEAL ANYTHING THAT MIGHT GIVE US AN EDGE.

YOUR QUANTUM ENGINES WOULD GIVE US THAT EDGE: OUR SCATTERED FORCES WOULD BE REUNITED IN *DAYS* IF OUR WARSHIPS COULD TRAVERSE THE ARGON NEBULAE IN THE BLINK OF AN EYE.

I THINK HE'S DOWN HERE... I HEARD SWOONING.

I CAN'T BELIEVE YOU'RE BEST FRIENDS WITH THUNDERCLASH.

SECRET BEST FRIENDS; SUBTLE DIFFERENCE.

NOW, RUNG, THIS *AUTOGRAPH...* YOU REMEMBER THE DEAL, RIGHT?

YOU GET THUNDERCLASH TO SIGN MY DATAPAD IF I PROVE TO YOU THAT MY *TRANSFORMATION COG* IS WORKING.

WAIT. LOOK OVER THERE...

WE HAVE TO *DO* SOMETHING.

LIKE WHAT? I'M THE *SECOND WEAKEST PERSON* ON THIS SHIP AND YOU'RE THE FIRST— AND WE'RE BOTH COMPREHENSIVELY *UNARMED.*

PERHAPS NOT...

THIS DOESN'T NEED TO GET *MESSY,* RODIMUS.

ORDER EVERYONE OFF THE *LOST LIGHT* AND I'LL BE ON MY W—

THWONK

boilerplate watermark: Lost Light Comic 6258. Reg #11

YOU CAN CHANGE BACK NOW, RUNG.

DID IT WORK?

"I DON'T KNOW *WHAT* I TURN INTO, IS THE SIMPLE ANSWER. NO ONE DOES."

WHEN THE *FUNCTIONISTS* CAME TO POWER THEY SUBJECTED ME TO EVERY EXAMINATION YOU CAN IMAGINE.

I DON'T BLAME THEM: THE BASIS OF THEIR ENTIRE PHILOSOPHY WAS FLAWED UNLESS THEY COULD WORK OUT WHAT I WAS *FOR*.

IN THE MEANTIME, THEY MADE ME WEAR A WHEEL TO GIVE THE IMPRESSION OF UTILITY.

AN *ANATOMICAL FEINT*, THEY CALLED IT.

DESIGNED TO REASSURE THE GENERAL POPULATION.

AFTER A THOUSAND MORE TESTS, THEY DECIDED TO *CHEAT*.

THEY INVENTED A NEW CATEGORY JUST FOR ME.

MY OLD I.D. CARD.

NAME: RONG OF THE PIOUS POOLS

FUNCTION: ORNAMENT

"UNTIL NEXT TIME, RODIMUS. AND LISTEN..."

...PERCEPTOR TOLD ME THAT USING YOUR QUANTUM ENGINES TO RE-ENERGIZE THE *V.V.* HAS SET YOU BACK *MONTHS*— FROM NOW ON YOU'LL BE JUMPING LESS OFTEN, AND COVERING SHORTER DISTANCES.

IF I FIND THE KNIGHTS BEFORE YOU DO, I HOPE FUTURE GENERATIONS REALIZE THAT IT WAS ONLY POSSIBLE BECAUSE OF YOUR *SELFLESSNESS* AND *INTEGRITY*.

YOU WERE AN *AUTOBOT IN NEED*—WHAT ELSE COULD I DO?

I TELL YOU, *REWIND*, I'M STARTING TO REGRET THE WHOLE "FULL ACCESS" THING...

WHY, WOULD YOU HAVE ACTED DIFFERENTLY HAD I NOT BEEN FILMING?

WHAT? DON'T BE RIDICULOUS.

BOR-*ING!*

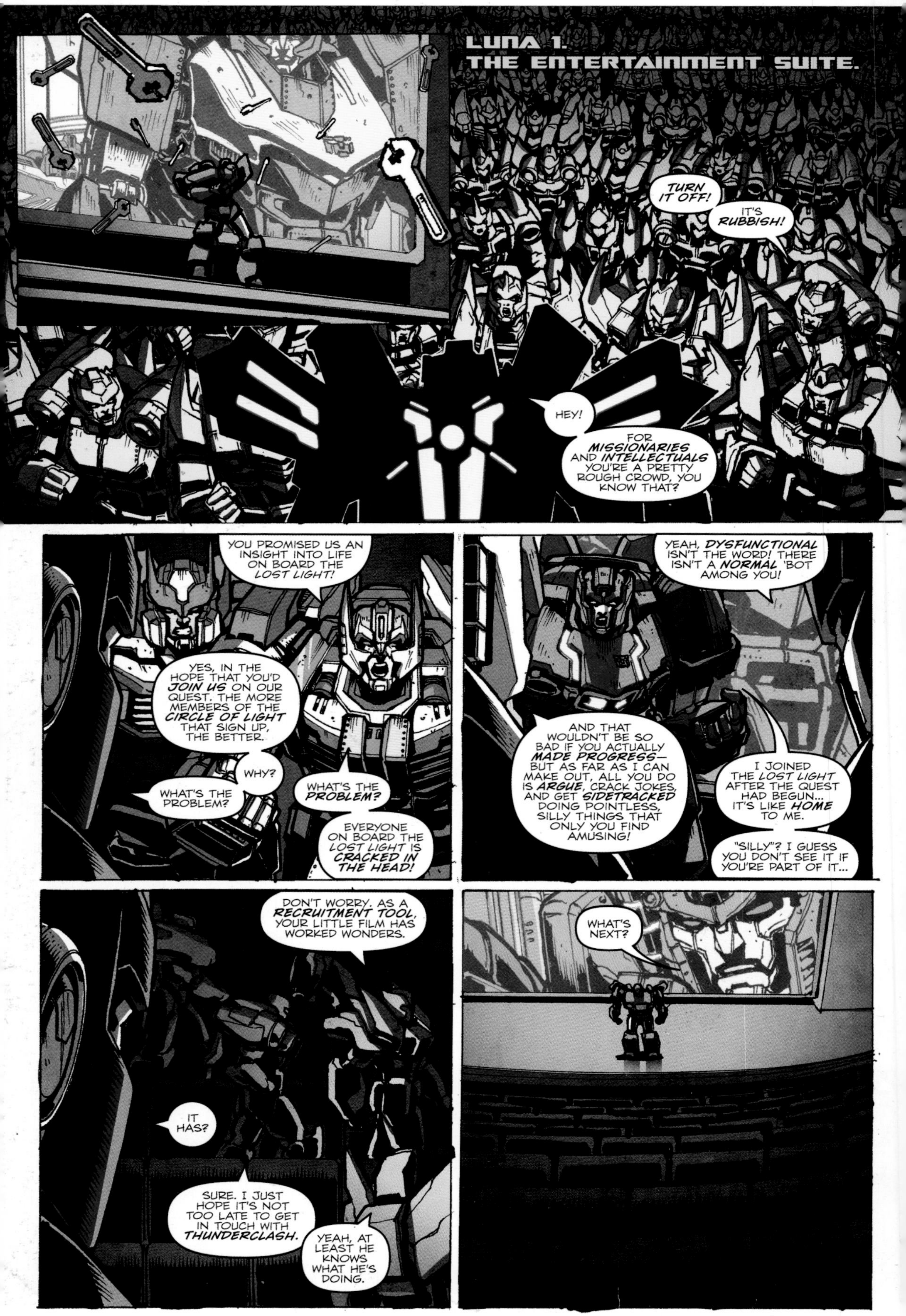
LUNA 1.
THE ENTERTAINMENT SUITE.
TURN IT OFF!
IT'S RUBBISH!
HEY!
FOR MISSIONARIES AND INTELLECTUALS YOU'RE A PRETTY ROUGH CROWD, YOU KNOW THAT?
YOU PROMISED US AN INSIGHT INTO LIFE ON BOARD THE LOST LIGHT!
YES, IN THE HOPE THAT YOU'D JOIN US ON OUR QUEST. THE MORE MEMBERS OF THE CIRCLE OF LIGHT THAT SIGN UP, THE BETTER.
WHY?
WHAT'S THE PROBLEM?
WHAT'S THE PROBLEM?
EVERYONE ON BOARD THE LOST LIGHT IS CRACKED IN THE HEAD!
YEAH, DYSFUNCTIONAL ISN'T THE WORD! THERE ISN'T A NORMAL 'BOT AMONG YOU!
AND THAT WOULDN'T BE SO BAD IF YOU ACTUALLY MADE PROGRESS— BUT AS FAR AS I CAN MAKE OUT, ALL YOU DO IS ARGUE, CRACK JOKES, AND GET SIDETRACKED DOING POINTLESS, SILLY THINGS THAT ONLY YOU FIND AMUSING!
I JOINED THE LOST LIGHT AFTER THE QUEST HAD BEGUN... IT'S LIKE HOME TO ME.
"SILLY"? I GUESS YOU DON'T SEE IT IF YOU'RE PART OF IT...
DON'T WORRY. AS A RECRUITMENT TOOL, YOUR LITTLE FILM HAS WORKED WONDERS.
IT HAS?
SURE. I JUST HOPE IT'S NOT TOO LATE TO GET IN TOUCH WITH THUNDERCLASH.
YEAH, AT LEAST HE KNOWS WHAT HE'S DOING.
WHAT'S NEXT?

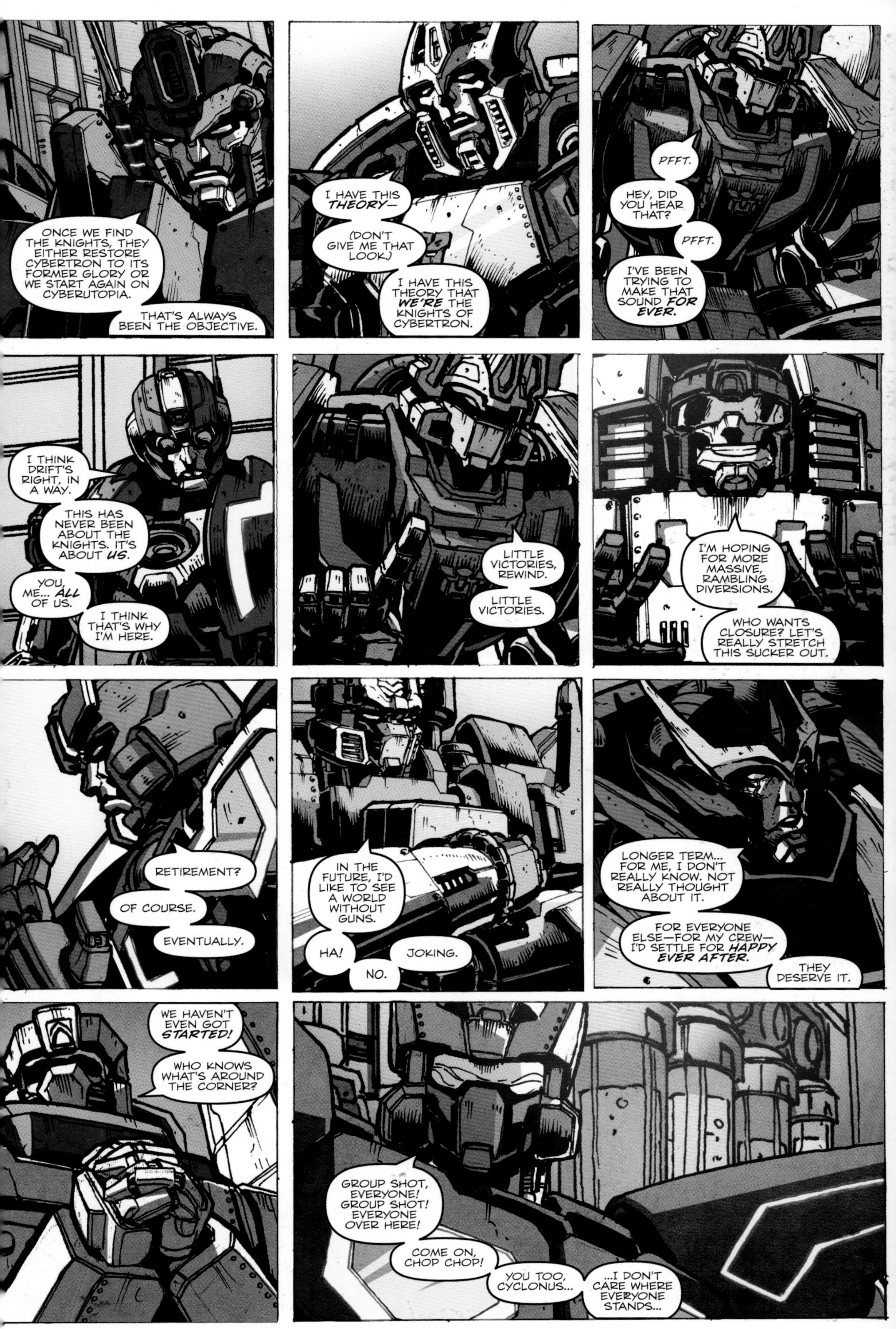
ONCE WE FIND THE KNIGHTS, THEY EITHER RESTORE CYBERTRON TO ITS FORMER GLORY OR WE START AGAIN ON CYBERUTOPIA.
THAT'S ALWAYS BEEN THE OBJECTIVE.
I HAVE THIS THEORY—
(DON'T GIVE ME THAT LOOK.)
I HAVE THIS THEORY THAT WE'RE THE KNIGHTS OF CYBERTRON.
PFFT.
HEY, DID YOU HEAR THAT?
PFFT.
I'VE BEEN TRYING TO MAKE THAT SOUND FOR EVER.
I THINK DRIFT'S RIGHT, IN A WAY.
THIS HAS NEVER BEEN ABOUT THE KNIGHTS. IT'S ABOUT US.
YOU, ME... ALL OF US.
I THINK THAT'S WHY I'M HERE.
LITTLE VICTORIES, REWIND.
LITTLE VICTORIES.
I'M HOPING FOR MORE MASSIVE, RAMBLING DIVERSIONS.
WHO WANTS CLOSURE? LET'S REALLY STRETCH THIS SUCKER OUT.
RETIREMENT?
OF COURSE.
EVENTUALLY.
IN THE FUTURE, I'D LIKE TO SEE A WORLD WITHOUT GUNS.
HA!
NO.
JOKING.
LONGER TERM... FOR ME, I DON'T REALLY KNOW. NOT REALLY THOUGHT ABOUT IT.
FOR EVERYONE ELSE—FOR MY CREW—I'D SETTLE FOR HAPPY EVER AFTER.
THEY DESERVE IT.
WE HAVEN'T EVEN GOT STARTED!
WHO KNOWS WHAT'S AROUND THE CORNER?
GROUP SHOT, EVERYONE! GROUP SHOT! EVERYONE OVER HERE!
COME ON, CHOP CHOP!
YOU TOO, CYCLONUS...
...I DON'T CARE WHERE EVERYONE STANDS...

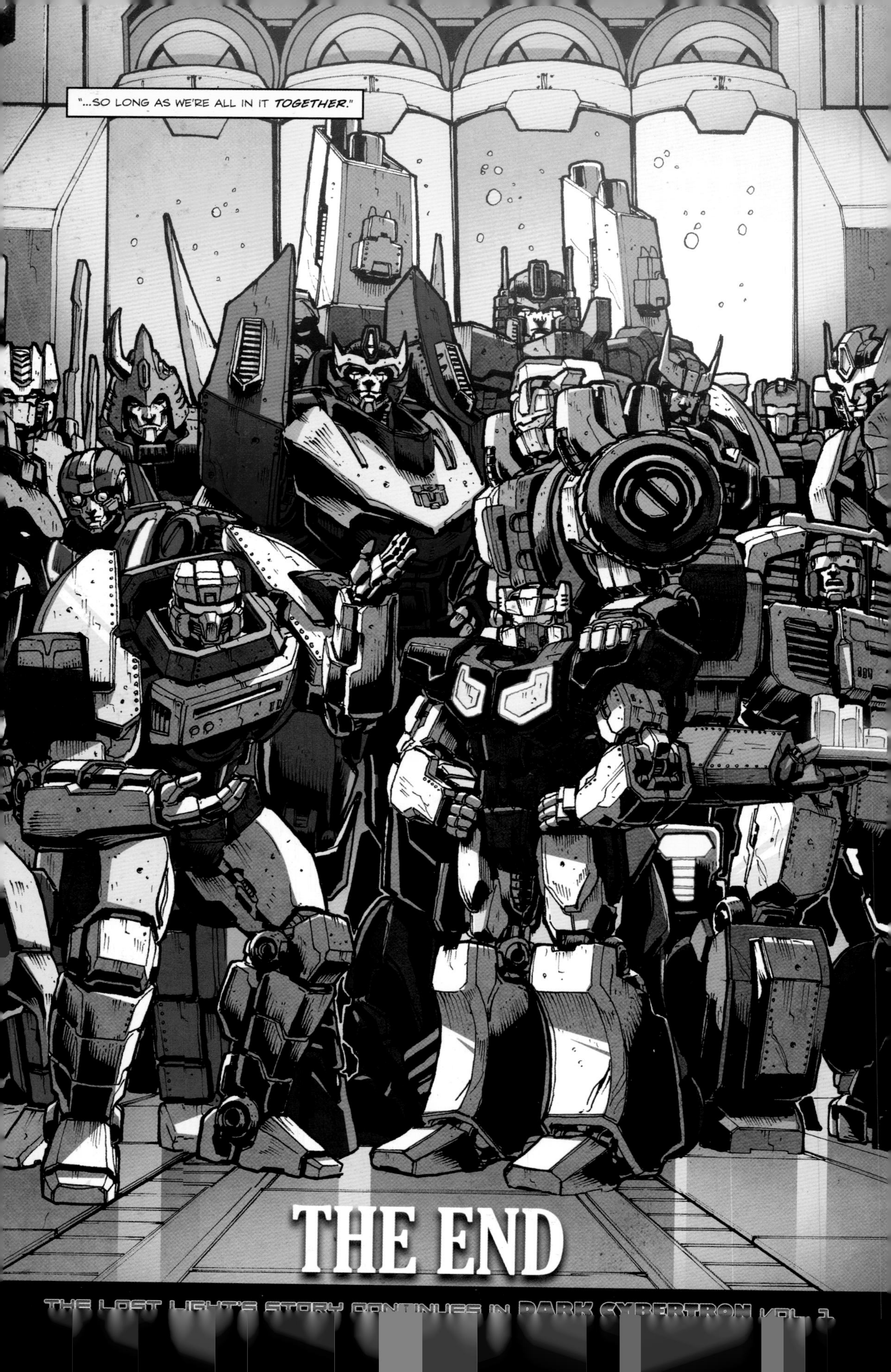
"...SO LONG AS WE'RE ALL IN IT TOGETHER."
THE END
THE LOST LIGHT'S STORY CONTINUES IN DARK CYBERTRON VOL. 1

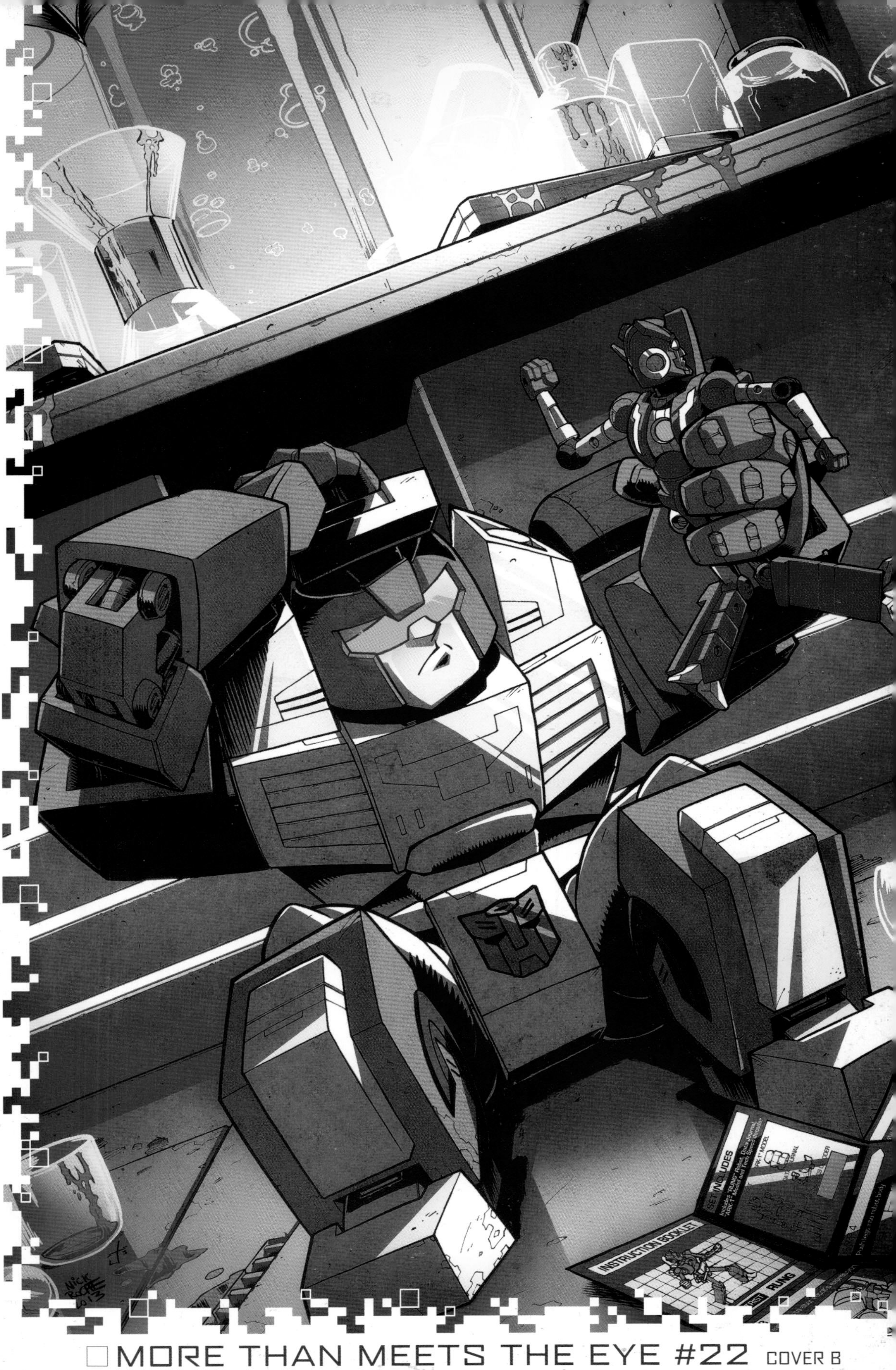
SET INCLUDES
INSTRUCTION BOOKLET
RUNG

MORE THAN MEETS THE EYE #22 COVER B

by **NICK ROCHE** Colors by **JOSH BURCHAM**

THE TRANSFORMERS

MORE THAN MEETS THE EYE

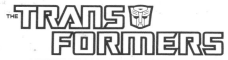

THE SOUND OF BREAKING GLASS

By James Roberts

"That is *pungent,*" said Minimus Ambus, tapping the side of his nose and recalibrating his olfactory sensors. "Is that the spacebridge?"

"The greater the distance covered," said Rodimus, "the stronger the smell. That's what Wheeljack says, anyway."

They were standing in Tyrest's Control Room, watching Brainstorm, Grapple, and Inferno sift through the wreckage of the spacebridge.

"Do you think Tyrest did it?" said Minimus. "A doorway to Cyberutopia?"

Rodimus tried to shrug, but his body—still tender after being pulverized by the Killswitch—was having none of it. "Dunno about Cyberutopia, but Skids says the portal took him *somewhere*. He's not making much sense, admittedly; it's all, 'I saw a giant spark and it spoke to me in feelings...'" He snapped his shoulder hydraulics back into position. "Rung thinks he experienced a form of trans-lingual synesthesia, whatever that is. In time, perhaps he'll—careful, Grapple! Set it down gently!"

"You're busy," said Minimus, stepping away. "We'll talk later."

Rodimus pressed his communicator to his ear. "Just let me make a few calls..."

Call 1: "Actually, Perceptor, I think finding Tyrest's communications room is a priority. He had a computer that would have—no, hear me out. If he could reach his Enforcer wherever he was in the galaxy, surely we can reach Cybertron?"

Call 2: "No, still no sign of... Ratchet, if we find Pharma's body I will tell you. I will call you. Yes. Yes, obviously. And what about Tailgate, any news? No, no, I understand. Keep me posted."

Call 3: "Just land outside, Max. Anywhere! What sacred ground? Oh, the hot spot. Okay, see the big tower by the smelting pool? Park alongside that."

Call 4: "I'm smiling. I am! I'm getting—Minimus is giving me a funny look because I'm standing here smiling. Nice one, Perceptor. Let me know as soon as you get it working."

It occurred to Minimus that Rodimus had given more orders in the space of three minutes than he had in the last 12 months. "You look like you're about to fall apart," he said, as Rodimus finally turned off his communicator.

"I'm fine."

Minimus tapped his leader's bicep. A hunk of machinery and buckled plating slid to the ground.

"Well I'm not about to bother Ratchet *now*, am I?" said Rodimus, stepping delicately out of the pool of his own body parts. "Not when he's got Tailgate to worry about."

In the 40 minutes since Tailgate's collapse, the team of engineers, medics and mechanics in Pharma's well-stocked medibay had discovered the cure to four infamous Cybertronian diseases. Under normal circumstances, an Autobot who solved the problem of form fatigue or static spark syndrome would have punched the air and yelped with delight. Today, with Tailgate's death clock creeping towards zero, they merely smiled, put the latest miracle formula to one side, and got back to work.

"You are tired, though," insisted Minimus. "Mentally, you're exhausted."

"I'm tired; other people are dead. Have you seen outside? There are hundreds of corpses out there—we're talking half the Circle of Light. Now, if I can't help them I can at least try to fix the spacebridge."

Rodimus rocked on his heels as Inferno barged past and fired foam into a section of the spacebridge that had caught fire. When the foam ran out Inferno stamped on the flames, and with a sad thud another chunk of Tyrest's precious patchwork portal hit the floor.

"Maybe it's better that the spacebridge isn't fixed," said Minimus slowly, seeing the look of horror on Rodimus's face. "If it was fixed, it might make people think that our losses were worthwhile: 'The ship was overrun and people died, but at least we found a way to get to Cyberutopia.' I don't want that. Do you?"

There was a sudden squeal of excitement, and Rodimus and Minimus turned to see Brainstorm skipping around the remains of the Killswitch, holding his briefcase above his head. Beaming behind his faceplate, the weapons engineer jogged out of the Control Room, pausing only to tug playfully at Minimus Ambus' moustache.

"Whatever happened to priorities?" muttered Rodimus, frowning with disapproval. "Now Minimus—sorry, Magnus—what was it you wanted?"

"I was, um, wondering if you'd found my outer shell?"

"The one without a head?" Rodimus pointed across the room. "Storage locker. I thought you'd come looking for it."

"Thank you," said Minimus, turning to leave.

"Magnus, wait. Listen. When it was all kicking off—when I was being wired into the Killswitch—you and I, we..." Rodimus paused to test the depth of a newly discovered dent in his forehead. "We came clean, didn't we? I told you about Overlord and... yeah."

Minimus waited for him to continue.

"I am going to do something about it, you know. I'm going to—"

"Make amends. So you said."

Rung looked up from the table at the sound of breaking glass and saw Fortress Maximus pulling his boot from the remains of a displaced engex canister. Max wasn't really to blame: it was impossible to walk across Swerve's ransacked bar without treading on something breakable.

"Thank you for seeing me," said Fortress Maximus, sitting down opposite Rung. He tilted his head and realized that the shards of tinted glass in font of the ship's psychiatrist bore a strong resemblance to Ark 5. "You know I'd have been happy to meet you in your office."

"My office is full of dead Legislators," said Rung, pushing a drink across the table.

Fortress Maximus swirled the room-temperature engex around the glass, watching the luminous pink liquid crest and collapse. "I've been made an offer. A new position. Rodimus was impressed by my handling of the Legislator invasion—which is ridiculous, frankly, because all I did was let them take over the ship…" He sipped his drink; it tasted bad. "Anyway. Yes. A new position."

"Congratulations. I'm pleased for you."

A second sip. "I don't know whether to accept."

Rung turned his friend's empty glass on its side; it made a decent rear thruster. "You don't think you've earned it?"

"Oh, I know I haven't 'earned' it. This isn't about 'earning' it. This is about whether I'm cured or not. The shooting spree—that's in the past. I mean—hell—it's easy for *me* to say that, but…" He slumped a little in his chair. "I feel like myself again. Like I did before Overlord attacked Garrus 9."

Rung swept the mosaic aside and put his elbows on the table. "You're not 'cured' because you were never diseased. But the fact you're asking these questions—of me, of yourself—is good, Max. It's really good."

"But do you think I might come unstuck again?"

"I think you're ready for whatever is around corner. As ready as the rest of us." Rung reached across the table and unclenched his friend's fist. "But promise me: if your thoughts run away with you, come find me. Ten floors down."

"Ten floors down?"

"My office is ten floors below the Bridge. I assume that's where you'll be, if you're going to be third in command?"

"Who said anything about being third in command? Rung, this new position—it means I have to leave the Lost Light."

As Rodimus stepped into his office he shielded his eyes—literally put his hand to his face—to avoid catching sight of the flames he'd had painted around the doorframe. As soon as he'd sorted out the current mess he'd ask Atomizer to help him redecorate. No more fire-rimmed entrances, garish pink walls or self-aggrandizing plaques: just a desk, a chair, some subdued lighting and a memorial to crewmembers killed by sparkeater, Legislator, or Overlord.

Overlord.

When his guard was down—when he wasn't showing off or doodling or spray-painting—the name made him think of the people who had died or lost loved ones because he'd been too scared to say no to Prowl. Overlord made him think of Pipes and Rewind and Chromedome and Lockstock and Lancet, but one face—Drift's face—kept crowding out all the others. It had been here, in his office, that they'd had their last proper conversation.

"An inquiry?" Drift stood in the doorway, looking incredulous. "An *inquiry*?"

Rodimus dragged him inside and locked the door. "I had to do *something!* People were asking questions! And what do you do if you want to stall things? You launch an inquiry." He slumped into his chair. "An inquiry into something *I'm* responsible for. Oh god. Oh god, I feel sick. I've messed up big time."

"I can sort this out, Rodimus. Honestly, I can fix this."

"This is my fault, not yours. We were standing in Prowl's office, and he was trying to convince me that bringing Overlord onboard was 'right and proper', and you called me an idiot for even

considering it."

"Was I that blunt?"

"I don't know why he even let you in on those discussions in the first place. It's not like he trusts you."

"I'll tell you exactly why he wanted me there: it was in case something like this happened. Need a scapegoat? Get an ex-Decepticon."

"Well it's not gonna happen. I'm taking the fall for this one. Your name doesn't have to come into it. It's taken you years to win back people's trust, and you're not throwing it all away on my behalf."

"Rodimus, if you tell the crew what you've done, then that's it. The quest's over. We'll never find the Knights."

"No, it just means someone else will take over. You, maybe? Ratchet? I dunno. Someone."

"But someone *doesn't* take over!"

Rodimus looked up sharply. "'Doesn't'?"

"Won't."

"You said 'doesn't.' What d'you mean, 'doesn't'?"

"It's hard to explain what I mean." Drift unclipped his Great Sword and placed it on the desk. "You remember when I nearly died, back on Cybertron? I was within feet of Vector Sigma."

"Yes…" said Rodimus slowly, unsure where this was going.

"When I put this sword through my spark, I saw something."

"What, like a vision?"

"Kind of. More a sense of how things would play out. It was abstract and it was fleeting, and every time I call it to mind it becomes harder to interpret, but something is around the corner, Rodimus—and a year from now, or 50 years from now, that something will arrive, and we won't be able to stop it unless we find the Knights. And I don't care if you think, 'Oh, that's just Drift being Drift,' because I'm convinced that you need to remain in charge. People can come and go—they can die—but you have to be here, otherwise we will fail. And so the simple solution—the only solution—is that I take the blame for this."

"I won't let you do this for me."

"I'm not doing it for you. I'm doing it for everyone else."

"Hey, what are you two doing in here? Are you… looting? I expected it of you, Fort Max, you light-fingered rogue, but *Rung?!*"

A grinning Swerve skipped across the room and went to vault over the bar. He caught his boot on an engex pump and fell face-first into the serving space on the other side. A second later, a solitary wheel rolled out from behind the bar, circled Rung's leg three times, and toppled over.

"Save your innermost energon," said Swerve, clambering to his feet. "I am unharmed!"

"You seem… reinvigorated," said Fortress Maximus.

"Saved a life, Max, saved a life. Tailgate! Lives! On!" He threw an energon goodie into the air and almost caught it in his mouth. "Who says you can't be a metallurgist *and* a bartender?"

Swerve's grin left his face as he saw a silhouette in the doorway: head, legs, arms, briefcase.

"I'd like a word with Chatterbot in private," said Brainstorm, fishing a barstool from the wreckage and sitting down. "You gonna do this place up, Swerve?"

"That's the plan, yeah."

"Good. Because people come here and they talk, and I need you to keep your ears open."

"For what? What am I listening out for?"

"I think…" Brainstorm looked over his shoulder to check that Rung and Fortress Maximus had left. "I think someone's tampered with the briefcase. It looks like someone's opened it, and I want to know who."

"Easy. Just look for the guy with no head."

Brainstorm laughed and clapped Swerve on the shoulder, agitating an old injury and making the bartender flinch. Brainstorm continued to laugh until Swerve joined in, at which point he grabbed him by the back of the neck and pulled him close. "It's not funny. Opening the briefcase when I'm not around is very far from being a sensible thing to do." He climbed off the stool. "So… any idle chatter and you come to me. Are we clear?"

Swerve nodded—but not, Brainstorm realized, in agreement. The nod was directing his attention downwards, to the green light escaping from his chest plate. Before Swerve could say anything, Brainstorm smothered the leaking light with his briefcase and fled the room.

Satisfied that the energon transfusion was having the intended effect and that the key points of articulation—waist, knees, elbows—were responding to his touch, Ratchet left Tailgate sleeping on the circuit slab. With the stab wounds in his chest and back patched up, the Waste Disposal Expert looked freshly forged. Sadly, that was just on the outside; before the anti-corrosives had forced it into remission, his rampaging cybercrosis had caused so much internal damage that when he'd collapsed in Tyrest's Control Room, it had sounded like someone punching a bucket of nails.

Before administering the anti-corrosives, Ratchet had bled Tailgate's body, opening the vents and traps designed to keep energon, oil and petrolex from escaping. Swerve had laid claim to the slops, saying he intended to run some tests. (It was nice that he was taking an interest, thought Ratchet, even if he wasn't prepared to give up his day job.) Now, all that was left was to wait for Tailgate's resurgent spark to build itself up until it could sustain him without the assistance of a life support machine.

Ratchet walked into the morgue, went to open one of the body-lockers, and stiffened as he sensed someone behind him. Minimus Ambus was standing in the doorway wearing the bottom section of the Magnus Armor, his wrist-thin legs plugged into a pair of massive kneecaps.

"Hello, Ratchet," said Minimus sheepishly, tottering into the room as if on stilts. "The armor's easy to take off but hell to put on, especially by yourself. I wondered if you could help. I can talk you through the process, give you instructions."

"I'm impressed you were able to sneak up on me," said Ratchet, kneeling down to examine the point where Minimus' right leg disappeared into the Magnus Armor. He tapped 13 hidden pressure pads in quick succession and the armor rose up and wrapped itself more tightly around Minimus's limb.

Minimus watched a confident Ratchet do the same—13 taps—with the other leg. "How long have you known?" he said quietly.

"About you and the armor? Ooh, quite a while now."

"But how? The armor is filled with these attention deflectors…"

"That work for all of five seconds." Ratchet climbed to his feet and wiped his hands. "You might as well use smoke and mirrors. And quite frankly, I'm a little insulted that you'd think I'd be fooled."

"You never said anything…"

"Why would I say anything? 'Hey, Ultra Magnus, I know your secret.' Why would I say that? What would that achieve? I didn't say anything to the others, either."

"You knew the other Magnuses?"

"Suture, Datum, Ramp, Blockus—all the way back to the original."

"What was he like?"

"He wasn't like you, that's for sure."

Minimus looked hurt. "Well, thanks for the assistance. I think I can put the rest on by myself."

"No two Magnuses are alike," continued Ratchet, worried that he'd said the wrong thing. "But because people assume they're the same person, they make allowances without realizing it. I've known you longer than any of your predecessors, and maybe that's why, to me—and I know this sounds strange—you're the true Ultra Magnus."

Minimus gave a nod of—what? Understanding? Gratitude? He wasn't sure, but he left the medibay feeling ten times taller, and it had nothing to do with the armor on his feet.

Ratchet turned back to the body-locker, slid a key in the lock, and braced himself. The body inside was different to all the other bodies in the morgue: it was alive.

"Anything?"

Rodimus pressed his foot gently against the lunar landscape as if testing the temperature of bath water. "No. Nothing." He pushed down harder—with his heel, this time. "Still nothing."

"Are you sure this is the place?" asked Getaway, who was standing on a Mobile Autobot Repair Bay that was hovering a few feet off the ground.

"Mountain range to the left," muttered Rodimus, flicking a thumb towards the horizon. He dropped to his hands and knees and pressed his cheek against the silver surface, hoping to detect weak heat or distant movement. "Last time, this whole place lit up the moment I stepped off the M.A.R.B. Millions of sparks, from here to the horizon. This—this sea of electric blue. VOMPF!"

"I'm no expert," said Getaway, "but hot spots don't normally blink in and out of existence. They ignite, they stay ignited."

"True, but they're not normally ignited by someone treading on them." Rodimus sat on the edge of Getaway's M.A.R.B. and scanned the resolutely un-illuminated landscape; the hot spot's stubborn dormancy registered as yet another personal failure. "Then again, you have to harvest surface sparks quickly, otherwise they… evaporate isn't the right word, but you know what I mean. Maybe we just missed our chance."

Getaway jumped to the ground, gave it a quick tap (why pass up an opportunity to find out if you were a Matrix-Bearer-in-waiting?) and sat down next to Rodimus. Sensing his despondency, he gave him a playful jab—"bomp"—on the upper arm. "What now, then?"

Rodimus reached into a compartment in his waist and pulled out the remains of the Matrix. "I don't know if this is the right thing to do," he said, scattering the cloudy fragments over the ground, "but I feel we should do something mark the passing of Luna 1's lost generation."

"I hope I don't have to arrest you for littering," came a new voice, and Rodimus and Getaway turned to see a second M.A.R.B. heading their way.

"Arrest me?" said Rodimus. "Does that mean what I think it means?"

Fortress Maximus skidded to a mid-air stop and smiled. "The newly-appointed Enforcer of the Tyrest Accord, reporting for service."

"Good decision, Max, good decision. Just because Tyrest lost the plot it doesn't mean there's not work to be done."

"Thank you for your faith in me."

"Happy to accept the thanks, but it was Magnus who wanted this to happen. He said his successor should..." His voiced trailed off as someone stepped out from behind Fortress Maximus.

"Red Alert?"

"Captain, I want to apologize for—"

"Stop right there. No apologies. Not on my ship."

"But I can't imagine the inconvenience I caused by my decision to, um, remove myself from the field of play."

"Nonsense. You were under tremendous pressure. Okay, so you didn't feel able to confide in me, but that says more about my failings as a leader than anything else." He pictured Ultra Magnus listening to him and nodding sagely at his words.

"Ratchet's brought me up to speed," said Red Alert. "I know that some of the Circle of Light are staying behind, and that you intend for Tyrest's body to remain here too, and I—"

"We've built a secure room in the medibay," interrupted Rodimus, pointing vaguely in the direction of what had been Tyrest's base of operations. "We've stabilized Tyrest but he won't be resuscitated until I've spoken to High Command—if I ever get to speak to High Command—and they've decided what to do with him."

"My point, Rodimus, is that I'd like to stay here." He held up a hand to forestall Rodimus's protests. "We all know there are pockets of rogue Decepticons out there. I can help the Circle of Light prepare for the possibility of attack. I'm already thinking that we could reprogram the... what are they called, Legislators? We could reprogram the Legislators to act as the moon's protectors."

"I think with you and Fort Max, Luna 1 is going to be in safe hands. Just promise to stay in touch!"

"Actually, Rodimus, that's why we're here. Perceptor's been trying to reach you."

Rodimus turned his communicator back on and nodded towards the hot spot. "Sorry, I was expecting to be busy with the..." He looked up. "What did Perceptor want?"

"You said you wanted to contact Cybertron as soon as I got this working," said Perceptor, gesturing to a monitor screen took up an entire wall of the Communications Room.

Rodimus craned his neck. "That. Is. Massive." He beckoned Getaway, Red Alert and Fortress Maximus over. "Who else wants one of these on the Lost Light?"

"I intend to replicate the comms system *without* the oversized monitor," said Perceptor, taking his seat at the operating console. "But first... dialing Kimia now, captain."

Rodimus clapped his hands. "Right! Good! Let's surprise Bumblebee!"

"I hope he's alright," said Red Alert, as the screen filled with static.

"'*Course* he's alright! I bet within 48 hours of us leaving Cybertron he'd talked the NAILs 'round, taught the 'Cons the error of their ways, and become Cybertron's first democratically-elected postwar leader. You'll see—any second now he'll be waving his little cane at us, telling us about the New Golden Age..."

Getaway was the first to detect a picture amongst the static. "What's that? Some kind of emblem? It's not an Autobot symbol, that's for sure." He read the words underneath the emblem as soon as they appeared. "'Welcome to the Republic of Cybertron.'"

"You see?" Rodimus turned to the others. "*You see? He's brought the whole planet together. Good old Bee. Good old brilliant Bee.*"

"That's not Bumblebee," said Fortress Maximus.

"Don't tell me Prowl is screening his calls..." Rodimus muttered, turning back to the screen.

Starscream looked down at him and grinned. "Well, well, well. What a *lovely* surprise."

⧖ POSTSCRIPT ⧖

Being entirely mechanical, Outrigger had never experienced breathlessness before, but running down half a mile of corridor and cutting across the hot spot put such a strain on his aging servos that when he crashed into Red Alert's office it took him a moment—bent in half and clamoring at the doorframe—before he was able to speak.

"He just moved!"

Red Alert helped Outrigger to his feet. Weren't members of the Circle of Light were supposed to be prime physical specimens? Weren't they supposed to be high-shine, chrome-coated überbots, their bodies and minds sharper and more deadly than the Great Sword they carried on their backs?

"Sorry, Red. I'd have called you, but I know you don't like using your communicator because you think it interferes with your—"

"Brainwaves, yes, yes. Forget that. Who just moved?"

"Tyrest!"

"I'm not saying I don't believe you," said Red Alert as they approached Luna 1's medibay a few minutes later. "But unless someone repairs him properly, Tyrest's going to be paralyzed forever. Maybe you saw the shadows move?"

"There are no shadows in the medibay," said Outrigger, pointing at the locked room in the corner. "Take a look. Tell me I'm seeing things."

Red Alert took a step closer, suddenly wary. "*How* did he move, exactly? Did he twitch? Was it a spasm?"

"No, nothing like that. It was very... considered."

Red Alert checked the door—still locked—and then put his eye against the peephole.

"It was his fingers," continued Outrigger. "The fingers on his right hand. It looked he was going to clench his fist."

"Get Fortress Maximus," said Red Alert, face still pressed against the door.

"Why? What should I tell him?"

"Tell him Tyrest has gone."

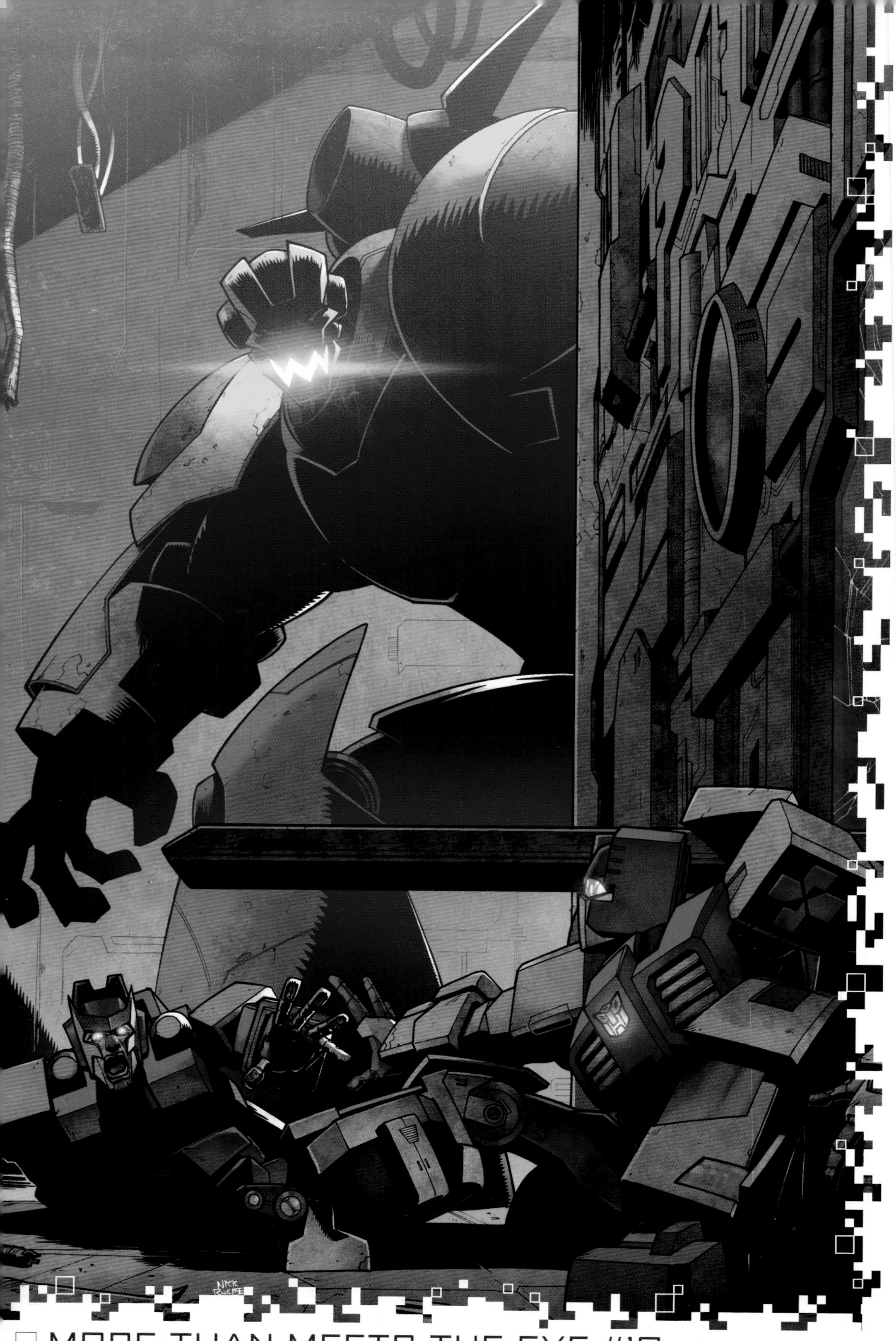
NICK ROCHE

MORE THAN MEETS THE EYE #18 COVER RI

by **NICK ROCHE** Colors by **JOSH PEREZ**

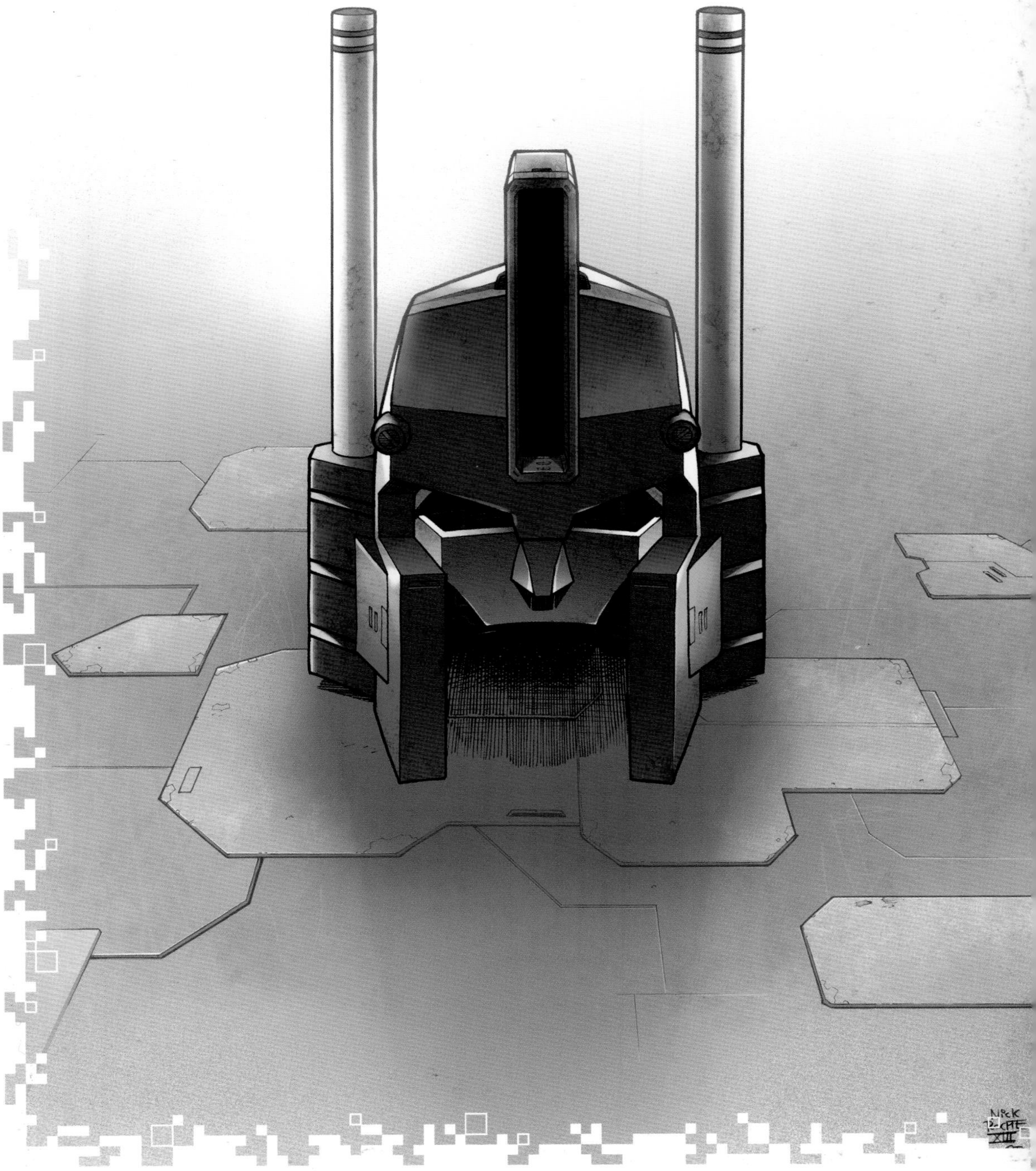

MORE THAN MEETS THE EYE #19 COVER RI

by **NICK ROCHE** Colors by **PRISCILLA TRAMONTANO**

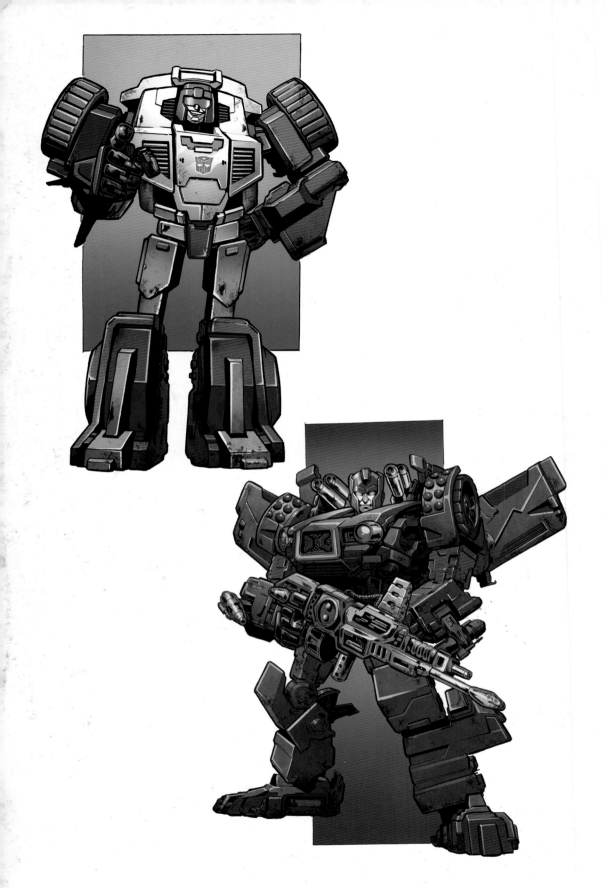

☐ MORE THAN MEETS THE EYE #20 & 22 COVER RI
by **PHIL JIMENEZ** Colors by **ROMULO FAJARDO, JR.**

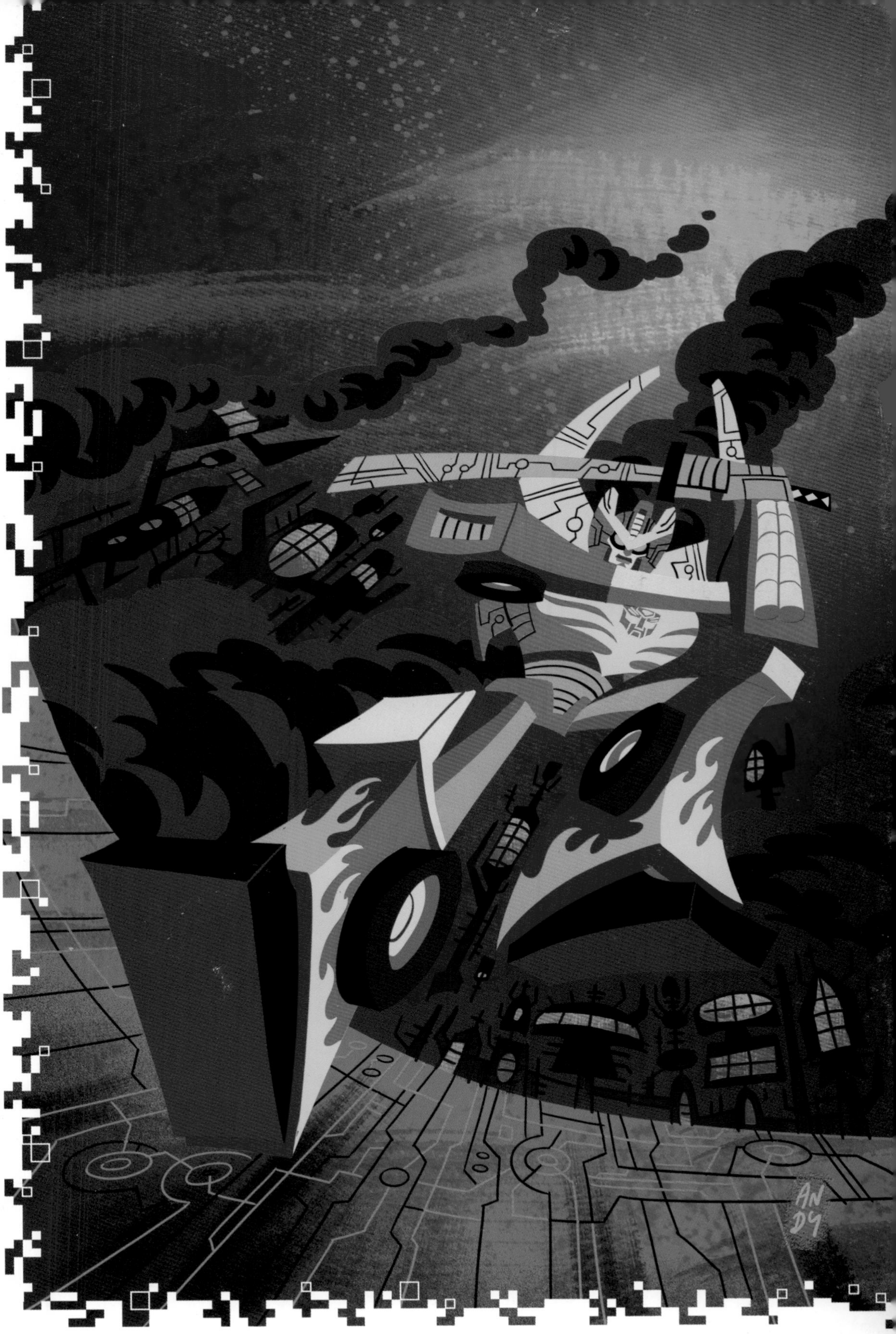
ANDY

MORE THAN MEETS THE EYE #21 COVER RI

by **ANDY SURIANO**

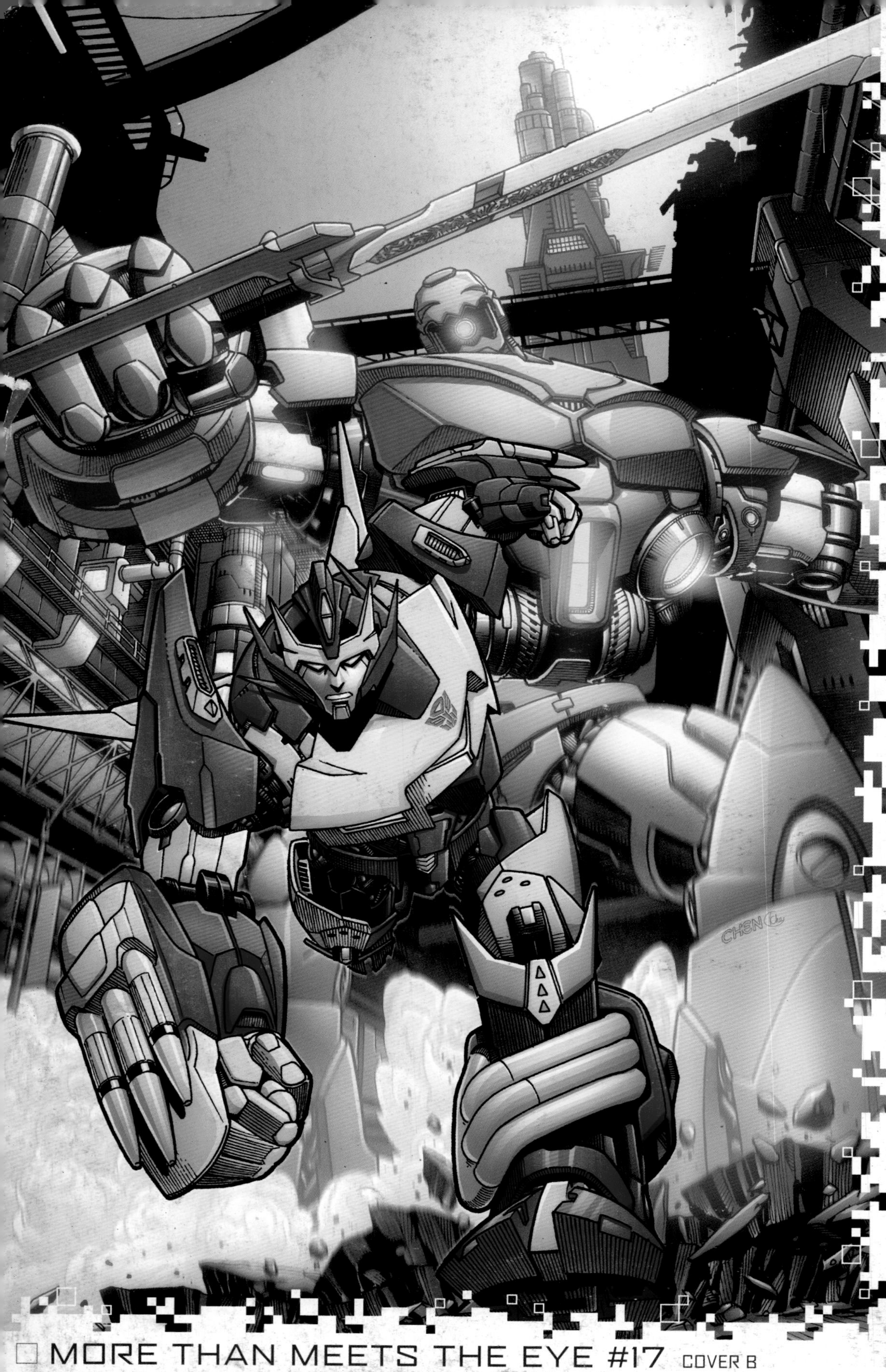

MORE THAN MEETS THE EYE #17 COVER B

by **SEAN CHEN** Colors by **TOM CHU**